AN INTRODUCTION TO THE NEW TESTAMENT

AN INTRODUCTION
TO
THE NEW TESTAMENT

BY

A. F. J. KLIJN

LEIDEN
E. J. BRILL
1980

Translated by Mrs M. van der Vathorst-Smit from the Dutch: *De Wordingsgeschiedenis van het Nieuwe Testament*, Aula-Boeken 207, Het Spectrum, Utrecht-Antwerpen, 1965.

First edition 1967.
Second impression revised in accordance with the Dutch Sixth impression.

TABLE OF CONTENTS

FOREWORD

I have often wondered why for some Americans the distance to the Netherlands seems so great, while for others it is so short. More than the Atlantic Ocean separates American churches from their Dutch cousins. It is apparent, too, that the distance when measured from west to east is much greater than when measured from east to west. They know our churches better than we know theirs. In fact, I believe the story of the Pilgrims has been studied more thoroughly by them than by us. At any rate, whatever the measure, we are ill-informed of their achievements, and this is nowhere truer than in theology. Apart from a few students who move from Grand Rapids or Holland, Michigan, to the Free University in Amsterdam, eastbound theological explorers seldom stop in the Lowlands. Some find the adjustment to Britain less taxing; others respond to the prestigious weight of German scholarship. Only a few seek out the Dutch faculties. When they do, they normally discover in the Dutch university a social climate as congenial as the British and an academic vitality as stimulating as the German. Yet the fact remains that the number of visiting students and teachers is too scanty to mediate the wealth available.

It is therefore of prime importance that more Dutch theology should be made available in English. The American ear does not readily conquer the venerable Dutch language, and professors in Holland continue to lecture in that alien medium, even though most could lecture readily in several other tongues. Translation is therefore essential. Nor should such translation be limited to an occasional best-seller written by a famous savant. If we are to understand the theological climate, we must become familiar with the staples of the curriculum, things like surveys of church history and introductions to the Bible.

It is as a representative of this last type that I welcome this small book by Professor Klijn. It covers what he considers to be the basic data needed by every student of the New Testament, presented in

brief compass and in lucid style. From his post on the theological
faculty in Utrecht he has lectured on this subject for many years,
yet he has written this book in English with American college and
seminary students in mind. His concern for them began when he
spent a term as visiting lecturer in Boston some years ago. What is
good for Utrecht and Boston should be good elsewhere. For so
succinct a book it would be silly to provide a verbose preface. I
therefore confine myself to a staccato "Thank you" to Professor
Klijn for this contribution to the theological conversation between
the Dutch and the American.

Paul S. Minear
Winkley Professor of Biblical Theology
Yale University

PREFACE

The Introduction to the New Testament deals with the data supplied by the New Testament concerning the origin and transmission of this book as a whole and of the writings of which it consists. In the present book these data have been conveniently arranged so that it may be used for purposes of study. As in other Introductions attention is given to the views of the early church on the subject of the origin and development of the New Testament. In this connection we have not limited ourselves to simple references to quotations from early Christian literature, but these quotations have been printed in full together with a translation.

The information supplied by the New Testament and by early Christian literature is open to different interpretations. This might lead to innumerable references to both old and more recent literature in which one or another interpretation is set forth. In the present book the different possibilities are pointed out, but without continually mentioning the names of particular persons or groups by whom the various views are held. The one or two references given will suffice to show the way to anyone wishing to go further into this matter. The author necessarily comes to his own decisions. For the student, however, it is more important to be acquainted with the various possibilities allowed by the facts than to follow the views expressed in any particular book.

As a stimulus to independent research a number of Appendices have been added, containing some important or disputed passages from the New Testament as well as from early Christian literature. The reader may thus acquire an insight into the nature of the evidence on which conclusions have to be based.

In the writing of this book the author has drawn largely on his experience as a lecturer on the subject of introduction at the University of Utrecht. In addition he was able to make use of knowledge gained during a stay at the Boston University School of Theology, where he had the opportunity, for a period of six months, of engaging in an intensive study of the historical problems of the New Testament with a group of students. While writing this book, the memory of those stimulating months was constantly in his mind. It is his hope that these results of study on both sides of the ocean may be of service to many students.

We gratefully acknowledge the permission of Uitgeverij Het Spectrum N.V., Utrecht/Antwerpen to translate the original Dutch version of this work.

CHAPTER ONE

INTRODUCTIONS TO THE NEW TESTAMENT

In an Introduction to the New Testament nowadays the following will be found:

a) an historical survey of the origins of the New Testament scripture,
b) an historical survey of the way in which these scriptures were combined into one volume,
c) a survey of the history of this volume both in manuscript and in printed form.

By no means all introductions, however, whether written at the present time or earlier, are strictly limited to these three topics. A short survey of the study of introduction will make this clear.

From an early date Christian authors have been concerned with what are customarily called introduction problems. As early as the first half of the second century Papias, bishop of Hierapolis in Asia Minor, was writing about the authorship of the gospels. Eusebius († 339) wrote a history of the church in which he expresses his own opinions about who wrote the various books of the New Testament as well as reporting the views of others. In the works of Origen († 253/4) we find frequent attempts to discover the original text of some New Testament passage. These authors were not inspired by pure scientific curiosity. Usually their object was to judge the apostolicity and thus the canonicity of a certain book on the basis of its authorship.

The so-called *introductores* dealt more systematically with the whole of the New Testament (cf. Cassiodorus, *Instit. div. lit.* I, 10, of the middle of the sixth century). These authors, however, treated more than just historical matters. They discussed the authorship, exegesis and hermeneutics of the New Testament scriptures. Their writings were intended to be of general assistance in understanding the New Testament correctly. This type of "introduction" continued to be written until after the Reformation both by Roman Catholic (e.g. Santes Paginus, *Isagogae ad Sacras Literas* 1536) and Protestant theologians (e.g. A. Rivetus, *Isagoge sive Introductio generalis ad Scripturan Sacram* 1627).

R. Simon, priest at the Oratory in Paris (1638-1712), tried to demonstrate by historical and critical means that the authority which the Protestants attributed to the New Testament was by no means infallible, since the text of the New Testament had been subject to alteration in the course of the centuries. His work resulted in four books which did not actually bear the title of "Introduction", but in which the New Testament was studied by a historical-critical method for the first time: *Histoire critique du texte du Nouveau Testament* 1689, *Histoire critique des Versions du Nouveau Testament* 1690, *Nouvelles Observations sur le Texte du Nouveau Testament* 1695 and *Histoire critique des principaux commentateurs du Nouveau Testament* 1693.

This historical-critical method of approach was taken over by the Protestants among whom it flourished greatly. J. D. Michaelis, *Einleitung in die göttliche Schriften des neuen Bundes* 1750, is still largely based on Simon, but the subsequent impressions of 1777 and 1778 show increasingly independent results. J. Ph. Gabler (1753-1826) and J. S. Semler (1725-1791) followed in Michaelis' footsteps. They called their writings "Introduction" although this name was initially used for a practical rather than a historical-critical approach of the New Testament. This gave rise to much discussion, in the 19th century, about the limits of what might be called an introduction. It gradually became accepted that it should cover the three topics mentioned at the beginning of this chapter.

This definition, however, has been continually disputed. There have been many scholars who believed that the 27 New Testament books represented an arbitrary choice from the far more extensive literature of the early Christian church, a choice not based on historical considerations but on an arbitrary decision made by the church. For this reason they wished to study the New Testament scriptures in the light of the whole of the literature produced by the early church, such as the writings of the Apostolic Fathers and the apocrypha. Representative for this approach is Ph. Vielhauer, *Geschichte der urchristlichen Literatur*, Berlin-New York 1975.

It is quite true that the 27 books of the New Testament represent an arbitrary choice. But surely this choice sprang from other considerations besides the belief that these books alone contained the revelation of God. These 27 books undeniably occupy a unique position on historical grounds. These are the scriptures that the church finally accepted as authoritative. These are the books that Christian writers of all times have quoted. It is not without good reason that their origin and history are considered the primary subjects for introduction studies.

The number of books to be discussed, is therefore no longer a subject of dispute. There is little unanimity, however, on the method of historical approach. The study of the origins of the New Testament scriptures has more and more made it clear that they are the literary product of the Christian community. We might say that every one of these books is inseparably bound up with the theological conceptions that existed in such great variety in this community. We continually find "Introductions" treating such subjects as "The life of Jesus", "The faith and life of the primitive church" and "The world in which the Christian church originated and developed". Against the background of these topics the various books of the New Testament are each given their place. Usually these books no longer bear the title "Introduction", but the aforementioned three topics are treated all the same. Some examples are: H. C. Kee and F. W. Young, *Understanding the New Testament*, London 1962, and R. M. Grant, *A Historical Introduction to the New Testament*, London 1963. An extensive treatment of theological subjects is found in *Introduction à la Bible* sous la Direction de A. Robert (†) et A. Feuillet, Tome II *Nouveau Testament* par C. Bigaré a.o. Desclée 1959. To these can be added C. F. D. Moule, *The Birth of the New Testament*, in: *Black's New Testament Commentary*, Companion Volume I, London 1962, although "it attempts no systematic investigation of the authorship, date, and composition of each writing ... it tries ... to investigate the circumstances which led to the making of the New Testament" (p. 1).

In the present book the theology of the primitive church, in which the writings originated, is not separately treated. Such a theology, after all, can not really be written until the various books of the New Testament have been extensively studied. This is what we have tried to do here. In each case we have paid some attention to the theological views of the author and if possible also to his place and significance in the early Christian church. In spite of all the apparent similarity between the authors it will be clear to anyone that it would be a hazardous undertaking to build up a picture of *the* primitive Christian church and its theology on the basis of demonstrable differences. We have therefore consciously restricted ourselves to a description of the particular character of each book of the New Testament. This method of approach is similar to that used by W. Marxsen in his *Einleitung in das Neue Testament*, Gütersloh 1963, translated by G. Buswell, *Introduction to the New Testament*, Oxford 1968, in which he keeps pointing out the significance of historical questions for exegetical practice. We have, however, refrained from direct discussion of this influence on exegesis. Marxsen was better able to treat this aspect because his views on historical questions were more definite.

In conclusion we list a number of Introductions with a brief description of each. As the first on the list we must mention H. J. Holtzmann, *Lehrbuch der historisch-kritischen Einleitung in das Neue Testament*, Freiburg 1892[3], and J. Mofatt, *An Introduction to the Literature of the New Testament*, Edinburgh 1927[3]. Both works are important because they contain an extensive discussion of 19th century literature. H. Appel. *Einleitung in das Neue Testament*, Leipzig 1922, gives few references but it is systematic and offers a clear picture of the state of affairs at the beginning of this century. A good survey of the sources is presented by Th. Zahn, *Einleitung in das Neue Testament*, Leipzig 1897, 1906-1907[2].

Of the new Introductions in German P. Feine, *Einleitung in das*

Neue Testament, 1913, is the most generally used. Later editions of this work were prepared, after 1936, by J. Behm and finally in 1963 by W. G. Kümmel (Heidelberg), translated by A. J. Mattill, Jr., *Introduction to the New Testament*, London 1965. This book aims at a certain degree of completeness, especially as regards the representation of the various views and the number of literature references. A book by W. Michaelis, *Einleitung in das Neue Testament*, Bern 1946, 1961³ is much used for study purposes. Essential passages are given in normal print and discussions of literature in smaller letters. The later editions place a great deal of stress on these dicussions. Somewhat older is the text-book by A. Jülicher and E. Fascher, *Einleitung in das Neue Testament*, Tübingen 1931³. This is a massive standard-work, in which the history of the canon in particular is given excellent treatment.

Representative for the English speaking world is E. J. Goodspeed, *An Introduction to the New Testament*, Chicago 1937. This contains some original ideas about, for instance, the letter to the Ephesians. K. Lake and S. Lake, *An Introduction to the New Testament*. London 1938, as representatives of English introduction scholarship, have rather less to offer than A. H. McNeile, *An Introduction to the Study of the New Testament*, Oxford 1927, with a revised edition in 1953 by C.S.C. Williams. This revision, however, has impaired the unity of the whole work. A. M. Hunter, *Introducing the New Testament*, London 1965², is a small but popular work. Equally concise is O. Cullmann, *The New Testament. An Introduction for the general Reader*, London 1968 (translated by D. Pardee from the French). A very extensive discussion of introduction questions is found in D. Guthrie, *New Testament Introduction, The Gospels and Acts* 1965, *The Pauline Epistles* 1963², *The general Epistles and Revelation* 1964, London. Two introduction by American scholars giving a thorough treatment of the subject are E. F. Harrison, *Introduction to the New Testament*, Grand Rapids 1964, and R. P. Martin, *New Testament Foundations*, vol. 1: *The Four Gospels*, Exeter 1975 (to be continued). In connection with the Synoptic problem we must mention the significant work by W. R. Farmer, *The Synoptic Problem. A Critical Analysis*, New York-London 1964.

CHAPTER TWO

THE SYNOPTIC GOSPELS

1. Introduction

The Greek word εὐαγγέλιον means "reward for the bringer of good tidings" or "good tidings". In the Greek version of the Old Testament the verb εὐαγγελίζειν occurs about 20 times. From the point of view of the New Testament use of the word, the occurrences found in Isa. 40, 9; 52, 7; 60, 6 and 61, 1 are the most important. The last of these is quoted by Luke 4, 18: . . . εὐαγγελίσασθαι πτωχοῖς ἀπέσταλκέν με . . . The noun εὐαγγελία occurs 4 times and εὐαγγέλιον only 3 times and always in the plural. As a noun the word "good tidings" has no religious significance. For this reason the New Testament use of the word εὐαγγέλιον is thought to have been influenced not so much by the Old Testament as by the usage of the Hellenistic world. There the word is frequently used in connection with the worship of the emperor, who has divine traits or is regarded as divine. His birth, and the beginning of each new phase of his life, are proclaimed to the people as a εὐαγγέλιον. Significant in this respect is the inscription found at Priene 150, 40:

ἦρξεν δὲ τῷ κόσμῳ τῶν δι' αὐτὸν εὐαγ- γελί[ων ἡ γενέθλιος] τοῦ θεοῦ	The day of the god's birth was the beginning of the good tidings given to the world through him.

This assumption is confirmed by the use of the word in the New Testament, where it is found especially in the writings of Paul (56 times). In the rest of the New Testament it occurs only 15 times altogether. By using the word εὐαγγέλιον, therefore, the Christian church probably meant to say that with the coming of Christ a new era began, that was to bring salvation to the world.

In the New Testament the word εὐαγγέλιον occurs only in the singular and in every case it means the proclamation of Christ. For

Christians, then, there was only one gospel. However when Paul warns against false teachings, he uses the expressions "another gospel" (Gal 1, 6 and II Cor. 11, 4) and "our gospel" (II Cor. 4, 3 and I Thess. 1, 5).

Although the church knew only one gospel, this might be presented in different forms. Mark, for instance, begins his book with the words "the beginning of the gospel of Jesus Christ". What he gives is a description of Jesus' life from his baptism by John the Baptist until the resurrection. But as the sources of the teaching concerning Jesus Christ gradually become restricted to the four gospels known to us, these books themselves come to be called "gospels". Something of the original meaning of the word may still be found in the designation of "The gospel according to (κατά) John" (Irenaeus, adv. Haer. III, 11 9). Justin, however, already speaks of the ἀπομνημονεύματα ἅ καλεῖται εὐαγγέλια (Apol. 66, 3), and Clement of Alexandria talks about passages ἐν τοῖς εὐαγγελίοις (Strom. I 136 1). This brings us to the usage by which the word "gospel" is used to denote one of the first four books of the New Testament.

The first three gospels are called the "synoptic gospels" because, as a rule, they are in mutual agreement to such an extent that they may be printed in columns of parallel text in a "synopsis".

The oldest known witnesses show no fixed order for the four gospels. Sometimes Matthew comes first, followed by Mark, Luke and John (B, Origen and minuscules), or by John, Luke and Mark (D W X e a b ff² f q). Or else John comes first, followed by Luke, Matthew and Mark (Ir., adv. Haer. III 11 8), or by Luke, Mark and Matthew, as for instance, in k.

With the gospels the early Christian church created a type of literature that cannot be compared to any literary genre of the Hellenistic world. It bears most resemblance to the *memorabilia* that were written about famous men. In the traditions concerning the life of Jesus, memory played an important part. By the regular breaking of the bread and drinking of the wine the death of the Lord was remembered (cf. I Cor. 11, 23-26). Jesus asks his disciples to keep certain happenings in mind (Mark 8, 19; Matt. 16, 9). At particular moments the disciples remember certain words (Matt. 26, 75) which Jesus instructed them to remember (Luke 24, 6-8, John 15, 20; 16, 4). This memory is continually called on (John 2, 17; 12, 16 and Acts 11, 16). Its purpose, however, is not to keep the past alive for posterity, but rather to establish the presence in the church of the living Lord. These memories do not proclaim a dead hero but the transfigured Christ, present in the church. The gospels, therefore, do not relate mere historical happenings. They tell of a phase in the existence of the Son of God that extends over all time. Biography and history have here been made subservient to the preaching of the church. We shall go further into this matter when we discuss the first three gospels separately.

2. THE SYNOPTIC PROBLEM

The first three gospels run parallel to a large extent, but even so there are a number of differences between them. The synoptic problem is the question of the mutual relationship of these gospels.

Quantitatively, the parallels and differences that appear in these gospels may be summed up as follows:

Mark has 661 verses, of which
> 600 are paralleled by Matthew
> 235 verses of Matthew are paralleled by Luke and
> 350 verses occur only in Matthew

Of the 661 verses in Mark,
> 350 are paralleled by Luke
> 235 verses of Luke are paralleled by Matthew and
> 548 verses are found only in Luke.

And so a synopsis shows passages where the three gospels agree, others where two are parallel (Mark-Matt., Mark-Luke or Matt.-Luke) and, finally, parts which are found in only one gospel.

The following are the similarities and differences found in the three gospels.

a. Similarities

The three gospels are very alike in structure. The following four parts may be distinguished:

1. The mission of John the Baptist, during which the baptism of Jesus and the temptation in the desert take place (Mark 1, 1-13/Matt. 3, 1-4, 11/Luke 3, 1-4, 13).

2. The public ministry of Jesus in Galilee, during which the call of the disciples and the greater part of the miracles take place. The climax of this period comes with the confession of Peter and the transfiguration on the mountain. (Mark 1, 14-9, 50/Matt. 4, 12-18, 35/Luke 4, 14-9, 50).

3. Jesus' journey to Jerusalem with discourses on the way and the healing of Bartimaeus (Mark 10, 1-52/Matt. 20, 1-34/Luke 9, 51-19, 28).

4. Jesus in Jerusalem, starting with the entry into Jerusalem and the cleansing of the temple. Disputes with the leaders of the Jewish people, discourse on the last things, institution of the Lord's Supper, Gethsemane, arrest, trial, death, resurrection and appearances (Mark 11, 1-end/Matt. 21, 1-end/Luke 19, 29-end).

The similarities between the gospels sometimes include the smallest details. Note, for example, the following pericopes:

Matthew	*Mark*	*Luke*	
8, 1-4	1, 40-44	5, 12-14	healing of a leper
9, 1-8	2, 1-12	5, 17-26	healing of a paralytic
17, 1-8	9, 2-8	9, 28-36	transfiguration on the mountain
19, 16-30	10, 17-31	18, 18-27	the rich young man
20, 29-34	10, 46-52	18, 35-43	the healing of Bartimaeus
21, 1-9	11, 1-10	19, 28-38	entry into Jerusalem
21, 23-27	11, 27-33	20, 1-8	the authority of Jesus

Matthew	*Luke*	
3, 7-10	3, 7-10	the preaching of John the Baptist
6, 24	16, 13	on serving two masters

6, 25-34	12, 22-31	on anxiety
11, 7-1	7, 24-28	testimony concerning John the Baptist
12, 43-45	11, 24-26	on the unclean spirits
24, 45-51	12, 42-46	on readiness

Matthew	Mark	
4, 18-22	1, 16-20	calling of the disciples
13, 53-58	6, 1-6	rejection of Jesus in Nazareth
20, 20-28	10, 35-45	on the sons of Zebedee
26, 6-13	14, 3-9	the anointing in Bethany
27, 27-31	15, 16-20	Jesus mocked by the soldiers

Mark	Luke	
1, 21-28	4, 31-37	rejection of Jesus in Capernaum
12, 38-40	20, 46-47	warning against the Scribes and Pharisees
12, 41-44	21, 1-4	the widow's small offering

b. Differences

Unlike Mark, both Matthew and Luke describe the birth of Jesus (1, 18-2, 23 and 1, 5-2, 52). Their stories of his birth, however, differ considerably. Both gospels give genealogies (Matt. 1, 1-17 and Luke 3, 23-38), but these are also different, and appear in different contexts.

Matthew and Luke both contain a large amount of parenetical matter, which Matthew has placed together in ch. 5, 6 and 7 (the Sermon on the Mount) but which in Luke is found scattered over chs. 6, 11, 12, 13 and 16. These chapters partly belong to Luke's so-called travel narrative, which relates Jesus' journey from Galilee to Jerusalem and is very extensive (9, 51-19, 27). Here, and in 6, 20-8, 3, Luke has collected all sorts of material, part of which he has in common only with Matthew and part of which occurs in no other gospel. Because of this, the structure of Luke differs somewhat from that of Matthew. The latter, like Mark, gives only a short travel narrative (19, 1-20, 34), while the material that is not found in Mark is scattered over the whole gospel.

Just as they have different beginnings, so the gospels end in completely different ways. After the resurrection Matthew tells of the Sanhedrin's order to say that the body of Jesus was stolen by his disciples, and of the Lord's command to preach the gospel (28, 11-20). Luke gives the story of the road to Emmaus, an appearance of the Risen One to the disciples and the Ascension (24, 13-53).

Apart from the passages that Matthew and Luke have in common but are not found in Mark, there are quite a number that occur in only one of these gospels. The most important of these are, in Matthew:

 5, 17-20   Jesus and the law
11, 28-30   "Come to me"
13, 24-30 and 36-43   parable of the darnel in the wheat
13, 44-46   parable of the valuable pearl
13, 47-50   parable of the net
17, 24-27   on the temple-tax
20, 1-16   parable of the labourers in the vineyard
21, 28-32   parable of the two sons
25, 1-13   parable of the wise and the foolish virgins
27, 3-10   the end of Judas

And in Luke:

 5, 1-11   the calling of Peter
 7, 11-17   the raising of a young man in Nain
 7, 36-50   the anointing of Jesus
10, 25-37   parable of the good Samaritan
10, 38-42   about Mary and Martha
11, 5-8   parable of a friend in the night
12, 13-21   the foolish rich man
15, 8-10   the lost silver piece
15, 11-32   the prodigal son
16, 1-13   parable of the dishonest steward
16, 19-31   the rich man and Lazarus the beggar
17, 11-19   the ten lepers
18, 1-8   parable of the unjust judge

18, 9-14   parable of the Pharisee and the tax-gatherer
19, 1-10   about Zacchaeus
22, 35-38   the two swords
23, 6-12   Jesus heard by Herod

Mark has very few passages that do not occur in either Matthew
or Luke. They are the following:

4, 26-29 parable of the seed that grows by itself
8, 22-26 healing of a blind man in Bethsaida

In addition, the passages Mark 9, 49; 3, 20-21 and 14, 51-52 are
not found in either Matthew or Luke.

Finally we may point out a few peculiarities in the gospel of
Luke. According to Luke, Jesus' first public teaching takes place
in the synagogue at Nazareth (4, 16-30). This passage runs parallel
to Mark 6, 1-6 and Matt. 13, 54-58, but the latter two gospels say
he first taught at Capernaum. In addition, Luke twice mentions a
sending forth of disciples by Jesus: the twelve in 9, 1-6 and the
seventy in 10, 1-20. In the other two gospels we find only one: the
sending forth of the twelve disciples (Mark 6, 7-13 and Matt. 10,
1-42) . In the passion narrative the denial of Peter is announced
during the meal (22, 31-34) and not after the meal as in Mark 14,
26-31 and Matt. 26, 30-35. In addition, Judas is pointed out as the
betrayer after the meal (22, 21-23) and not before as in Mark 14,
17-21 and Matt. 26, 20-25.

3. HISTORY OF THE RESEARCH INTO THE SYNOPTIC PROBLEM

Ever since Augustine people have been interested in the problem
of the similarities and differences between the first three gospels.
In his *De consensu evangelistarum I,* Augustine says that Mark
depends on Matthew, and Luke on Matthew and Mark. Since the
end of the eighteenth century there has been continuous research
into the relationship of the synoptic gospels. At that time *G. E.
Lessing* [1] suggested that the first three gospels all went back to an

---

[1] G. E. LESSING, *Neue Hypothese über die Evangelisten als bloss menschliche
Geschichtsschrieber betrachtet,* 1778.

original Aramaic "Gospel of the Nazarenes". This theory fails to do justice to the differences between the gospels. For that reason, more varied sources were looked for.

E. *Schleiermacher*[1] assumed that the gospels were based on what he called "Diegesen" — writings in which eye witnesses had recorded stories of miracles and parables, and the narrative of the crucifixion and resurrection. From these the evangelists composed the gospels. This point of view was further developed by *J. C. L. Gieseler*[2], who assumed oral traditions behind the gospels. These hypotheses did account for the differences between the gospels, but they did not explain why the latter are in literal agreement on so many points.

H. *J. Holtzmann*[3] thought the solution to the problem was to be found in the assumption of a common source as well as mutual dependence. The common source consisted mostly of sayings of Jesus and was used by Matthew and Luke. The dependence consists in the use of Mark as a source by both Matthew and Luke. This is represented in the following diagram:

$$\begin{matrix} \text{Mark} & & \text{Q(uelle)} \\ \text{Matthew} & & \text{Luke} \end{matrix}$$

This hypothesis explains the similarities between Matthew, Mark and Luke, as well as the extra material that Matthew and Luke have in common as opposed to Mark.

Using this diagram as a starting-point, all sorts of variations are possible. Since Luke generally follows Mark closely, but fails to include the passage Mark 6, 45-8, 26, it has been assumed, for instance, that Luke used a so-called "proto-Mark".

There have also been suggestions concerning a 'proto-Luke', that is the gospel of Luke less the passages that have parallels in Mark. This hypothesis is based on the fact that the material from Mark

---

[1] E. SCHLEIERMACHER, „Über die Zeugnisse des Papias von unseren Evangeliën", in: *Stud. und Krit.* V 1832, p. 735-768.

[2] J. C. L. GIESELER, *Historisch-kritischer Versuch über die Entstehung und die frühesten Schicksale der schriftliche Evangelien*, Leipzig, 1818.

[3] H. J. HOLTZMANN, *Die synoptischen Evangelien*, Leipzig, 1863.

is found in Luke in "blocks". These "blocks" of material from Mark were thought to have been inserted in an already existing gospel. Finally, the two-sources hypothesis (i.e. Mark and Q) has been expanded into a 'four-sources theory'. The material that is found only in Mark or in Luke is there called M and L. [1] This gives:

This theory has found fairly general acceptance. However a number of questions still require answers. It does not explain the origin of Mark. The use made of Q, as well as the contents of this source, remain quite obscure. What is more, the hypothesis runs counter to tradition as first recorded by Papias, who speaks of a gospel of Matthew originally written in Aramaic (see Appendix A).

This last difficulty led to a statement published by the Papal Biblical Commission on June 26, 1926, which said that, for research purposes, hypotheses might be framed concerning oral or written sources, and that one evangelist might be regarded as dependent on another, as long as the traditional data were adhered to. Tradition speaks of the 'substantial oneness' of the Greek gospel and its original in Aramaic, and of a certain chronological order in which the gospels were written. This means that the gospel of Matthew, which according to tradition was originally written in Aramaic, is the oldest.

This statement did not greatly alter the views of those who were engaged in research in this field. Many assumed that the originally Aramaic source Q was the Aramaic gospel of Matthew. Chronologically, this was then placed before the writing of Mark. Others tried to follow tradition even more closely by supposing that this Aramaic source was also used by Mark.[2]

---

[1] Cf. B. H. STREETER, *The Four Gospels*, London 1926.
[2] Cf. J. SICKENBERGER, *Kurzgefasste Einleitung in das Neue Testament*, Freiburg 1935[5-6], p. 79 and L. VAGANAY, *Le Problème synoptique*, in: *Biblioth. de Théol.* III 1, Paris 1952.

While some were reflecting on the statement of the Papal
commission, with its threat to the almost classic two or four
sources theory, others had already begun to develop a less schematic
approach to the problem.

About 1920 three important books were published by *K. L.
Schmidt*[1], *M. Dibelius*[2], and *R. Bultmann*[3]. These were concerned
with the use that the primitive church made of the material
found in the gospels. Schmidt proved such use by showing that
a particular pericope may occur in identical form in different
gospels, but that the frames in which it appears are usually
different. Take, for example, the feeding of the four thousand
in Matt. 15, 32-39/Mark 8, 1-10. The two gospels give practically
identical stories, but Matthew begins with the words: "Jesus
called his disciples and said to them...", and Mark writes:
"There was another occasion about this time when a huge
crowd had collected and, as they had no food, Jesus called his
disciples and said to them ..." A similar difference may be
observed in Matt. 16, 24-28/Mark 8, 34-9, 1/Luke 9, 23-27,
the passage about following Jesus. Matthew begins with:
"Jesus then said to his disciples..", Mark: "Then he called
the people to him as well as his disciples, and said to them...",
and Luke: "And to all he said ..." Often, these introductions
contain a rudimentary indication of time. They obviously serve to
join originally isolated stories together to form more or less one
narrative. Tradition furnished the evangelists with the isolated
stories, but they themselves are responsible for the introductions.

This would mean, then, that the isolated stories without indication of place or time came first. Bultmann and Dibelius occupied
themselves with the structure of these isolated stories. They noted
that parables, sayings, or miracle stories, for instance, each have
their own particular form. These forms were borrowed from the
surrounding world, where miracle stories, sayings and parables

[1] K. L. SCHMIDT, *Der Rahmen der Geschichte Jesus*, Berlin 1919.

[2] M. DIBELIUS, *Die Formgeschichte der synoptischen Tradition*, Tübingen 1919.

[3] R. BULTMANN, *Die Geschichte der synoptischen Tradition*, in: *Forsch. z.
Gesch. u. Rel. des A.u.N.T.* 22 1921.

were also used. These stories were used for purposes of preaching, instruction and apologetics.

These studies have undoubtedly created a livelier picture of the origin of the gospels. This method of "form criticism", however, could not explain quite as much as some of those who employed it would have wished. Too much was attributed to the activities of "the church", while the factor of tradition, which plays such an important part in Judaism, was too little taken into account. The fact that this tradition had its starting point in the person of Jesus was often neglected.[1]

Another error resulting from the method of "form criticism" was the degradation of the evangelists to mere collectors of isolated stories. It has been found that, although the evangelists did use traditional material, they definitely put their personal stamp on it. This is evident not only from the way the material is arranged but also from innumerable small alterations made to it. It is the history of the editing of this material ("Redaktionsgeschichte") that is at present the focus of interest.

A study of the traditions that go back to Jesus himself, and which existed in the first instance in the still Aramaic-speaking church has brought to light the Jewish element in the gospels. Both the structure of the story and the choice of words continually suggest that this material was not translated into Greek till a later stage. [2]

4. From Jesus to the Gospels

We shall take the two-sources theory as a basis for our discussion. It has been established that both Matthew and Luke used the gospel of Mark as a source. The classic proof of this is the fact that there is no instance where Matthew and Luke both run counter to the order found in Mark. In other words: the three gospels all have the same order or else either Matthew and Mark, or Luke and Mark, run parallel. When Matthew or Luke diverge from Mark in this respect

---

[1] Cf. H. RIESENFELD, *The Gospel Tradition and its Beginning*, in: *Studia Evangelica*, in: *Texte u. Unters.* 73 1959, p. 43-65 and B. GERHARDSON, *Memory and Manuscript*, Uppsala 1961.

[2] See M. BLACK, *An Aramaic Appraoch to the Gospels and Acts*, Oxford 1946.

there is always an obvious reason for the difference. In the gospel of Luke the calling of the disciples does not follow directly on the temptation in the desert as in Mark, 1. 16-20. It does not take place until Luke 5, 1-11. Luke devotes the first part of his account of Jesus' ministry to his teaching at Nazareth (4, 14-30), based on Mark 6, 1-6, and at Capernaum (4, 31-41), based on Mark 1, 21-39. Luke thus immediately calls attention to Jesus' teaching and its rejection in his own environment.

Matthew likes to place similar material together. After the Sermon on the Mount in ch. 5—7 he gives a series of miracles in chs. 8 and 9. He collected these miracles from material that is found scattered in Mark:

Matthew		*Mark*
8, 1-4	healing of a leper	1,40-44
8, 5-13	healing of the centurion's servant	—
8, 14-17	various healings	1, 29-34
8, 18-22	on following Jesus	—
8, 23-27	the storm on the lake	4, 35-41
8, 28-34	healing of two possessed	5, 1-20
9, 1-8	healing of a paralytic	2, 1-12
9, 9-13	calling of Matthew	2, 14-17
9, 14-17	on fasting	2, 18-22
9, 18-26	raising of the daughter of Jairus	5, 22-43
9, 27-31	healing of two blind men	(10, 46-52)
9, 32-34	healing of a dumb demoniac	—
9, 35-38	conclusion of the part concerned with healings	6, 34

A second piece of evidence for the dependence of both Matthew and Luke on Mark may be found in the difference in style and contents between the three gospels. These can only be explained by assuming that Matthew and Luke depend on Mark. Out of many possible examples we will here cite only Matt. 20, 29-34/Mark 10, 46-52/Luke 18, 35-43:

Mark says that "they came to Jericho" and that "as he was leaving the town with his disciples and a large crowd, Bartimaeus,

son of Timaeus, a blind beggar, was seated at the road-side".
Matthew omits the superfluous coming into Jericho, and Luke
changes the whole sense by saying that they were approaching
Jericho. Matthew makes the miracle even greater by talking of
two blind men and Luke leaves out the name, which he apparently
found unnecessary. According to Mark the blind man hears Jesus approaching. Luke makes the story livelier by saying that the blind
man asks who is coming. Mark continues his narrative with a
hebraism: ἤρξατο κράζειν καὶ λέγειν. Matthew avoids this by using
the paraphrase ἔκραξαν λέγοντες and Luke by writing ἐβόησεν λέγων.
The pleonastic comparative ὁ δὲ πολλῷ μᾶλλον ἔκραζεν in Mark
becomes οἱ δὲ μεῖζον ἔκραξαν λέγοντες in Matthew. According to
Mark, Jesus calls the blind man to him. Luke, again, makes this
livelier by saying: σταθεὶς δὲ ὁ Ἰησοῦς ἐκέλευσεν αὐτὸν ἀχθῆναι πρὸς
αὐτόν.

Both Luke and Matthew, however, omit the passage in Mark
where the blind man is told to keep heart and he throws away
his garment. When Jesus speaks, his words are introduced by
a hebraism: καὶ ἀποκριθεὶς αὐτῷ ὁ Ἰησοῦς εἶπεν which Matthew
shortens to καὶ εἶπεν and which Luke changes into better Greek:
ἐπηρώτησεν αὐτόν.

The hebraism ῥαββουνι used by Mark becomes κύριε in Luke and
Matthew. Jesus' command ὕπαγε is corrected by Luke to ἀνάβλεψον,
while Matthew tells us that Jesus actually brings about the cure:
σπλαγχνισθεὶς δὲ ὁ Ἰησοῦς ἥψατο τῶν ὀμμάτων αὐτῶν.

It is possible, of course, that the text of Mark which Matthew and
Luke used was not quite identical with the one we have at present.
In this connection, the absence of Mark 6, 45-8, 26 in Luke
has been pointed out. Although this is not easy to explain,
there is not much reason to assume a "proto-Mark". In any case,
when studying the synoptic problem we have to accept the present
text of Mark as a working hypothesis. Only when concentrating on
certain details will we sometimes be obliged to assume that Matthew
and Luke used a different text of Mark from the one we have. This
applies particularly to those instances where Matthew and Luke are
obviously based on Mark and both show the same deviation from the

latter. Thus we read in Matt. 9, 7/Luke 5, 25 εἰς τὸν οἶκον against Mark 2, 12; in Matt. 17, 5 / Luke 9, 35 the addition λέγουσα against Mark 9, 7; in Matt. 22, 37 / Luke 10, 27 ἐν ὅλῃ τῇ καρδίᾳ against Mark 12, 30: ἐξ ὅλης τῆς καρδίας σου; in Matt. 21, 38 / Luke 20, 14 the addition ἰδόντες against Mark 12, 7; and greater deviations in Matt. 13, 11 / Luke 8, 10 ὑμῖν δέδοται γνῶναι τὰ μυστήρια against Mark 4, 11: ὑμῖν τὸ μυστήριον δέδοται and the addition in Matt. 26, 28 / Luke 22, 64 τίς ἐστιν ὁ παίσας σε against Mark 14, 65. Such instances of agreement in differing from Mark may be the result of chance but they remain interesting for the study of the relationship between the synoptics.

Unlike the book of Mark, the source Q no longer exists as such. Certain striking instances of agreement between Matthew and Luke, however, indicate that they must have used the same material. Matt. 3, 7-10 and Luke 3, 7-9 have, after γεννήματα ἐχιδνῶν, 66 words of which only one is not the same in the two texts (δόξητε instead of ἄρξησθε in Matt. 3, 9 and Luke 3, 8). Such parallels are by no means exceptional. This would warrant the assumption that their source was a written one and in the Greek language. The possibility that Matthew and Luke used different versions of this source is not excluded. Thus Matt. 25, 14-30 and Luke 19, 12-27 give similar parables which, however, differ in various points. Perhaps Luke's own hand may be discerned in his version, but even so the two evangelists probably used different versions of the parable.

From the examples we have given it is clear that Q contains a variety of material. It includes all that Matthew and Luke have in common concerning the preaching of John the Baptist and the temptation in the desert (Matt. 4, 3-10 and Luke, 4, 3-10), and it consists for a large part of material of a parenetical character which is to be found in Matt. 5-7, and is in Luke scattered over chapters 6, 11, 12, 13 and 16. To this material also belong the teachings concerning the future missionary work of the church (Matt. 10, 1-16 and Luke 10, 1-12), warnings against Pharisees and scribes (Matt. 23, 1-36 and Luke 11, 39-52) and sayings about the second coming (Matt. 24, 26-28; 37-41 and Luke 17, 23-24; 17, 37 and 17, 26-27 and 34-35). From this we may deduce that the contents of Q were of a distinctly parenetical nature. It was intended for the edification of the church and to give directives for the daily practice of being a Christian, for both inward and outward use (preaching), and for both present and future.

How large this source Q actually was is not so easy to determine. We may wonder, for instance, whether Q contained more about John the Baptist than only some of his sayings. It is not always clear, moreover, whether Matthew and Luke derived their so-called own material from Q or from another source, since there is no reason to suppose that both included the whole of Q in their writings.

While discussing the manner in which Mark was used by Matthew and Luke we noted that Luke borrowed his material from Mark in "blocks". We may therefore expect Luke to have used a similar method in borrowing from Q. This results in a number of doublets where Mark and Q contain identical material. In Luke 9, 1-6 the sending out of the twelve is found exactly as in Mark 6, 7-13. In Luke 10, 1-20, the sending of the seventy contains material from Q. This material is also used by Matthew in his pericope concerning the sending out of the disciples (10, 1-42), which thus shows a combination of Mark and Q. The same happens to the pericope Mark 4, 21-25. This is found in Luke 8, 16-18. Matthew did not follow Mark in this case, since the passage also occurred in Q. This passage from Q is found in Matt. 5, 15; 10, 26; 7, 2 and 25, 29. Luke gives the passage again, now taken from Q, in 11, 33; 12, 2; 6, 38 and 19, 26.

Another result of Luke's method is that he takes over unconnected passages from Q, whereas Matthew works them into stories derived from Mark. Thus Matthew 12, 25-35 consists of a passage from Mark (3, 23-30), supplemented with material from Q that Luke gives in a different context in 12, 10 and 6, 43-45. Since Luke reproduces whole blocks of borrowed material, while Matthew rearranges what he borrows so as to place similar material together, Luke's text remains closer to the original version of Q.[1] But, in spite of this, Matthew often uses the material from Q in the same order as Luke.

---

[1] V. TAYLOR, "The Original Order of Q", in: *New Testament Essays . . . in memory of T. W. Manson*, Manchester 1959, p. 246-269.

Let us take for example Luke 6, 20-47. When we compare this with Matthew the result is as follows:

Luke	Matthew
6, 20-23	5, 3, 5, 6, 11, 12
6, 27-30	5, 39-42
6, 31	7, 12
6, 32-36	5, 44-48
6, 37-38	7, 1-2
6, 41-42	7, 3-5
6, 43-45	7, 16-20
6, 46	7, 12
6, 47-49	7, 24-27

The material found placed together in Luke occurs in the same order in Matthew, though interwoven with Matthew's own material. Concerning the origin, nature and extent of Matthew's own material (M) and Luke's (L) nothing can be said with any certainty.

This means that the assumption of a source Q provides an excellent working hypothesis. But if we prove that Mark and Q served as sources for Matthew and Luke, this takes us only one step back on the way to the origin of the tradition in the gospels. Between the person of Jesus, at the beginning, and Mark and Q as a stage on the road to Matthew and Luke, there is still a long way. We have already seen that the stage previous to the writing of Mark was one of isolated pericopes. These separate pericopes must have shown a tendency to combine into blocks of similar material. Sayings concerning the last things as found in Mark 13, will undoubtedly have been combined into one whole at an early date. Discussions about the sabbath, as in Mark 2, 23 — 3, 6, must also already have formed a whole when Mark encountered them. Such grouping together of similar data must have taken place at a very early stage where the Passion narrative is concerned. As far as we know, however, Mark was the first to combine this material, which was becoming more and more consolidated, into a gospel built around the framework of the works of Jesus, starting in Galilee and ending in Jerusalem.

Possibly such a geographic framework on which to base teaching concerning Jesus was traditional. The Acts of the Apostles may, of course, have been influenced by the gospel of Luke but the notable fact remains that in Acts 10, 37-40 the life of Jesus is represented as beginning with his baptism by John and ending with the appearance of the Risen One. It thus includes his ministry in Galilee, his trial in Jerusalem and the crucifixion.[1]

Between Jesus and the gospels, undoubtedly, lies the preaching of the church. This church drew on traditions concerning Jesus, but shaped them according to its own needs and emphasized various aspects of them according to the circumstances. The traditions were grouped around certain subjects, such as the keeping of the sabbath, life as a Christian in a Jewish society, proving to Jews and Gentiles that Jesus was indeed the Christ, and showing that the Passion was necessary. In the following stage, these traditions were assembled into a "life of Jesus", of which the oldest known example is the gospel of Mark. We cannot tell with any certainty whether this is in fact the earliest attempt. Luke, at least must have known of the existence of several written sources concerning Jesus. This is evident from the very first words of his gospel, where he says that "Many writers have undertaken to draw up an account of the events that happened among us" (Luke 1, 1).

5. MARK

a. Contents

The gospel of Mark describes the life of Jesus from the appearance of John the Baptist (1, 1-8) until the Resurrection (16, 1-8). Between these two events, a large number of pericopes describe events that took place during his life. Initially there is strong emphasis on Jesus' activity in word and deed, as for instance in his teaching in the synagogue at Capernaum (1, 21-28), the healing of a leper (1, 40-45) and of a paralytic (2, 1-12). This

---

[1] Cf. C. H. DODD, *The Apostolic Preaching and its Developments*, London 1936, but also D. E. NINEHAM, "The Order of Events in St. Mark's Gospel-an examination of Dr. Dodd's Hypothesis", in: *Stud. in the Gospels in mem. of R. H. Lightfoot*, Oxford 1955, p. 223-239.

brings a multitude of people to him but it also immediately puts him in conflict with the Pharisees (2, 7), who disapprove especially of his transgressions of the Jewish law (2, 18-22; 2, 23-28; 3, 1-6). Jesus then gathers 12 disciples around him (3, 13-19). People are unsure whether his activities are inspired by God or by the devil (3, 20-30). Through parables Jesus explains that not every one will receive the Word (4, 1-34).

Although Jesus gives proof of his power by new miracles he is rejected in Nazareth (4, 35 — 6, 6). Disciples are then sent out to proclaim the Kingdom (6, 7-13), but the death of John the Baptist shows that to serve Jesus is a matter of life or death (6, 14-29). After some miracles (6, 45, 56), more arguments with the Pharisees are recounted (7, 1-23). Jesus retires to the neighbourhood of Tyre (7, 24 — 8, 10) but once more he comes into conflict with the Pharisees (8, 11-21).

In the northern part of Palestine, in Caesarea Philippi, Peter recognizes him as the Messiah. At the same time, however, Jesus announces his passion (8, 27 — 9, 1). This is directly followed by his transfiguration on a mountain (9, 2-13). After another announcement of his passion (9, 30-32) they leave Galilee.

On the way to Jerusalem they talk of how one should follow Jesus, and the obedience required from his disciples (10, 1-52).

The entry into Jerusalem is a glorious one (11, 1-10). Jesus casts the traders out of the temple (11, 11-26). Now the conflict with the leaders of the Jewish people really breaks out (11, 27 — 12, 44).

After a discourse about the last things (13, 1-37) the narrative continues with the anointing of Jesus by a woman and Judas' betrayal of him (14, 1-11). During the passover meal Jesus institutes the Lord's Supper (14, 12-31). Jesus then goes to Gethsemane with his disciples and is arrested there (14, 33-52). The Sanhedrin condemns him (14, 53-65) and Peter denies him (14, 66-72). Pilate has Jesus crucified (15, 1-41). After his death, Jesus is buried (15, 42-47).

Striking aspects of this gospel are that it repeatedly insists that Jesus is capable of miraculous deeds but on the other hand goes to his death of his own free will, and that great multitudes come to him but desert him in the end. A subject that keeps returning throughout the gospel is that of Jesus' arguments with the scribes and Pharisees.

b. Nature

It is clear from the contents of this gospel that the author did more than merely compile traditional accounts of events from the life of Jesus. Right from the beginning, the author puts it beyond doubt that Jesus was an exceptional person, recognised by demons as the "Holy One of God" (1, 24), but that he will come into conflict with the leaders of the people (2, 7: "He speaks blasphemies"). A climax occurs in 8, 27 — 9 13, where Peter's confession, the announcement of the passion and the transfiguration on the mountain are given side by side. Jesus' teachings are coupled by the author with his journey to Jerusalem, which provides an appropriate context for subjects such as the following of Jesus and suffering in his service.

It is clear that the author deliberately places side by side and contrasts Jesus' glory and his Passion. While doing so, he describes the reactions of the bystanders. The manifestations of his glory cause astonishment, dismay and even fear (1, 27; 2, 12; 4, 40; 5, 15; 5, 33; 6, 50; 9, 6, cf. also 10, 24; 10, 32 anf 16, 8). When Jesus enters on his Passion, however, bewilderment and incomprehension prevail (4, 13; 4, 40; 7, 18; 8, 17; 8, 33; 9, 6; 9, 19; 9, 32; 10, 24, cf. also 14, 37-41).

Astonishment, fear and bewilderment are all a part of the pattern on which the author builds his description of the life of Jesus in glory and suffering. The remarkable thing is, however, that the writer continually shows that Jesus intended the bystanders to be so astonished, afraid and bewildered. Instead of allowing full emphasis to be placed on his glory, Jesus according to this gospel forbade his remarkable deeds to be made known (1, 43-45; 5. 43; 7, 36).

When the demons recognize him, they are forbidden to speak about it (1, 23-25; 1, 34; 3, 11-12). When Peter recognizes him as the Messiah, he is not allowed to say anything about it (8, 30), and the transfiguration on the mountain must remain a secret (9, 9).

Since the beginning of this century, this striking aspect of Mark's description of Jesus' life has been referred to as the "Messianic Secret". Why Mark puts such special stress on this aspect is a question, however, to which as yet no satisfactory answer has been given. The oldest explanation, by W. Wrede, has long been abandoned. [1] According to him the author combined very old material, in which Jesus was not regarded as the Messiah during his lifetime, with the preachings of the later church, which recognized Jesus as the Messiah after his resurrection. Now that the gospels have come to be regarded as a reflection of the beliefs of the church, it is assumed that the author had in mind the empirical fact that the preaching concerning Jesus the Messiah is not accepted by everyone. Mark, it is thought, wished to show that there is no need to feel disappointment on this score, since Jesus desired the situation to be so. Few only are chosen to know Jesus (cf. 4, 11). [2]

There is a drawback to the latter explanation, however. The evangelist talks of concealment during Jesus' lifetime and of disclosure after the resurrection: "On their way down the mountain, he enjoined them not to tell anyone what they had seen, until the Son of Man had risen from the dead" (9, 9). Evidently the secret of Jesus' Messiahship, and the fact that Jesus himself deliberately keeps it concealed, is connected with the way that Jesus, according to Mark, is following. Before Jesus' transfiguration, the Passion awaits him. What Mark especially brings out is the incomprehensibility of this course of things. In spite of his suffering he cannot keep his greatness hidden, and as the Son of God he cannot escape suffering. For this reason it has rightly been said that the problem is not determined by the question whether Jesus

---

[1] W. WREDE, *Das Messiasgeheimnis in den Evangelien . . .*, Göttingen 1901 (reprint in 1963).

[2] Cf. H. EBELING, *Das Messiasgeheimnis und die Botschaft des Marcus-Evangelisten*, in: *Beih. Zeitschr. neut. Wissensch.* 19 1939. See for more recent literature: G. H. BOOBYER, "The Secrecy Motif in St. Mark's Gospel", in: *New Test. Stud.* 6 1960/61, p. 225-235, and T. A. Burkill, *Mysterious Revelation*, Ithaca 1963.

is the Messiah, but rather by the question whether or not this Messiah must suffer. [1]

Regarded from this point of view, the description of Jesus' successful activity alternating with the continually recurring conflict with the Jews has a clear purpose. Even more important is the contrast between what happens in Galilee and in Jerusalem. In Galilee, Jesus' power is revealed through healings and the casting out of demons, with the transfiguration on the mountain as a climax following on the confession of Peter. In Jerusalem, Jesus dies on the cross. The significance of the former place receives the more stress since it is there that the Risen One appears to his disciples (14, 28 and 16, 7). When Jesus appears in glory it is not in a public place like Jerusalem, but in an outlying part of the country. This again is certainly a part of the "Messianic secret". There is also, however, an polemic element in it, directed against the Jews who, in their capital, see only a humiliated Messiah.

The gospel of Mark shows a well-considered plan. In a world that regarded a crucified Messiah as a "stumbling-block" and a "folly" (I Cor. 1, 23), it tried to show that the glory of the Crucified One cannot remain concealed.

c. *Author*

The oldest testimony concerning the author comes from Papias (see Appendix A). From what he says it appears that the gospel was based on the testimony of Peter. There may be a historical foundation for this assertion, but it may also be a result of the desire to provide an apostolic basis for this gospel.

John Mark was the son of that Mary in whose house the Christians of Jerusalem used to gather (Acts 12, 12). Together with his uncle Barnabas he accompanied the apostle Paul on the latter's first missionary journey (Acts 13, 5). Mark accompanies them only as far as Cyprus (13, 13), but later he is again found in Paul's company (Philem. 24, Col. 4, 10 and II Tim. 4, 11). He appears to have had connections with Peter (I Peter 5, 13).

---

[1] See T. W. MANSON, ,,Realized Eschatology and the Messianic Secret", in: *Studies . . . in mem. of R. H. Lightfoot*, Oxford 1955, p. 209-222.

d. *Place and time of origin*

From the information supplied by Papias it cannot be inferred with any certainty that the gospel was written in Rome. Arguments for its origin in a Latin speaking environment have been found in certain Latinisms in the Greek text, for instance λεγιών in 5, 9 and 15 and ἱκανὸν ποιῆσαι in 15, 15 (*satisfacere*). These, however, are by no means conclusive arguments. The fact that Matthew and Luke used this gospel as a source would rather suggest an origin in a more easterly part of the Roman empire.

Since the gospel contains no reference to the destruction of Jerusalem, it must have been written before A.D. 70. It is usually assumed to date from between 60 and 65.

e. *The conclusion of Mark*

In the mss. א B k sys armᶜᵒᵈᵈ, and according to Clement of Alexandria, Eusebius and Jerome, the gospel ends with 16, 8. Many manuscripts add 16, 9-20 (C K D G etc.) while in others the so-called short conclusion is inserted between 16, 8 and 16, 9-20: "And they delivered all these instructions briefly to Peter and his companions. Afterwards Jesus himself sent out by them from east to west the sacred and imperishable message of eternal salvation" (LΨ etc.). Evidently the lines originally occupied the place of 16, 9-20, as may still be seen in the Latin ms. k.

It is commonly agreed that both passages following 16, 8 are secondary in origin. The long conclusion is a summary of the appearances described in Matthew, Luke and John and its style differs from that of the rest of the gospel.

Somewhat more difficult is the question whether the gospel originally closed with the words ἐφοβοῦντο γάρ. It may be that, initially, these were followed by the description of some appearances. In that case these were deliberately removed, for which there seems to be no reason, or else accidentally omitted. The latter is possible but not likely. We will have to assume, therefore, that the gospel did in fact end with the words "for they were afraid". This is not impossible, for these words are the same as were used in 9, 6—ἔκφοβοι γὰρ ἐγένοντο—in connection with the transfiguration on the mountain. They sum up the emotions of a man to whom it is given to see the Humiliated One transfigured.

a. *Contents*   6. MATTHEW

The book begins with a genealogy of Jesus (1, 1-17), after which the birth of Jesus and the events directly following it are described (1, 18-2, 23). The narrative continues with a more extensive version of Mark's account of John the Baptist, the baptism of Jesus and the temptation in the desert (3, 1-4, 11). Jesus teaches for the first time in Capernaum (4, 12-17). This is followed by the calling of the disciples and a few healings (4, 18-25). Chs. 5, 6 and 7 constitute the so-called Sermon on the Mount, containing material of a parenetical nature. Chs. 8 and 9 (8, 1-9, 38) are largely devoted to healings. The sending out of the disciples (10, 1-42) is given, not as in Mark in connection with the death of John the Baptist, but with an appraisement of the latter (11, 2-15), Jesus' contemporaries are reprimanded (11, 16-24) but "all who labor and whose load is heavy" are invited to come to him (11, 25-30). Chapter 12 (1-50) gives an account of various actions of Jesus that are disapproved of by the Pharisees and the bystanders. Chapter 13, 1-58 gives a number of parables. These are followed by a large number of isolated episodes (up to 16, 12) including the death of John (14, 1-12), the first miraculous feeding (14, 13-21) and disputes with the Pharisees (15, 1-9). The confession of Peter, the announcement of the passion and the transfiguration on the mountain are placed together (16, 13-17, 13). The healing of an epileptic (17, 14-21) and the second announcement of the passion (17, 22-23) are followed by some parenetical material on subjects such as forgiveness (18, 21-35), divorce (19, 1-12) and service (20, 20-28).

Here, too, the entry into Jerusalem (21, 1-11) is followed by the casting out of the traders in the temple (21, 12-17). Next comes another parenetical passage, partly consisting of parables (21, 28-32; 21, 33-46; 22, 1-14) and partly of disputes with the leaders of the Jews, culminating in a long sermon directed against them (23, 1-39). A lengthy passage concerning the last things is accompanied by relevant parables on the subject of watchfulness (24, 1-25, 46).

The anointing of Jesus, the announcement of Judas' treachery, the institution of the Lord's Supper. Gethsemane and Jesus' arrest are given together, as in Mark (26, 6-56). The remainder of the gospel also follows the same lines as Mark: Jesus before the Sanhedrin (26, 57-68), the denial of Peter (26, 69-75), Jesus brought before Pilate (27, 1-10), condemnation (27, 11-26), Jesus mocked by the soldiers (27, 27-32), crucifixion (27, 33-44), death and burial (27, 45-66).

Finally, the resurrection is described (28, 1-10). The Sanhedrin gives orders that it should be put about that Jesus' body has been stolen (28, 11-15). The gospel concludes with Jesus' instructions to his disciples to preach the gospel to the whole world (28, 16-20).

Clearly the framework of this gospel is similar to that of Mark. It is evident, however, that the parenetical nature of Jesus' preaching is given special emphasis in all sorts of ways (in sayings, parables and disputes).

b. *Nature*

It has been supposed by some that the structure of this gospel might betray something of its nature. The narrative is interrupted five times by a similar formula: ,,When Jesus had finished "these words" 7, 28; 19, 1; "all these words" 26, 1; "these parables" 13, 53; "his instructions to the twelve disciples" 11, 1. This has been viewed as a conscious attempt to create a division analogous to the five books of Moses, in which case one might infer that the author regarded Jesus as the "new Moses". A drawback to his point of view, however, is the fact that this division must surely have escaped the attention of any ordinary reader. We may also note in this connection that the formula, with its characteristic variations: "these words", "all these words", "these parables" and "his instructions to the twelve disciples", would seem to be a part of the method commonly employed by a writer who places similar material together. [1]

---

[1] See B. W. BACON, *Studies in Matthew*, New York 1930 and W. D. DAVIES, *The Setting of the Sermon on the Mount*, Cambridge 1964, p. 14-25.

If we wish to understand the nature of this gospel, we must start from those passages where Mark and Matthew run parallel. Comparison will show us what end Matthew may have had in view in altering Mark's text.

In the first place it will strike us that Matthew shortens the narrative element in Mark. The story of the possessed in the country of the Gerasenes in Matt. 8, 28-34 is much shorter than that of Mark 5, 1-20. The same is true of the pericope concerning the daughter of Jairus and the woman who suffered from haemorrhages in Matt. 9, 18-26 and Mark 5, 21-43. Two miracles in Mark 7, 31-37 and 8, 22-26 are not given at all by Matthew.

On the other hand, Matthew does expand certain of Mark's stories by adding parenetical matter. When Mark describes how Jesus walks on the lake, the story is obviously intended as an illustration of Jesus' glory (Mark 6, 45-52). Matthew (14, 22-33) adds that Peter also walks on the lake but that he is seized by fear and sinks. Jesus consequently rebukes him for his "little faith". This incident gives the story a parentical character: when in distress, a man should look to Jesus. Related to this is the story of the storm on the lake (Mark 4, 35-41), where Jesus, as the cosmic Lord, shows his power over the elements. Matthew 8, 23-27 slightly changes the purport of the story by substituting "Lord" for "master" and "ye of little faith" for "cowards". Again the pericope is changed into a lesson for the faithful: in Jesus' presence there is no place for fear. [1]

The relationship between Jesus and his disciples, as these stories show, is one between "the Lord" and "the faithful" or "those of little faith". This relationship leaves far less room for fear, bewilderment and ignorance than is present in Mark's versions. This is in conformity with the fact that in the gospel of Matthew there is no question of a "Messianic secret". In Mark 1, 34 Jesus forbids the demons to make him known, but this is left out in the pericope Matt. 8, 16-17. In Mark 3, 11-12 Jesus again insists that the spirits

---

[1] G. BORNKAMM, „Die Sturmstillung im Matthäus-Evangelium", in: *Überlieferung und Auslegung im Matthäus-Evangelium*, in: *Wissensch. Monogr. z. A. u. N. T.* 1 1960, p. 48-53.

should not make him known. This time Matthew follows Mark but he regards the incident as a fulfilment of Isaiah's prophecy (Isa. 42, 1-4) that the voice of the servant of the Lord shall not be heard in the streets. When the madman in the country of the Gerasenes is cured, Matthew does not say that the people are afraid (Mark 5, 15 and Matt. 9, 34). The same applies to the story of the woman who suffered from haemorrhages (Mk. 5, 33). When the disciples see Jesus transfigured on the mountain they are terrified according to Mark 9, 6, but according to Matthew they are seized with terror only when God's voice is heard from the cloud (Matt. 17, 6). Jesus' rebuke when the disciples do not understand his parbles in Mark 4, 13 is left out in Matt. 13, 18. When Peter, on the mountain, suggests the building of three shelters, Matthew does not add that he did not know what he was saying (Mark 9, 6 and Matt. 17, 4). When Jesus announces his passion for the second time, Matthew (17, 23) no longer says that "they did not understand what he said" (Mark 9, 32). In Matthew's version, the disciples are not amazed to hear that it will be hard for the wealthy to enter the kingdom of God (Mark 10, 24 and Matt. 19, 23).

Matthew thus profoundly alters the character of the gospel of Mark. Since the relationship of Jesus with his disciples is not disturbed by bewilderment and lack of faith to the extent it is in Mark, there is room for development of the faith assumed to be present in the disciples. This Matthew achieves by his extensive instructions on how to live a Christian life, as in the Sermon on the Mount. The disciples are not simply sent out, but they are told what is expected of them, how they should behave and what fate awaits them (Matt. 10, 1-42). The sermon on the last things is followed by some parables, such as the parable of the wise and the foolish virgins and that of the talents (25, 1-30), which give to Christians a practical indication of how they should conduct themselves while awaiting the Second Coming of Christ.

It is clear that this book was written with an eye to the church. Its contents are determined by the theological views of the church. This is especially true of those passages where the author points out that some event in the life of Jesus is a fulfilment of what is written in the Old Testament (1, 23; 2, 6-7; 2, 15; 2, 17-18; 2, 23; 4, 14-16; 8, 17; 12, 17-21; 13, 35; 21, 4-5; 27, 9-10). These "formula quotations" (in German "Reflexionszitate") are the expression of a church that saw its own already-existing faith reinforced and confirmed by the Old Testament. These quotations are probably derived from oral tradition. The same will have to be assumed with regard to Matthew's "own" material.

The author of this gospel is, therefore, a part of the Christian community. This community must have known the gospel of Mark as well as other written (Q) and oral traditions. The Old Testament was the Scripture which confirmed their belief in Jesus. The gospel of Matthew, using Mark as a basis, combines all this material into one whole.

c. *Destination*

As was noted above, the numerous quotations from the Old Testament are a characteristic feature of the gospel of Matthew. Even if these quotations form no conclusive proof for its origin in a Jewish-Christian community, there are other passages which indicate that both the author and the readers of this gospel still had relations with Judaism. The passage Matt. 17, 24-27, which is found only in Matthew, shows that the question of paying temple-tax was an important one for Christians. Pharisees and Scribes are reprimanded for their wide phylacteries (23, 5) and for the way they carry out the Law (23, 24). Christians are enjoined to be more righteous than is customary for the Pharisees (5, 17-20). Three classical Jewish works of righteousness are discussed in the Sermon on the Mount: giving alms, praying and fasting (6, 1-18). It is made emphatically clear that Jesus did not come to abolish the Law but to fulfil it (5, 17).

Other passages, however, show that the relations between Jews and Christians were not so close that they actually formed one group. The expression "your (or: their) synagogue" is continually used in this gospel (4, 23; 9, 35; 10, 17; 12, 9; 13, 54; 23, 34). The service of the temple is a thing of the past since the curtain was torn at the death of Christ (27, 51). Certain remarks even indicate a rejection of the people of Israel: "those who were born to the kingdom will be driven out" (8, 2); "the kingdom of God will be taken away from you, and given to a nation that yields the proper fruit" (21, 43); the blood of Christ is on the Jews (27, 25).

If this is a Jewish-Christian community, it apparently leads an existence quite separate from the Jewish people. It is doubtful, however, whether this community is an exclusively Jewish-Christian one. There are some striking universalistic passages: "this gospel will be proclaimed throughout the earth as a testimony to all nations" (24, 14), "make all nations my disciples" (28, 19). Obviously the church is regarded as a world-wide community. But this gospel also contains the sharpest attacks on the "heathens" (7, 6; 5, 47; 6, 7; 10, 5, 18; 12, 18; 18, 17; 24, 9; 24, 14; 25, 32).

This leads us to suppose that the author and readers of this gospel lived in an environment where the church was regarded as a community of people of Jewish and heathen origin. These people, however, had regular connections with the Jews among whom they lived and from whom they derived their members.

d. *Author*

Tradition, with Papias as the earliest witness (see Appendix A) designates Matthew as the author. Matt. 9, 9 mentions a tax-gatherer called Matthew, who follows Jesus. The parallel text of Mark 2, 14, however, mentions a man called Levi, son of Alphaeus, while Luke 5, 27 speaks of Levi the tax-gatherer. The lists of apostles also include a Matthew (Matt. 10, 3-4/Luke 6, 14-16/Mark 3, 17-19/Acts 1, 13). These also mention a son of Alphaeus called James. It is not possible to provide a satisfactory answer to the questions that arise from these variations. Why does Matt. change the name of Levi into Matthew? Is Matthew (or Levi) the tax-gatherer the same man as the disciple mentioned in the lists? What is the connection between James, son of Alphaeus, and Levi, son of Alphaeus?

Whatever the true facts may have been, according to tradition the evangelist, the disciple and the tax-gatherer are one and the same person. According to the same tradition, this gospel was originally written in Hebrew, which is, however, certainly not true of the book now known as the gospel of Matthew.

This fact places Matthew's authorship in grave doubt. On the other hand we may safely assume that in the environment where this gospel was written Matthew the apostle was highly esteemed. Possibly he even had a personal influence in these circles.

Although many questions concerning the author and the authorship of this gospel remain undecided, they are not really important for us at the present moment. For none of the other gospels bear less the personal imprint of their authors than does this one. We saw that the book was written for the church community, which really means that it also proceeded from this community. The study of the scriptures is no private matter but takes place in the community; similarly, the ethics were not drawn up by any single person but evolved from the life of the community. What we find in Matthew, therefore, is a reflection of the views and beliefs existing in a particular community.

e. *Place and time of origin*

The contents of this gospel allow no decisive answer to the question of its place of origin. Since the environment appears to have been Jewish, Antioch or some place near Antioch would seem likely.

In view of the fact that the author made use of the gospel of Mark, we must assume the gospel of Matthew to have been written after A.D. 60. A date sometime after A.D. 70 seems most plausible, for in 22, 7 it is said that the king will "set their town on fire". This comparatively late date is confirmed by the fact that the author appears to be unfamiliar with the details of life in Palestine at the time of Jesus. In the gospel of Luke we find the sayings of Jesus addressed on the one hand to the Scribes (Luke 11, 45, 46 and 52) and on the other hand to the Pharisees (Luke 11, 39, 42, 43-44). In Matthew's text they are addressed to both Scribes and Pharisees (Matt. 23, 13, 15, 23, 25, 27, 29). This shows either that the author

did not know the exact difference between these two groups or else
that this difference was no longer significant in his time. [1]

7. LUKE

a. *Contents*

The contents of the gospel of Luke are to a large extent the
same as those of Mark and Matthew. The main difference between
Luke and the other two lies in the fact that Luke inserts a large
proportion of his "own" material together with material derived
from Q in his extensive narrative of Jesus' journey from Galilee
to Jerusalem.

The prologue (1, 1-4) is followed by the accounts of the birth of
John the baptist and of Jesus (1, 5-2, 20). Luke then relates some
stories of Jesus' childhood (2, 21-52). The ministry of John the
Baptist, the Baptism of Jesus and the temptation in the desert
(3, 1-4, 13) are interrupted by a genealogy of Jesus (3, 23-38).

Jesus' first teaching takes place in the synagogue of Nazareth
(4, 14-30), in Capernaum (4, 31-41) and "in the synagogues of
Judaea" (4, 42-44).

The calling of some disciples by the Lake of Gennesaret (5, 1-11)
is followed by healings (5, 12-26), the calling of Levi (5, 27-32) and
conflicts with the Jews (5, 33-6, 11).

The names of the twelve disciples are given (6, 12-19) and Jesus
teaches them (6, 20-49).

Two healings are described in 7, 1-17. Then comes a passage
concerning the relation between Jesus and John the Baptist
(7, 18-35). In 7, 36-50 we are told how Jesus is anointed by a sinful
woman. Of the short pericopes that follow as far as 9, 17, some
are found also in Mark and some are only found in Luke. Among
those that are also present in Mark are the parable of the sower
(8, 4-15), the pericope about true listening (8, 16-18), the storm on
the lake (8, 22-25), the passage about the daughter of Jairus
(8, 40-56) and the feeding of the five thousand (9, 10-17).
Peculiar to Luke is, for instance, the passage about Jesus and the
women in 8, 1-3.

---

[1] A. F. J. Klijn, „Scribes, Pharisees, Highpriests and Elders in the New
Testament", in: *Nov. Test.* 3 1959, p. 259-267.

The confession of Peter and the transfiguration on the mountain (9, 18-36) are a climax in this gospel. After another healing and some discussions we are told that Jesus sets out for Jerusalem (9, 51). From here onwards the narrative consists mainly of sayings of Jesus, discussions and parables. To a large extent these may also be found in Matthew. There are some important passages, however, which are found only in Luke. These include the parable of the good Samaritan (10, 25-37), the story of Mary and Martha (10, 38-42), the parable of the foolish rich man (12, 31-21), the passage about the eighteen Galileans murdered by Pilate (13, 1-5), the parable of the barren fig-tree (13, 6-9), two healings on the sabbath (13, 10-17 and 14, 1-6), the parables of the lost silver piece, of the prodigal son (15, 8-32), of the dishonest bailiff (16, 1-9) and of the rich man and poor Lazarus (16, 19-31), the healing of ten lepers (17, 11-19), the parable of the unjust judge (18, 1-8), and the conversion of Zacchaeus (19, 1-10).

Beginning with 19, 28, the entry into Jerusalem, Luke continues with the same narrative as Mark and Matthew. We have already noted above a few details in which Luke's passion narrative differs from the other two synoptic gospels.

b. *Nature*

In a prologue composed in very good Greek the author gives a summary of his intentions. He tells us that many have tried to set down in writing what "happened among us", following the traditions handed down by the original eyewitnesses and servants of the Gospel. Now he too will write this down in the form of an ordered narrative for a certain Theophilus, who is unknown to us. Before writing his book he went over all the sources again to ascertain their authenticity.

In Acts, 1, 1-5, the author gives, again for Theophilus' benefit, a short summary of the gospel. This summary has the form that is usual in classical literature whenever a book consists of more than one volume. It appears, therefore, that the gospel and the Acts together formed one work which was, for technical reasons, published in two volumes. And so in determining the nature of the gospel

we shall have to take the book of Acts into account. Compared with Mark, whom he used as a source, this author wrote
a far more extensive work. It covers a period of time beginning
with the birth of John the Baptist and ending with the preaching
of the gospel in Rome. This is not quite true, however, for the
real break in the history of salvation comes with the beginning of
Jesus' ministry. The author deliberately brings the period of
John the Baptist to a close in 3, 20 by saying, at this early stage,
that John has been put in prison. "Until John, it was the Law
and the prophets; since then, there is the preaching of the gospel"
(Luke, 16, 16). This gospel manifests itself in the person of Jesus
Christ and in the preaching of the primitive church in Jerusalem.

Since the author of Luke-Acts described the effects of Jesus'
work in the primitive church, he did not need, like Matthew, to
actualize Jesus' preaching. For this reason Luke is more of an
historian than the other evangelists. It is as an historian, in fact, that
he presents himself in the prologue of Luke 1, 1-4. We must keep in
mind, however, that the material that was used by the author was
not to serve a biographical purpose. As we have said above, this
material served the preaching of the gospel in the widest possible
sense.

In writing this book the author kept in view the geographical
object of the gospel, Rome. As a result, we continually find
allusions to the mission to the heathen. The genealogy of
Jesus, the Son of God, is taken right back to Adam, the Son of
God (3, 23-28). The birth of Jesus is placed in the reign of emperor
Augustus (2, 1). In addition to the twelve disciples that are sent
out (9, 1-6) another 70 (or 72), probably symbolizing the 70 nations
of the world (cf. Genesis 10), are sent out in Luke 10, 1-20.

Since the author viewed his material as an historian he was
concerned not only with the heathen, for whom the gospel is
ultimately meant, but also with the Jews among whom Jesus
was born. The author emphatically insists that Jesus came for
the Jewish people: "He has ranged himself at the side of Israel
his servant . . ." (1, 54), "he would deal mercifully with our fathers,
calling to mind his solemn covenant . . ." (1, 72-73); ". . . I have

good news for you: there is great joy coming to the whole people . . ."
(2, 10). But we are shown, repeatedly, how Israel rejects the
Messiah. In the parable of the talents (19, 11-27) it is said that the
"citizens" do not want their lord to be king over them. As a result,
this gospel predicts in an extraordinarily severe manner the judgment on Israel (13, 22-30; 13, 34-45; 19, 39-44). This is corroborated
by the contents of Acts, where the question of the relations between
Jesus, Jews and heathens, is continually raised.

The way in which the life of Jesus is given a place in the history
of salvation, therefore, is characteristic of this gospel. This historical
setting goes side by side with the geographical framework in which
Jesus' life is placed by the gospel of Mark which Luke used as a
source. Jesus' ministry can no longer be divided into one part
taking place in Galilee and another part in Judaea. Right from the
beginning Luke has the whole land of the Jews in view. Jesus
preaches in the synagogues of Judaea (4, 44); people come to Jesus
from Galilee, Judaea and Jerusalem (5, 17); after he has raised a boy
in Nain, the story of what he has done runs through all Judaea
(7, 17); Pilate is told that Jesus is sowing unrest among the
people by his teaching in the whole of Judaea, beginning in Galilee
(23, 5). So, when Jesus goes south, his journey leads not to Judaea
(Mark 10, 1/Matt. 19, 1) but to Jerusalem (Luke 9, 51). In Jerusalem, the heart of the Land of the Jews, the fate of the Jews is to be
decided. In contrast to Jerusalem there is Rome, the heart of the
heathen world. These two cities represent stages in the history of
God and the world.

Thus we see that this gospel, however faithfully it reproduces
its sources, has a character of its own.

c. *Sources*

Since more than one third of the material in this gospel is not
found in any of the other gospels, we may conclude that the author
drew on a rich source of tradition. It has even been suggested
that this source alone contained sufficient material to com-
pose a gospel. Material from Mark would later have been added
to this so-called proto-Luke. According to this view, these "blocks"

of material from Mark would then consist of Mark 1, 21-3, 6/Luke 4, 31-6, 11; Mark 4, 1-9, 40/Luke 8, 4-9, 50; Mark 10, 13-52/Luke 18, 15-43 and Mark 11, 1-14, 16/Luke 19, 28-22, 13 [1]. There is little evidence, however, to support this supposition. When the passages from Mark are omitted, the remaining gospel does present a "life of Jesus" but relates hardly any of his miracles. In the second place, it is evident that the gospel of Mark served as a framework into which the other material was inserted. This latter observation is confirmed by the fact that in the two instances where Luke follows Q and his own source only (6, 20-8, 3 and 9, 51-18, 14) he leaves out two passages from Mark (3, 20-30 and 9, 42-10, 12).

Of far more importance than the supposed proto-Luke, for which very few supporters are still to be found, is the question whether Luke used another source besides Mark in the passion narrative. We have already noted peculiar differences between Luke on the one hand and Mark and Matthew on the other. Some instances of transposition were pointed out above. Equally important in this respect are certain additions: the two swords (22, 35-38) and Jesus before Herod (23, 6-16). We may also regard as additions the special ways in which Peter's denial is announced (22, 31-34) and the institution of the Lord's Supper is described (22, 15-20). Although we cannot conclude with any certainty that Luke knew a complete passion narrative besides that of Mark, we can at any rate be certain that he drew on traditions that went back to a source we no longer possess. It remains remarkable, moreover, that Luke keeps diverging from Mark here, in contrast to his usual procedure [2].

If Luke's passion narrative presents a problem, his narrative of the births of John and Jesus in chapters 1 and 2 is no less of a mystery. In the whole of the New Testament there is no passage of a similar length containing so many hebraisms. We may wonder

---

[1] See J. Jeremias, *Die Abendmahlsworte Jesu*, Göttingen 1960³, p. 92.

[2] Deviations go back to Luke according to J. Finegan, *Die Überlieferung der Leidens- und Auferstehungsgeschichte Jesu*, in: *Beih. Zeitschr. neut. Wissensch.* 15 1934. Luke used an extra source according to J. B. Tyson, "The Lukan Version of the Trial of Jesus", in: *Nov. Test.* 3 1959, p. 249-258 and F. Rehkopf, *Die Lukanische Sonderquelle*, in: *Wissensch. Unters. z. N. T.* 5 1959.

whether this passage was translated from a Hebrew (or Aramaic) original, or whether it was perhaps deliberately written in the style of the Greek version of the Old Testament. [1] Even then we still face the problem of the origin of these traditions. They may well at least in part be derived from circles going back to the group of disciples that had gathered around John the Baptist. Quite apart from this, it is remarkable how closely the style of this gospel approaches the Hebrew. So closely, in fact, and particularly in those passages that are peculiar to Luke, that some scholars have been led to suppose that Luke drew on a source that was in any case not far distant from the Christian community in Jerusalem. [2] Additional evidence for this assumption might be found in the fact that this particular gospel places special emphasis on the privilege of the poor (cf. 4, 18; 6, 20; 14, 13; 14, 21; 18, 22; 19, 8 and 21, 2). We know that the church in Jerusalem was conspicuous for its poverty (cf. Acts 2, 45; Rom. 15, 26; II Cor. 9, 1 and 9; Gal. 2, 10).

And so there is as yet little agreement on the subject of Luke's sources.

d. *Author*

Ever since Canon Muratori (see Appendix E) tradition has designated Luke as the author of this gospel. This Luke is known as Paul's companion in Col. 4, 14, Philem. 24 (and II Tim. 4, 11). According to Eusebius, *H.E.* III 4 6, Luke came from Antioch. As a curious variant in Acts, 11, 28, the text of D reads: "When we had gathered (in Antioch) . . ." Possibly, however, this variant was inspired by traditions such as are related by Eusebius.

There are few factual objections to Luke's authorship. It is

---

[1] Cf. P. WINTER, "Some Remarks on the Language of the Birth and Infancy Stories in the third Gospel", in: *New Test. Stud.* 1 1954/55, p. 111-121; N. TURNER, "The Relation of Luke I and II to Hebraic Sources and to the Rest of Luke-Acts", in: *New Test. Stud.* 2 1955/56, p. 100-109 and P. WINTER, "On Luke and Lucan Sources, a Reply to the Rev. N. Turner", in: *Zeitschr. Neut. Wissensch.* 47 1956, p. 217-242.

[2] Cf. E. SCHWEIZER, in: *Theol. Zeitschr.* 4 1948, p. 469-471; 5 1949, p. 231-233 and 6 1950, p. 161-185 and J. JEREMIAS in 5 1949, p. 228-231, but also H. F. D. SPARKS, "The Semitisms of St. Luke's Gospel", in: *Journ. Theol. Stud.* 44 1943, p. 129-138.

true that much depends on our evaluation of the so-called "we" passages in Acts (see below, Ch. IV). But the fact that Luke was a heathen Christian and not one of the apostles does not in itself make the tradition of his authorship unacceptable.

e. *Place and time of origin*

The gospel is generally believed to have been written after the destruction of Jerusalem (cf. Luke 19, 39-44). This would mean that it was written around A.D. 80.

Not much can be said about a possible place of origin. We should expect the Christian community of such a place to have been mainly of heathen extraction. In addition it must be a place where the gospel of Mark was known. Caesarea would perhaps satisfy these conditions, but Rome is also a possibility.

8. SUMMARY

In these gospels and the gospel of John we find four different ways of relating the "life of Jesus". These books show us that there existed a certain, limited number of traditions concerning Jesus' work. This argues in favour of the reliability of these traditions. It is remarkable that these traditions showed no tendency to develop into legends of a miraculous character. We may note, in this connection, that there is no evidence of any desire to multiply the number of miracles performed by Jesus. Development of tradition took place in the theological field. It should also be pointed out that the "life of Jesus", that is its historical side, presented a problem. The past had to be made relevant to the present. Mark is the one who takes this problem least into account. This depends, however, on our evaluation of the so-called "Messianic secret". If Mark's approach to the life of Jesus was really inspired by his experience that the preaching of the gospel did not succeed in making everyone a believer, then Mark also actualized his story in a way. Actualization of Jesus' life is most clearly discernible in Matthew. He repeatedly shifts the setting of certain past happenings to the present church. This has the disadvantage of practically turning past into present. It is a justifiable procedure, however, in that the church was not concerned with an historical personage, but with someone who was with the church "always till the end of the world" (Matt. 28, 20). Luke, again, places Jesus in an historical setting. He can do so, however, only by adding the Acts of the Apostles in which he shows that the history of Jesus is presupposed by the existence of the church. In conclusion we may make some observations about the gospel of John. As we shall see, John also wrote history, but by adding an extra dimension actualized it. Miracles are not mere historical happenings, they are signs of something that is of all times. "Reality" lies behind the veil of temporality.

It is evident that each gospel should be explained in relation to the intention with which it was written. In dealing with parallel pericopes we should realize that they are parallel only on purely literary grounds.

From a theological point of view each pericope in each separate gospel has its own place in the totality. It is this place which determines the explication that should be given for each pericope.

CHAPTER THREE

THE GOSPEL OF JOHN

1. Contents

No satisfactory division of this gospel is possible. The various happenings are situated in a particular place or occur at the time of some Jewish feast. For this reason place and time of occurrence are added in each case in the following table of contents.

Unbelief and doubt in Galilee and among the brothers of Jesus; Peter's confession 6, 60-7, 9.

Jesus goes to Jerusalem for the Feast of Tabernacles and asks for a fair judgment 7, 10-36.

Discourse on "whoever is thirsty, let him come to me" 7, 37-44.

Nicodemus defends Jesus 7, 45-52.

The woman caught in adultery 7, 53, 8-11.

Discourse of Jesus on "I am the light of the world" 8, 12-20.

Controversy with the Jews leading to the discourse "You belong to this world below, I to the world above" 8, 21-59.

Healing on the sabbath of a man born blind 9, 1-41.

Discourse on "The good shepherd" 10, 1-21.

At the festival of the Dedication of the Temple an attempt is made to stone Jesus 10, 22-39.

Departure of Jesus to the other side of the Jordan 10, 40-42.

Before the Jewish Passover: raising of Lazarus at Bethany and decision by the leaders of the people to have Jesus put to death 10, 40-57.

At Bethany Jesus is anointed 12, 1-11.

Entry into Jerusalem 12, 12-19.

Jesus announces his death because the people are obdurate 12,20-50.

Jesus washes the disciples' feet 13, 1-20.

Jesus is warned 13, 21-30.

Words of parting and warning to Peter 13, 31-38.

Promises for the future; the Comforter 14, 1-31.

About the "real vine" 15, 1-8.

The hate of the world and the appeal to persevere 15, 18-16, 4.

The Spirit of truth 16, 5-15.

"High-Priestly prayer" 17, 1-26.

Arrest of Jesus and interrogation by the High Priest 18, 1-27.

Before Pilate 18, 28-19, 15.

The crucifixion 19, 16-37.

The burial 19, 38-42.

The resurrection, appearances and first conclusion 20, 1-31.

Appearances by the Sea of Tiberias and second conclusion 21, 1-25.

2. Comparison with the Synoptic Gospels

a. *Differences*

In the synoptic gospels Jesus at first stays in Galilee, after which he goes to Jerusalem to celebrate the Passover and dies there. His ministry, therefore, can have covered a period of no more than one year, of which his stay at Jerusalem occupies only one week. The gospel of John mentions two Passover feasts (2, 13 and 11, 55), while the "festival" in 5, 1 is also often regarded as a Passover. This means that Jesus' ministry extended over at least two years. When Jesus comes to Jerusalem for the last time he celebrates the festival of Tabernacles (7, 10) and the festival of Dedication (10, 22). On the feast of the Passover he dies. This means that he was in Jerusalem for the last six months of his life.

Instead of the sayings that are characteristic of Jesus in the synoptic gospels, the gospel of John has long discourses on certain themes (Chs. 4; 5; 6; 9; 11: 17).

Parables such as are given in the synoptic gospels are not found here. We do, however, find metaphors "I am the good shepherd" (10, 11), "I am the door of the sheepfold" (10, 7), "I am the true vine" (15, 1), and "I am the bread of life" (6, 48).

The gospel of John contains certain events not mentioned in the other gospels: the changing of water into wine at the wedding at Cana (2, 1-11), the healing of a paralytic at Bethesda (5, 1-9), the healing of a man born blind (9, 1-7), the raising of Lazarus (11, 43-44), and conversations with Nicodemus (3, 1-21) and the Samaritan woman (4, 1-42).

b. *Similarities*

The similarities between the synoptic gospels and the gospel of John are the following:

The ministry of John the Baptist (1, 19-28),—but in this gospel it is John who bears witness to Jesus and designates him as the Messiah.

Calling of the disciples (1, 35-52), in which Nathanael plays a part not found in the synoptic gospels.

Cleansing of the temple (2, 13-25); here at the beginning of Jesus' ministry and not in the passion week.

Healing of the son of an official (4, 46-54), related to Luke 7, 1-10 which, however, tells of the healing of a servant.

Feeding of the five thousand (6, 1-15).

Jesus walks on the lake (6, 16-21).

Peter's confession (6, 67-71).

Unbelief of Jesus' brothers (7, 1-9).

Jesus anointed at Bethany (12, 1-11) by Mary, the sister of Martha. These two are also mentioned as sisters in Luke 10, 38-42.

Entry into Jerusalem (12, 12-19).

Warning to Judas (13, 21-30).

Warning to Peter (13, 36-38).

In the passion narrative the gospel shows great similarity to the synoptic gospels (from 18, 1 onwards). There are some deviations, however:

There is no institution of the Lord's supper.

The prayer at Gethsemane is not mentioned.

No interrogation by the Sanhedrin, but by Annas and Caiaphas.

Jesus is shown to the people by Pilate with the words "Behold the Man".

The breaking of Jesus' bones.

The part played by Nicodemus at the burial.

The appearances also bear some resemblance to those in the synoptic gospels, but the appearances to Thomas and those by the Sea of Tiberias (Ch. 21) are found only in the gospel of John.

As we said above, the discourses of Jesus are characteristic of this gospel. These contain, however, a large number of sayings that are also to be found in the synoptic gospels

2, 19: Destroy this temple . . . . . . Mark 14, 58 and parallels.

3, 3: On being born again, Matt. 18, 3.

3, 35: The Father loves the Son, Matt. 11, 27.

4, 44: A prophet is not honoured in his own country, Mark 6, 4 and parallels.

13, 20: He who receives any messenger of mine receives me, Matt. 10, 40.

15, 20: A servant is not greater than his master, Matt. 10, 24 and parallels.

16, 23: Ask and you will receive, Matt. 7, 7.

18, 11: Sheathe your sword, Mark 14, 36 and parallels.

20, 23: If you forgive any man's sins, they will be forgiven, Matt. 18, 18.

3. Interpolations, Transpositions and Sources

In addition to the variants where some word is added, left out or changed, there are two extensive additions to the text which have found their way into modern translations. The first of these is found in 5, 3b-4: . . . ἐκδεχομένων τὴν τοῦ ὕδατος κίνησιν. ἄγγελος γὰρ κυρίου κατὰ καιρὸν κατέβαινεν ἐν τῇ κολυμβήθρᾳ καὶ ἐτάρασσε τὸ ὕδωρ· ὁ ουν πρῶτος ἐμβὰς μετὰ τὴν ταραχὴν τοῦ ὕδατος ὑγιὴς ἐγίνετο, ᾧ δήποτε κατείχετο νοσήματι.

This passage occurs in L, K A Θ pl. it vg [cl] sy[p] Tert. The healing virtue of the water is here ascribed to an angel's doing. This is an old gloss, possibly at first placed in the margin and later included in the text.

The second addition is in 7, 53-8, 11, the long passage about the woman detected in adultery, in K D pm. b c e ff² f vg sy[pal]. The same passage is found in different places: after 7, 36 in 225, after 21, 24 in 1 and others and after Luke 21, 38 in fam. 13. The story in question is a very old one; Eusebius says that it was known to Papias (*H.E.* III 39 17):

. . . ἐκτέθειται δὲ καὶ ἄλλην ἱστορίαν περὶ γυναικὸς ἐπὶ πολλαῖς ἁμαρτίαις διαβληθείσης ἐπὶ τοῦ κυρίου, ἣν τὸ καθ' Ἑβραίους εὐαγγέλιον περιέχει.	(Papias . . .) also gave another story about the woman who was accused to the Lord of many sins, as is told in the gospel of the Hebrews.

And so it is plain that the story originated in Jewish-Christian circles. This is confirmed by the fact that this story is used in the *Constitutiones Apostolicae* II 24 and in the Syrian *Didascalia 7*, both of which contain other evidence as well of having been influenced by Jewish-Christian ideas. This story, which appears to have been circulating among certain groups, was given a place in the gospel of John by some copyist or other. [1]

In this connection we may finally mention ch. 21. This passage is indeed found in all the manuscripts, but the contents indicate that it must have been added at a later date by someone other than the author of chs. 1-20. This conclusion is based on the fact that 20, 30-31 is obviously intended as a conclusion to the gospel and that 21, 24 was written by someone who recommends the author of the preceding chapters. The reasons for this addition will be discussed later.

Many who have studied the gospel of John have supposed that the present order is not the original one. Indeed the transference of some passages to a different context does eliminate abrupt transitions. One such transposition is supported by manuscript evidence. The passage in question is 18, 12-27, which occurs in sy[s] in the order: 12-13, 24, 14-15, 19-23, 16-18 and 25-27. In the latter case the narrative runs as follows: Jesus is taken to Annas (12-13). Annas sends Jesus to Caiaphas (24), Peter follows Jesus there (14-15), Caiaphas interrogates Jesus (19-23), Peter betrays his Lord (16-18 and 25-27).

Another well known transposition is the placing of ch. 6 between chs. 4 and 5. The narrative at present goes thus: Jesus goes from Judaea to Galilee by way of Samaria (4, 1-4), he travels to Jerusalem (5, 1) and crosses the Sea of Tiberias (6, 1). This would become: Jesus goes to Galilee (up to 4, 54), he crosses the lake (6, 1) and goes to Jerusalem (5, 1). This transposition is found as early as the Diatessaron of Tatian.

Other such transpositions are: 3, 22-30 and 2, 12 (connecting Capernaum in 2, 12 and Jerusalem in 2, 13) and 7, 15-24 after 5, 47.[2]

It is very hard to judge whether these transpositions are warranted. It is quite possible, of course, that loose leaves of papyrus

---

[1] I. BECKER, *Jesus und die Ehebrecherin*, in: *Beih. Zeitschr. neut. Wissensch.* 28 1963.

[2] Cf. C. K. BARRETT, *The Gospel according to St. John*, London 1956, p. 18-21.

got into disorder. In such considerations, however, we are led by the assumption that this gospel was intended as a finished narrative in both a topographical and a literary respect. And this is just the point. The work is built up around a number of particular events, such as a healing or a certain Jewish feast, or a given theme such as the discourse about the good shepherd. The suggested transpositions are, whether consciously or unconsciously, based on the geographical pattern of the synoptic gospels. For a right understanding of this gospel, therefore, it is better to leave the sometimes abrupt transitions intact.

As in the case of the synoptic gospels, the question arises what sources were used by the author. In the first place we may think of the synoptic gospels. Of these, Mark seems the most likely source. In this connection some people have pointed out a parallel series of events in Mark and John:

John 1, 19-36: The ministry of John the Baptist, Mark 1, 4-8.
    4, 3 3 : Departure for Galilee, Mark 1, 14.
    6, 1-13 : Miraculous feeding of the 5,000, Mark 6, 34-44.
    6, 16-21: Jesus on the lake, Mark 6, 45-52.
    6, 68-69: Peter's confession, Mark 8, 29.
    7, 10-14: Jesus goes to Jerusalem, Mark 9, 30.

However it is doubtful whether this identical order is in fact a result of the use of Mark by the author of John. The only really remarkable similarity is in the order — the feeding, Jesus on the lake and the confession of Peter. Tradition may have grouped these three together at quite an early date. Now that our attention has been drawn to the way stories of Jesus' life were employed for purposes of preaching in the church, the use of data derived from tradition seems very probable.

This would also explain some striking instances of similarity to the gospel of Luke. We may mention as the first of these the anointing in John 12, 1-8. Unlike Matthew and Mark, Luke also speaks of Jesus' feet being moistened and afterwards dried with the woman's hair. In John, this all takes place at the house of Lazarus, Martha and Mary. Mary and Martha are mentioned also in Luke 10,

38-42. Another instance of agreement between John and Luke is found in John 4, 46-54 and Luke 7, 1-10: the healing of the son (Luke: servant) of an official. Finally, there is a remarkable resemblance to the passion narrative as told by Luke, which deviates from that of the other synoptic gospels on a number of points. Points of similarity in this case are the statement that it was Satan who drove Judas to his betrayal (Luke 22, 3 and John 13, 2 and 27), the warning to Peter during the meal and not afterwards (Luke 22, 31-34 and John 18, 36-38), the cutting off of the right ear of the high priest's servant (Luke 22, 50 and John 18, 10), and the fact that Jesus' interrogation takes place in the house of the high priest and not before the Sanhedrin (Luke 22, 54 and John 18, 12-13). Finally, both gospels say that there were two angels present at the grave after the resurrection (Luke 24, 4 and John 20, 12).

These similarities are not to be explained by assuming that John used Luke as a source. The solution must once more be sought in the use of similar traditions.

In addition to using the synoptic gospels, the author of John has also been supposed to have drawn on a "sign-source". This source is thought to have enumerated the signs that should lead to faith, but which the Jews did not appreciate at their true significance. Remmants of this source, it is said, are to be found in 2, 11: "This deed . . . is the first of the signs . . ."; 4, 54: "This was now the second sign . . . ."; and 12, 37: "In spite of the many signs which Jesus had performed in their presence they would not believe in him . . . .". The conclusion of this gospel is also said to derive from this source: "There were indeed many other signs that Jesus performed in the presence of his disciples . . ." (20, 30). Other passages mentioning "signs" are found in 2, 11; 2, 18; 2, 23; 3, 2; 6, 2. 14. 26. 30; 7, 31; 9, 16; 10, 41; 11, 47; 12, 18.

Besides this "sign-source", the author is thought to have used another one: a "discourse source". This source is supposed to have contained the many discourses found in this gospel. [1]

---

[1] Cf. R. BULTMANN, "Johannesevangelium", in: Rel. in Gesch. u. Gegenwart III 1959, c. 840-851.

The trouble with accepting two sources is that this gospel has a uniform style which gives no indication of any use of sources. The "discourse source" theory, therefore, has found very little favour. This uniformity of style is, of course, equally an obstacle to the theory of a "sign-source". If he used such a source at all, the author must have thoroughly rewritten the material he derived from it. [1]

In this connection we may finally mention the part played by a possible editor. It will not do to deny this possibility without further investigation. Chapter 21, at least, was added by someone other than the author of chs. 1-20. It is hard to say, however, where the hand of a editor might be detected. Some regard as editorial additions the numerous short remarks that are found throughout the gospel as a sort of commentary (2, 21-22; 4, 2; 3, 24 and other; see also below). The editor is also sometimes held responsible for certain supposed irregularities in this gospel. For example, he is thought to have added some passages that mention a future eschatology (5, 28-29; 6, 39-40; 12, 48). Such theories, however, are based on a preconceived opinion concerning the theology of the gospel of John before which all contrary indications must yield.

Research into the sources of this gospel has therefore certainly not resulted in universally accepted hypotheses. The great obstacle continually proves to be the uniformity in the use of words and in matters of style generally, as well as the similar trains of thought.

These considerations do not, however, exclude the possibility of sources. The author depended, in any case, on traditional material, but he assimilated this to such an extent that the transition from traditional material to the author's own thoughts can no longer be detected. This is an author with very definite ideas of his own.

---

[1] Cf. E. Ruckenstuhl, *Die literarische Einheit des Johannesevangeliums*, Freiburg 1951, B. Noack, *Zur johanneischen Tradition*, Kopenhagen 1951 and D. Moody Smith, *The Composition and Order of the Fourth Gospel*, New Haven and London 1965.

[2] Cf. L. van Hartingsveld, *Die Eschatologie des Johannesevangeliums*, Assen 1962.

These ideas are however not only his, but also those of the circle to which he belonged, for chapter 21, which was written by a different hand, exhibits the same characteristics as the rest of this gospel.

4. NATURE

A characteristic feature of this gospel is the author's continually interrupting the narrative to insert his own comments, additions and explanations. Explanations are found in 2, 21-22 (the temple is his body); 4, 2 (Jesus himself was not baptizing); 7, 39 (the Spirit had not yet been given); 8, 20 (nobody seized him, for his hour had not come yet); 18, 9 (to fulfil a text of Scripture). We may regard as commentary: 2, 11 (the beginning of the signs); 2, 23-25 (Jesus knew the Jews); 3, 24 (John had not yet been thrown into prison); 4, 9 (Samaritans do not associate with Jews); 12, 6 (Judas was a thief). A few times it is emphatically stated that the author was an eyewitness to all this (1, 14 and 19, 35).

Another characteristic feature of this gospel is the fact that those who come into contact with Jesus continually fall victim to misunderstandings. They keep looking at the outside of things without seeing the truth. In 2, 20 the audience does not realize that Jesus is speaking of the temple of his body; in 3, 3 Nicodemus does not understand what it is "to be born over again"; in 4, 4 the Samaritan woman does not see that Jesus is talking about living water; in 8, 22 the Jews think when Jesus leaves that he is going to commit suicide; in 11, 13 people think that Lazarus is asleep when Jesus means to say he is dead, and in 13, 36-38 Peter does not understand the consequences of following Jesus.

Misunderstandings where Jesus is concerned are found particularly among the Jews. The latter are constantly placed opposite Jesus. They murmur disapprovingly when he speaks (6, 41); persecute him (5, 16); want to put him to death (5, 18 and 7, 1) and to stone him (10, 31-33 and 11, 8); do not believe him (9, 18); take him prisoner (18, 12) and hand him over to Pilate (18, 36). Jesus' followers also constantly have trouble with the Jews (7, 13; 9, 22 and 20, 19).

What is done by the Jews, however, is only a symptom of what is done by the "world". Jesus was sent into this world as a light (1, 9; 3, 19; 9, 5; 8, 12; 12, 46), but the world does not recognize him (1, 10), although he is its Saviour (4, 42). The world hates Jesus and those who follow him (15, 8).

This continual opposing of light and dark, truth and falsehood, Jews and Jesus and his followers, gives this gospel its own particular colour. The meeting of Jesus and the Jews results in a clash of two worlds which are totally different and which do not understand one another because they speak different languages. It is necessary to be born anew to share in the world of Jesus.

Attempts have been made to relate this antithetical way of thinking to all sorts of writings, such as the Dead Sea scrolls, Hermetic literature, the writings of Philo, and the Mandaean writings. [1] The resemblance to these writings is indeed striking in some instances, but it does not touch the core of the matter. Such similarities as there are, are mainly matters of terminology which go with the antithetical way of thinking that is present also in these writings. They must be explained as deriving from a Jewish-syncretic world which, however, accounts for the form rather than the content of the gospel of John.

5. Purpose

The purpose of this gospel is clearly stated in the first con-clusion: ". . . . . these (signs) are written that you may be-lieve that Jesus is the Christ and that believing you may have life in his name" (20, 30-31). The gospel is thus intended to convince the reader that Jesus is the Christ. This is a theme we continually meet in the Acts, when the Jews are addressed in the synagogue (cf. Acts 17, 2-3; 18, 5; 18, 28; 9, 20 and 22). In Acts it is the scriptures that serve this purpose,

---

[1] Cf. C. H. Dodd, *Interpretation of the Fourth Gospel*, Cambridge 1955, p. 10-30.

as they also do in this gospel (5, 39). But here further testimony
is added: the Samaritan woman (4, 39), the works of Jesus (5, 36
and 10, 25), the "Comforter" (15, 26), the eyewitness (19, 35), God
(5, 31 and 37; 8, 18).

It is beyond doubt that this preaching is addressed, among
others, to the Jews as in Acts also. This is evident not only from the
ever recurring conversations between Jesus and the Jews, but also
from the continual allusions to what will be the consequences
for the Jews if they believe in Jesus: they will be thrown out of the
synagogue (9, 22; 12, 42 and 16, 2). A number of places (7, 35;
10, 16; 11, 51-52 and 12, 20) which refer to the Dispersion and to
Jews living in the Dispersion, may indicate that the book is especially meant for them. [1]

In assuming that this book is intended as proof of the fact that
Jesus is the Christ, we should not overlook the evidence of the polemic
directed against certain movements which apparently also claimed
to bring salvation. In this connection it is interesting to note
that Irenaeus considered the gospel to be directed against the
followers of Cerinthus and Nicolaus, who represented gnostic
principles (adv. Haer III, 11, 1). The expression "The Word has
become flesh" (1, 14) and the fact that the author was an eyewitness
at Jesus' death (19, 33-35) suggest a refutation of those who thought
that Jesus was only "in appearance born" and "in appearance
died".

Also striking is the continual assurance that Jesus is the true
vine (15, 1), the true light (1, 9), and the true bread (6, 32), which
seems to indicate a rejection of a salvation which the author did not
consider to be "true". And in the discourse about the good shepherd
there are references to climbing in by some other way (10, 1),
to following a stranger (10, 4) and to persons who came before
Christ, who were thieves and robbers (10, 8).

It is also plain that the gospel is opposed to over-estima-
tion of John the Baptist. It is emphatically stated that
he is not the light (1, 8), that he is not the Christ (1, 20)

---

[1] See W. C. VAN UNNIK, "The Purpose of St. John's Gospel", in: Studia
Evangelica, in: Texte und Unters. 73 1959, p. 382-411.

and that when the followers of John fell into a dispute with the followers of Jesus, John testified that Jesus must grow greater and he must grow less (3, 22-26).

The preaching concerning Jesus who is the Christ thus appears to take place in a very special situation, where faith in Jesus was certainly not the only way to salvation being advocated.

In conclusion we may note an old notion, found as early as Clement of Alexandria (Eusebius, *H.E.* VI 14 7) according to which this is a "spiritual gospel" as opposed to the synoptic gospels which only write about the external facts (τὰ σωματικὰ). In other words: whatever its specific intention, this gospel was written to supplement the synoptic gospels.

This point of view presupposes that the author knew the synoptists. But this is doubtful. It does not, however, exclude the possibility that he knew traditions similar to those used by the synoptists. In that case it must be said that he deliberately gave this material a profounder meaning. The "signs" continually get an extra dimension. The resurrection of Lazarus points to "resurrection and life" (11, 25), the miraculous feeding to the true bread (6, 32), and the water that is drawn on the last day of the feast of Tabernacles stands for the Spirit (7, 39). This might be regarded as a supplementing of traditions that exclusively concern historical facts. Detached traditions concerning the life of Jesus are made into signs with a general, ever valid, meaning. This was not done deliberately, though. There is a very definite Johannine theology at the back of this interpretation.

6. AUTHOR

In the gospel itself the author's name is not mentioned. He represents himself as an eyewitness (1, 14) and in 21, 24 the person who is publishing the gospel writes that "it is this same disciple who attests what has here been written". He is referring to verse 20 which speaks of "the disciple whom Jesus loved". These are the same words that are used to describe a disciple of Jesus in a few other places (13, 23; 19, 26 and 20, 2). They are used to designate a particular disciple, who cannot be Peter, since the two are mentioned together in 20, 2. And so the possibilities are reduced to ten names if we leave out Judas Iscariot and assume the man in question to have been one of the twelve disciples. Of this we cannot be quite sure, however, since John uses the word "disciple" not solely to mean one of the twelve (4, 1; 6, 66).

Another difficulty is that we cannot be certain that the "we" of 21, 24 knew who this disciple was. Very likely they did, for their style of writing indicates a close connection with the circles in which this gospel was written. The only possibility that remains, in that case, is that in certain circles the expression: "the disciple whom Jesus loved" was so well known that no further indication of his name was necessary.

Did Irenaeus, perhaps through old traditions, know to whom this expression referred or was he relying on church traditions which were themselves based on a wish to attribute an apostolic origin to this gospel? Irenaeus says that it was written by John (Ir. *adv. Haer.* III 1 1, quoted by Eusebius, *H.E.* V 8 4):

ἔπειτα Ἰωάννης ὁ μαθητὴς τοῦ κυρίου, ὁ καὶ ἐπὶ τὸ στῆθος αὐτοῦ ἀναπεσών, καὶ αὐτὸς ἐξέδωκεν τὸ εὐαγγέλιον, ἐν Ἐφέσῳ τῆς Ἀσίας διατρίβων.	Subsequently a gospel was also published by John, the disciple of the Lord who rested at his bosom, when he was staying at Ephesus in Asia (Minor).

In any case the tradition is an old one, for it is also found in *Canon Muratori*. Eusebius, finally, tells us that Polycrates of Ephesus (c. 190) wrote in a letter to bishop Victor of Rome that the disciple who lay at Jesus' bosom was John (*H.E.* V 24 3). It is not necessary here to cite any more sources, since after A.D. 190 no one doubted John's authorship.

We must admit, however, that there are a number of difficulties attached to ascribing the gospel to John:

How can someone who is a Jew by birth write against the Jews in such a polemic fashion?

Why does a Jew of Palestine quote from the Greek version of the Old Testament?

May we suppose that a Galilean fisherman was capable of

acquiring the style and the language that are typical of syncretic Judaism in the Dispersion?

Before going into these questions any further, we must note another possible way of determining the authorship of this gospel.

There is such a close relationship between this gospel and the three Johannine letters that we may assume one author for all these writings. In II and III John, the author calls himself "elder" (πρεσβύτερος). "Elder" need not be a title of office and it may even refer to an apostle, as we see in I Peter 5, 1, where Peter calls himself a "fellow elder". Certain traditions, however, seem to indicate that there was a presbyter called John who was not the same man as the apostle. This elder would have lived at Ephesus.

Irenaeus tells us that Papias, bishop of Hierapolis, had met the disciple John (Ir., *adv. Haer.* V 33 4 and Eusebius, *H.E.* III 39 1). Eusebius doubts the truth of this assertion on the basis of Papias' own words, which he quotes (*H.E.* III 39 3-4):

οὐκ ὀκνήσω δέ σοι καὶ ὅσα ποτὲ παρὰ τῶν πρεσβυτέρων καλῶς ἔμαθον καὶ καλῶς ἐμνημόνευσα, συγκατατάξαι ταῖς ἑρμηνείαις, διαβεβαιούμενος ὑπὲρ αὐτῶν ἀλήθειαν. οὐ γὰρ τοῖς τὰ πολλὰ λέγουσιν ἔχαιρον ὥσπερ οἱ πολλοί, ἀλλὰ τοῖς τἀληθῆ διδάσκουσιν, οὐ δὲ τοῖς τὰς ἀλλοτρίας ἐντολὰς μνημονεύουσιν, ἀλλὰ τοῖς τὰς παρὰ τοῦ κυρίου τῇ πίστει δεδομένας καὶ ἀπ' αὐτῆς παραγινομένας τῆς ἀληθείας· εἰ δέ που καὶ παρηκολουθηκώς τις τοῖς πρεσβυτέροις ἔλθοι, τοὺς τῶν πρεσβυτέρων ἀνέκρινον λόγους, τί Ἀνδρέας ἢ τί Πέτρος εἶπεν ἢ τί Φίλιππος ἢ τί Θωμᾶς ἢ Ἰάκωβος ἢ τί Ἰωάννης ἢ Ματθαῖος ἢ τις ἕτερος τῶν τοῦ κυρίου μαθητῶν ἅ τε Ἀριστίων καὶ ὁ πρεσβύτερος Ἰωάννης τοῦ κυρίου μαθηταί, λέγουσιν· οὐ γὰρ τὰ ἐκ τῶν βιβλίων τοσοῦτόν με ὠφελεῖν ὑπελάμβανον ὅσον τὰ παρὰ ζώσης φωνῆς καὶ μενούσης.

I shall not hesitate to assemble for you exactly what I have learnt and remembered of the elders, and to add the explanations with which the truth may be confirmed. For I found no pleasure in those who speak much, as do most, but in those who taught the truth: and not in those who record strange commandments but in those who transmitted what the Lord showed us to keep and what arises from the truth itself. Whenever arrived a follower of the elders I would ask him about the words of the elders, what Andrew said, or Philip or Thomas or James or John or Matthew or another of the disciples of the Lord and what Aristion and the elder John say, for I considered that what was contained in the books could not profit me as much as the living word that endures (or: still exists).

Eusebius rightly infers from this that Papias is speaking of two persons by the name of John: one the disciple of the Lord and the other an elder, and that Papias only knew the latter. According to Eusebius this would confirm what some people say of two persons by the name of John who were both living at Ephesus and of two sepulchral monuments in Ephesus both bearing the name of John.

It is a very attractive solution, of course, to regard an otherwise unknown elder John as the author of the fourth gospel. But our very ignorance of this person constitutes an obstacle to such an assumption.

If this possibility is rejected, there remains only the choice between the apostle John and an unknown author. The arguments against John's authorship are indeed powerful, but they do not prove that John was not the most prominent figure in a community of Christians where this gospel originated.

7. TIME AND PLACE OF ORIGIN; DESTINATION

We know that the gospel was written before A.D. 120, for a piece of papyrus, dating from that year, has been found containing a few verses from the gospel of John (P[52]). [1]

Further determination of the date and the place of origin of this gospel will depend on our assumption concerning who was the author. If we regard the apostle John as the author, we will have to accept the traditions that connect John with the town of Ephesus (Irenaeus, *adv. Haer.* III 1 1, Eusebius *H.E.*; III 23 6; V 8 4; V 24 3). In that case we can hardly fix the date any later than A.D. 80.

If we do not accept these traditions, or not fully, we are obliged to rely on the data furnished by the gospel itself. These point to an environment where Jews play a rather prominent part. For this reason some have thought that this gospel originated in the Syrian-Palestine region. If so, the community which produced it must have led a rather secluded existence. This may be inferred from the great difference between this gospel on the one hand and the synoptic gospels and Paul on the other. Evidently this com-

---

[1] C. H. ROBERTS, "An unpublished Fragment of the Fourth Gospel in the John Ryland's Library", in: *Bull. of the John Ryl. Libr.* 20 1936, p. 45-55.

munity was dominated by a forceful personality. Either the disciple John was greatly admired by this group or it was he who laid the foundations for this community of Christians. [1]

In conclusion something may be said about the manner in which the work was published. It is a curious fact that someone at a later date added to this gospel a passage recommending it and adding that the author's testimony is true. He says, moreover, that the author is the one who is designated in the gospel as "the disciple whom Jesus loved". This indicates that the gospel is being recommended to certain persons outside the group in which it originated. In view of the fact that the last chapter especially mentions Peter and his appointment as shepherd of the church, we may suppose that this gospel was presented to a group of Christians who held Peter in special esteem. Chapter 20, 3-10 also mentions Peter and the disciple whom Jesus loved. It is quite possible, therefore, that it is the Johannine community which through this gospel presents itself to the outside world. Since Peter was held in particular esteem in Antioch, perhaps that is the place to which this gospel was addressed.

---

[1] Cf. J. A. T. Robinson, "The Destination and Purpose of St. John's Gospel", in: *New Test. Stud.* 6 1960, p. 117-131.

CHAPTER FOUR

THE ACTS OF THE APOSTLES

1. Contents

In 1, 8 the disciples receive Jesus' instruction to bear witness for him in Jerusalem, all over Judaea and Samaria and to the ends of the earth. The book may be more or less divided according to the preaching of the gospel in these various territories.

Chapter 1 harks back to the first part of this work, the gospel of Luke (1, 1-5). It relates the Ascension of Jesus and how Matthias was assigned the place of the twelfth apostle. Chapter 2 describes the descent of the Holy Spirit and Peter's speech.

After 2, 41 a number of events are described that take place in Jerusalem. Of these we may mention: the healing of a paralytic (3, 1-10), a speech by Peter (3, 11-26), Peter and John interrogated by the Sanhedrin (4, 1-31), the transgression of Ananias and Saphira (5, 1-11) and conflicts with the Jewish leaders (5, 17-42).

Events around the seven "hellenists", of whom Stephen is the most prominent, are recounted in 6, 1-8, 3. Stephen's speech and his death are described at length.

The episode in Samaria starts with 8, 4. Here Philip and Simon Magus play a part. The passage from 9, 1 to 9, 31 tells of the conversion of Paul. In 9, 32-43 we hear of Peter's activities in Joppa. An extensive account is given of the baptism of Cornelius by Peter (10, 1-11, 18). The proclamation of the gospel is extended to Cyprus and Antioch (11, 19-30). There follows a passage about the death of James, the imprisonment and liberation of Peter and the death of Herod (12, 1-23).

Beginning with 12, 24 the narrative continues with the ministry of Paul. From Antioch he goes by way of Cyprus to the southern part of Asia Minor, accompanied by Barnabas and John Mark (up to

14, 28). On his return to Antioch he is invited to come to Jerusalem to discuss with the disciples the question whether heathens who are converted ought to be circumcised (15, 1-21). Paul, Barnabas, Judas and Silas carry the decisions to Antioch and the southern part of Asia Minor (15, 22-16, 3). This is the beginning of Paul's second missionary journey which takes him and his companions to Macedonia, Athens, Corinth, Ephesus and back to Caesarea and Antioch (up to 18, 22).

From Antioch Paul starts on his third missionary journey (from 18, 23), which takes him by way of Asia Minor to Ephesus, Macedonia and Greece (up to 20, 2). He then travels back by way of Macedonia, stopping at Miletus to speak with the elders of Ephesus, and goes on to Caesarea and Jerusalem (21, 15).

In Jerusalem, Paul is arrested on the accusation of having taken a gentile into the temple (21, 17-39). Paul makes a speech before the Jews and appears before the Sanhedrin (21, 40-23, 11). When the Jews conspire to kill him, the authorities are obliged to transfer Paul to Caesarea (23, 12-35). There he appears before Felix and his successor Festus, in front of whom he appeals to the emperor (24, 1-25, 12). After a speech before king Agrippa (25, 13-26, 32) follows the journey to Rome. On the way they are shipwrecked on the island of Malta (27, 1-28, 10). The book ends with Paul's arrival in Rome and the information that he stays there for two years at his own expense.

2. NATURE

In our discussion of the gospel of Luke we saw that the Acts are the second part of a book that begins with the foretelling of the birth of John the Baptist in the temple of Jerusalem and ends with Paul preaching the gospel in Rome. The significance of Jerusalem and Rome as stages in the history of God and the world is thus made clear: the gospel must first be preached in Jerusalem (Luke 24, 47). This takes place at Pentecost. The gospel is to be carried to "the ends of the earth" (Acts 1, 8). The expression "the ends of the earth" is generally used for the world of the gentiles. This is evident from Acts 13, 47-48, where Paul in quoting Isa. 49, 6 "salvation to the

ends of the earth" is referring to the proclamation of the gospel to
the gentiles. As Jerusalem is the centre of judaism, so Rome is the
centre of the gentile world. The purpose which Jesus has set the
apostles is thus fulfilled when the gospel reaches Rome. While the
gospel is on its way to Rome, however, the Jewish people retain
their significance. "When God raised up his Servant, he sent him
to you (Jews) first . . . ." (Acts 3, 26). Everywhere the preaching is
first addressed to the Jews (Acts 13, 14; 14, 1; 17, 1-2; 18, 4; 19, 8
and 28, 23). It is "necessary that the word of God should be de-
clared to you (the Jews) first" (Acts 13, 46). When the gospel has
reached Rome, however, that is when the tidings of Jesus Christ
have been brought not only to the gentiles but also to the Jews
dispersed "to the ends of the earth", the moment has come to
draw up the balance of this preaching. It appears that the Jews have
everywhere rejected the Messiah, which confirms the words of
Isaiah (6, 9-10, in Acts 28, 26-27). Paul's conclusion is: "Therefore
take notice that this salvation of God has been sent to the gentiles:
the gentiles will listen" (Acts 28, 28). Thus the Jewish people appear
to have lost the first place which they used to occupy before
God. From now on God addresses Himself to Jews and gentiles alike.
Salvation has been transferred from Jerusalem, which has been
destroyed as Jesus predicted (cf. Luke 19, 39-44), to Rome, that is,
from Jews to gentiles. What happened in fact — the development of a
community consisting of Jews into a church of which the majority of
members were of gentile origin, is given an explanation in terms of
"Heilsgeschichte" in the book of Acts.

This train of thought on the part of Luke fits in with two striking
characteristics of the book of Acts: the emphasis placed on the
significance of the twelve apostles in Jerusalem and the defence
of the Christian faith against the gentiles.

In Acts the significance of the apostles is expressed more strongly
than in any other book of the New Testament. The eleven who
remain must be supplemented by the appointment of Matthias
(1, 12-26); the apostles, by laying their hands on them, place the
seven "hellenists" under their authority (6, 6); the preaching of the
gospel beyond the actual boundaries of the Jewish country, in

Samaria, is made legitimate by the apostles' coming from Jerusalem to lay their hands on the baptized Samaritans (8, 14-17); the apostles in Jerusalem decide on the procedure to be followed in admitting gentiles into the church (15, 1-21). Paul expresses the difference between the apostles and himself when he calls them "witnesses" but says that he himself has been called to proclaim the gospel (13, 31-32). It is a notable fact that Paul is called an apostle only once (14, 14). Gradually, however, the significance of the apostles fades. They are not named but only James, the leader of the congregation in Jerusalem, when Paul is in Jerusalem for the last time (21, 17-26). This again is a reflection of the transition from "Jerusalem" to "Rome".

As the Christian tidings proceed through the gentile world it is continually stated that the gentiles cannot object to this preaching. It is not against the emperor's laws to say that there is another king, namely Jesus (17, 7). The Jews may accuse Paul, but Gallio the proconsul does not listen to their accusations (18, 12-17). The town clerk of Ephesus cannot accuse Paul and his followers of robbing the temple or of blaspheming against the goddess Diana (19, 37). Paul's trial, beginning in Jerusalem and ending in Rome, shows all the time that there is no crime of which Paul can be accused (23, 29; 25, 25; 26, 32; 28, 18). Finally Paul can live in Rome freely and without hindrance.

In this last aspect we may perhaps detect apologetic motives. These are certainly not totally absent. As a whole, however, it fits into the great pattern which the author has in view. The way in which the Jews treat the Christians and particularly Paul, and the way the gentiles treat them, are a reflection of the theme of this book: Jerusalem cedes its place to Rome.

3. SOURCES

With a book encompassing such a large body of material, we may well wonder where the author derived it all from. This question is especially important for the speeches, the description of the events in Jerusalem, and the surroundings and happenings around Paul.

The speeches take up a large part of this book. It is doubtful whether these can be derived from tradition. We can hardly expect that the speeches made by Peter at Pentecost, or by Paul in the court of Areopagus, were considered of such great weight that they were written down on the spot. We can only conclude that the author followed classical usage in having his personages make speeches at decisive moments. This would seem to detract greatly from the authenticity of the contents of such speeches, but that is only partly true. We must realize that the original speakers and the author of Acts belonged to the same Christian tradition, which determines both contents and form. The speeches clearly represent typical preachings as they were certainly held. They are therefore invaluable as a record of the way in which Jews and gentiles were addressed not only in general, but also in particular by such men as Paul and Peter. We can be sure that 13, 15-41 is an example of how a Christian preached to the Jews and 17, 22-34 of how he preached to the gentiles. A remarkable speech is that of Stephen (7, 1-53). Each speech has a style of its own, which must have been typical, long before the Acts were written, of the way in which the various groups were addressed. [1]

The events in Jerusalem and surroundings (up to and including chapter 12) cannot have been witnessed by the author himself. He draws on traditions which some have thought to have been contained in several written texts with similar though slightly different contents. In practice, however, any attempt at dividing the text into sections derived from different sources meets with grave difficulties, even on a purely literary level. Furthermore it is hard to imagine what purpose such traditions may have served in the church. It would seem more likely that the author drew on oral traditions which were not concerned with the life of the primitive church but with the doings of particular persons. A characteristic feature of the first part of Acts is the grouping of the various stories

---

[1] M. DIBELIUS, "Die Reden der Apostelgeschichte und die Antike Geschichtsschreibung", in: *Sits. ber. Heidelb. Ak. Wissensch., phil.-hist. Kl.* 1949, also in: *Aufsätze zur Apostelgeschichte*, herausgeg. v. H. GREEVEN, Göttingen 1951, p. 120-162.

around a small number of persons, such as Peter (and John),
Stephen and the "hellenists", Philip and James. The primitive
church must have been interested in the activities of these
people. This interest is evident also in John 21, 21-23 where
Peter inquires about the fate of the disciple John. The author of
Acts places these traditions in a framework: the life of the Christian
community in Jerusalem. This he effects by interrupting his
descriptions of the adventures of certain persons to give what are
sometimes called "Sammelberichte" ", that is short pericopes
containing general information about the life of the church (2,
41-47; 4, 32-37; 5, 12-16; 5, 41-42; 8, 1-3; 11, 19-30; 12, 24). [1]

Finally we come to the source from which the part describing Paul's travels is derived. A striking feature here is the presence
of four passages where the author changes to the first person
plural, the so-called "we passages". These are: 16, 9-18, Paul
goes from Troas to Philippi on his second journey; 20, 4-16,
from Philippi to Miletus on the third journey; 21, 1-18, from Miletus
to Jerusalem; 27, 1-28 from Caesarea to Rome. Possibly these
passages are derived from a particular source. It is not necessarily
the author himself speaking here, since the passages in question
may record the reminiscences of any companion of Paul's at all.
However there is no noticeable difference in style between the "we-
passages" and the remainder of the description of Paul's travels. For
this reason, and also because Luke did accompany Paul during the
periods described by these passages, it seems a plausible inference
that the "we-passages" are Luke's own story.

And so it is quite possible that large sections of the second half
of Acts are based on the author's own experiences. This does
not mean that he gives a precise account of what actually took place.
Such a procedure would not only run counter to the rules of classical
prose-writing, but also to those of the author himself, who makes

---

[1] About the sources in Acts: H. HAENCHEN, "Tradition und Komposition
in der Apostelgeschichte", in: *Zeitschr. Theol. u. Kirche* 52 1955, p. 205-225,
R. BULTMANN, "Zur Frage nach der Quellen der Apostelgeschichte", in:
New Test. Essays in mem. of T. W. Manson, Manchester 1959, p. 68-80,
and J. DUPONT, *Les Sources des Actes*, Desclée de Brouwer 1960.

both his sources and his own story subordinate to the aim he has in view in writing his book.

In a discussion of this book, therefore, we cannot speak of sources in the same way as in our discussion of the gospels. The author is not working with material that was used for preaching in the church. Traditions that lived among the people concerning certain important personages, examples of preaching to outsiders and personal experiences have been combined into a book which is intended to show how the good news was taken from Jerusalem to the "ends of the earth".

4. AUTHOR

Both the style of writing and the choice of words make it clear that the gospel of Luke and the book of Acts are by the same author. Thus, if we assume that Luke wrote the gospel we must also accept his authorship of Acts.

5. TIME AND PLACE OF ORIGIN

This book must have been written directly after the gospel of Luke. For that reason we shall have to accept a date circa A.D. 80. The place of writing may have been Caesarea or Rome.

6. THE TEXT OF ACTS

The text of this book has come down to us in two distinctly different forms. In the mss. ℵ B A C P[74] and in the Byzantine text we have the form that is found in the printed editions of the Greek New Testament. In D, the Old Latin, the Old Syriac, the marginalia of the Syra Harclensis and in some papyrus fragments we find a text that deviates greatly from the others, containing as it does numerous additions. The differences are so striking that some have believed that Luke published two different versions of his text. Some have supposed the text of D to be the original. [1] At present the text of B, etc. is generally regarded as the original one.

---

[1] Cf. A. C. CLARK, *The Acts of the Apostles*, Oxford 1933.

It is possible to explain the text of D on the basis of B, but not the other way around. This can be seen in the apostles' decree in 15,29, where the original ceremonial restrictions have been changed into ethical precepts. This was effected by leaving out καὶ πνικτῶν and by adding the rule: "refrain from doing to others what you would not like done to yourselves". There is also an antijudaic tendency to be discerned in D. [1]

An important problem is the question why this book in particular has been so extensively revised in a number of the manuscripts. A possible explanation may be that it was included in the canon rather late, but for this there is no evidence. Chance circumstances may also have played a part here, since a single copyist may well be responsible for a whole tradition with a deviating text.

---

[1] Cf. E. J. Epp, "The theological Tendency of Codex Bezae Cantabrigiensis in Acts", in: *Society for N,T. Studies, Monograph Series 3*, Cambridge 1966.

CHAPTER FIVE

PAUL AND HIS LETTERS

1. THE NUMBER OF PAUL'S LETTERS

The New Testament contains 13 letters that mention Paul
as their writer. The letter to the Hebrews, in which the name of
Paul does not occur, was regarded as Pauline in Alexandria during
the early centuries of our era. Later (towards the end of the
fourth century) this view was shared in western countries, but
nowadays it is rejected practically everywhere.

Doubts concerning Paul's authorship of certain letters have been
expressed ever since the eighteenth century. The criteria used to
judge their authenticity were mostly based on particular views concerning the structure of the primitive church, with which some
letter or other did not fit in. The so-called Tübingen school (of which
the most important representative was F. C. Baur 1792-1860) believed that the church was originally divided by a conflict between
Pauline and Jewish factions. For this reason they only accepted
those letters as authentic that showed some evidence of this
conflict. As a result, Galatians, I and II Corinthians and Romans
were thought to be authentic. The Netherlands radical school
(represented by Naber, Loman, van Manen) saw no room even for
these letters in their reconstruction of the first century of church
history and relegated them to the second century.

At the present time we take a more differentiated view of the
primitive church. For that reason certain letters which were not
thought authentic at one stage or another can again be given a place
in the life of Paul. Even so, the authenticity of II Thessalonians,
Colossians, Ephesians and the pastoral letters is often doubted. The
structure of the church no longer furnishes the main criteria for

rejection. Usually the authenticity of a letter is judged by comparing it with another one. The aspects that are taken into account in such a comparison are choice of words, style, theological views, organization of the church and the false teachings that are attacked. Since the letters in question were all written for special occasions, it is very difficult to evaluate the differences between them. Often the acceptance or rejection of the authenticity of a certain piece of writing will depend on the individual scholar. It will be clear from the following chapters that the only serious objections put forward here concern the authenticity of the pastoral letters.

If a certain letter is considered not to have been written by the person mentioned as its author, we must not fail to take into account the background of the times in which it was written. First of all we should remember that so-called pseudepigraphy was a normal phenomenon in the Jewish world. All sorts of writings were published under the names of well-known persons (Enoch, Baruch, Aristeas), in order to give authority to their contents. It must also be remembered that practically every letter was written through an intermediary, a secretary, who in many instances put his own stamp on the choice of words and the style in general. Finally we should also keep in mind that individual and community were very closely related in classical times. In view of this fact we cannot regard it merely as forgery if some disciple of Paul's attempted to preserve or elaborate the Pauline heritage under the name of Paul.

In addition to the letters that are known to us, Paul also wrote others. I Cor. 5, 9 and II Cor. 2, 4 mention letters that are not found in the New Testament. In our discussion of the letters to the Corinthians we shall see that parts of such letters may have been incorporated in I and II Corinthians. In Col. 4, 16 there is a reference to a letter to the Laodiceans which may perhaps be identified with the letter to the Ephesians.

Of a later date are those letters which, under Paul's name, sometimes propagated doctrines that deviated from generally accepted views. These are the letters to the Laodiceans, III Corinthians, the Alexandrians and an exchange of letters between Paul and Seneca. [1] Letters such as these must have been written even during Paul's lifetime, for in II Thess. 2, 2, Paul complains about a disturbance in the church of Thessalonica, caused by a letter purporting to come from him.

2. The Nature of Paul's Letters

All of Paul's letters deal with concrete situations in various Christian communities. Some are replies to questions asked by some community or occasioned by some piece of information concerning such a community. The letters to the Romans and the Ephesians are of a more general nature, but even so they must be viewed in connection with the situation in Rome or in the western part of Asia Minor. Since, in many cases, we are not acquainted with the situation, and since it was not necessary for Paul to go into details on such matters, it is often very difficult to arrive at a correct interpretation of Paul's intentions. In view of the nature of the letters it is hazardous to base general conclusions on some isolated remark of Paul's, the more so when we note Paul's tendency to carry his opponents' ideas to their logical consequences, thus intentionally creating an absurd or caricatured picture. In such cases it is often scarcely possible to tell where Paul himself and where his opponents are speaking.

As far as their form is concerned, the letters are written on the model of the hellenistic letters that have been found in Egypt. These begin with a prescript giving the name of the writer and that of the person addressed as well as a greeting. They end with greetings and wishes. It is worth noting, however, that the words used in the beginning and the end of a hellenistic letter (an example of which is to be found in Acts 15, 23-29) differ from those used in Paul's letters, χαίρειν becomes χάρις καὶ εἰρήνη and Ἔρρωσθε is replaced by Ἡ χάρις τοῦ κυρίου.

A striking aspect of these letters is the stereotyped manner in which elements of traditional faith are expressed (I Cor. 11, 23 and

---

[1] See L. Vouaux, *Les Actes de Paul et ses Lettres apocryphes*, Paris 1913.

I Cor. 15, 3: received . . . . delivered), the manner in which virtues and vices are enumerated (cf. Phil. 4, 8; I Cor. 5, 11; 6, 9-10; II Cor. 12, 20; Gal. 5, 19-22), and the way instructions are given concerning the mutual relations in a family (cf. Eph. 5, 22-6, 9 and Col. 3, 18-4, 1). These are all formulas that were widely known throughout the church.

3. CHRONOLOGY OF PAUL'S LIFE

There is only one instance of an intentional dating of an event in the New Testament: the calling of John the Baptist in Luke 3, 1-2. For the dates of Paul's life and letters we have to rely on incidental remarks about historical events or personages. The book of Acts supplies us with some chronologically uncertain data, for instance Acts 11, 27-30 and 12, 20-23 (the death of king Agrippa and the famine in Palestine), Acts 13, 7 (the proconsulate of Lucius Sergius Paulus), Acts 24, 27 (the accession to office of Porcius Festus). Acts 9, 23-26 in combination with II Cor. 11, 32 also gives some information (Aretas IV, King of Nabatea). The mention of Gallio in Acts 18, 12-18 is the only piece of information which offers a real possibility of determining a date.

In Acts 18, 12-18 it is said that Paul has to answer for himself before Gallio. In Delphi fragments of an inscription were discovered which informs us in which years this took place. The emperor Claudius directs himself to the inhabitants of Delphi in this inscription. He apparently reacts upon a letter written by Gallio about a shortage of inhabitants in Delphi. Claudius' answer to Delphi was given after Gallio's departure from the city. The answer was given, according to the inscription, when Claudius was acclaimed emperor for the 26th time (see Appendix C). We do not know the exact date of this acclamation. From information given by other inscriptions it may be inferred that the 27th acclamation was published before the 1st of August 52 and the 24th before the 24th of January 52. The 25th and the 26th acclamation, therefore lie between the 25th of January and the 1st of August 52. We know furthermore, that a proconsul held office only for the time of one year, from May to May. If the inscription was written just after Gallio's departure, he must have been proconsul in Achaia from May 51 until May 52. From Acts 18 we know that Paul appeared before Gallio at the beginning of the latter's period of office. We may therefore assume that Paul left Corinth in the summer of 51.

Since Acts supplies very few data concerning the length of Paul's stays in the various towns he visited, the dates of his life can only be superficially determined. The main points may be summed up as follows (see also the more detailed list given in Appendix B):

30/31 Conversion of Paul
46-48 First missionary journey
    48 Conference at Jerusalem
48-52 Second missionary journey
57-59 Third missionary journey
    59 Arrival in Rome
    61 End of Paul's stay in Rome.

We do not know for certain whether Paul was killed in 61 or whether he started out on another journey. This question will be treated more fully below when we discuss the pastoral letters.

4. The Place of Paul's Letter in the Early Christian Church

The letters of Paul are the oldest documents known to us from the early Christian church. Nevertheless, Paul's first letter dates from almost 20 years after this church was founded. It may be inferred that the primitive church apparently felt no great need to put its new faith down in writing. There could be various reasons for this. In the first place the church was expecting the Second Coming of the Lord at an early date, which made it unnecessary to record its faith in writing for future generations. In the second, the church consisted of people who were not accustomed to expressing themselves in writing. But the main reason lies in the nature of the Christian faith itself. This faith is not based on fixed rules but on direct communion with the Risen Lord. People live in his community and speak by his authority. Quite in keeping with this situation is the practice of writing letters, through which the dispersed members of the church encourage, lead and admonish each other, according as the circumstances demand (cf. Acts 15, 23-29). Paul's letters derive their authority from the fact that the writer is a person who feels himself called by Christ (cf. Rom. 1, 1 and the prescripts of the other letter) and who can admonish on the strength of this calling (cf. I Cor. 7, 10). The epistolary genre is characteristic of the Christian church, and in Paul it found its representative *par excellence.*

Paul's letters are unique in the Christian church not only on account of their form. As a person, too, Paul has unique significance. This is evident from the numerous misunderstandings that have arisen from his preaching. On the one hand he was distrusted by those who felt themselves closely bound to the Jewish people, a point of view which led to making circumcision compulsory for Christians. On the other hand he was also distrusted by those who, prompted only by the Spirit, broke away from all traditions. In the midst of these people Paul adhered to tradition by maintaining the connection with the church in Jerusalem while dissociating the Christians from the Jewish people by making circumcision not compulsory. This position was made possible by the fact that the territories of their activities were kept strictly separate: Paul went to the gentiles and Peter and his followers to the Jews (Gal. 2, 7-8). This difficulty was removed when, after the destruction of Jerusalem in A.D. 70, the church in Jerusalem lost all contact with the Christians of the Greek and Roman world. From that moment onwards Paul could be regarded as *the* apostle to the gentiles since it was no longer necessary to take into account his ideas concerning the relations with the Jewish-Christian church. It is not too much to say that many Christians did not accept Paul during his lifetime, but that after his death he was accepted because he was misunderstood. [1]

---

[1] See J. MUNCK, *Paulus und die Heilsgeschichte,* in: *Acta Jutlandica* 26 1, København 1954 and H. J. SCHOEPS, *Paulus,* Tübingen 1959.

CHAPTER SIX

THE LETTER TO THE ROMANS

1. Origins of the Christian Community in Rome

In the letter to the Romans Paul addresses a community which he did not found himself (cf. 1, 8-15). He does not say how this community came into being, and so we shall have to look to other data for information concerning its origin.

A starting-point is furnished by a quotation from Suetonius,

Claudius 25:	He (Claudius) expelled the Jews
Iudaeos impulsore Chresto assidue	from Rome because on the instiga-
tumultuantes Roma expulit.	tion of Chrestus they were conti-
	nually causing disturbances.

This edict was published in 49 A.D. If the name Chrestus refers to Christ, as is generally assumed, it follows that:
a. there was a Christian community in Rome as early as 49 A.D.,
b. that this community was so closely connected with the Jewish one that disturbances among the Christians had their repercussions among the Jews.

The data from Suetonius are confirmed by Acts 18, 1-2, where it is said that Aquila and Priscilla had to leave Rome and take refuge in Corinth because of Claudius' edict.

Three early Christian traditions concerning the origins of the church in Rome must also be noted:

a) Irenaeus (*c.* 190) *adv. Haer.* III 1 1, writes that Peter and Paul founded the community.
b) Dionysius, bishop of Corinth, writes in a letter to the church in Rome at the time of bishop Soter (*c.* 160-174), quoted in part by Eusebius, *Hist. Eccl.* II 25 8, that Peter and Paul "together instructed Italy" (καὶ εἰς τὴν Ἰταλίαν ὁμόσε διδάξαντες).

c) In a dialogue with Proclus, written at the time of bishop
Zephyrinus of Rome (*c.* 198-217) also quoted by Eusebius,
II 25 7, Gaius says that Peter and Paul founded the church in
Rome (. . . . τῶν ταύτην ἱδρυσαμένων τὴν ἐκκλησίαν).

These traditions must be regarded as attempts to attribute an
apostolic origin to the community in Rome. They are incompatible
with the following facts:

a) The letter to the Romans shows that Paul is not the founder of
their community.

b) It is impossible that Peter should have founded the community
before the year 49. According to Acts Peter was in or near Jerusalem until the time of the persecution by Herod (Acts.12, 1-5).

This persecution took place "about the time of the great famine"
(Acts 11, 28 and 12, 1) which must have occurred around A.D. 47/8
While the persecution lasts Peter goes "elsewhere" (12, 17). He is
back in Jerusalem when the conference of the apostles is held there
in A.D. 48 (15, 7). This leaves only a period of one year, before
A.D. 49, during which Peter might have travelled to Rome. It is
most unlikely, however, that he could have travelled all the way
from Jerusalem to Rome and back and also found a community,
all in the time of one year. Lastly, it may be doubted whether, only
one year after it was founded, such a community could attract so
much attention that Claudius had to take measures against it.

Claudius' edict, therefore, remains the only definite piece of
evidence. The data which it furnishes agree with what we are told
by the unknown writer of a commentary on the letters of Paul,
usually referred to as Ambrosiaster. Some time during the fourth
century he writes (*Comm. in Ep. ad Rom.*, in: Patrol Lat. (Migne)
XVII, c. 46A):

. . . *nulla insigna virtutum videntes, nec aliquem apostolorum, susceperant fidem Christi rite licet judaico, in verbis potius quam in sensu; non enim expositum illis fuerat mysterium crucis Christi.*	. . . while they (the Christians of Rome) saw no signs at all of their deeds, nor any of the apostles, they accepted the faith of Christ, albeit according to the Jewish rites, though more in letter than in spirit, for the mystery of the cross had not been explained to them.

Neither the exact meaning nor the source of this information are known, but we may infer from it that the first Christians in Rome were of Jewish origin and that they did not know the apostles. The community probably came into being through incidental preaching by Jewish Christians to Jews.

2. COMPOSITION OF THE CONGREGATION

The above assumptions concerning the composition of the community would seem to be inconsistent with the contents of the letter, which appears to be addressed to gentile Christians. This can be seen in the following quotations:

> I, 5: . . . the gentiles, yourselves among them.
> I, 13: . . . among you . . . as elsewhere among the gentiles.
> II, 13: . . . I speak to you, gentiles (cf. 15, 16).

On closer investigation, however, it is found that the gentile Christians are continually viewed in their relation to Jews and Jewish Christians. In this letter Paul unfolds his ideas about the future of Israel (ch. 9-11). In 4, 1 Abraham is called "our ancestor". The Christians are addressed as people who are "dead to the law" and "discharged from the law" (7, 4-6). In 13, 1-7 Paul speaks of obedience to the authorities, which reminds the reader of the disturbances that had occurred among the Christians in Rome. Towards the end of the letter Paul speaks about the "weak", who attach much importance to the observance of certain feast-days and who will not eat certain foods (14, 4-6). He is referring to "impure" foods (14, 13-23), which the "strong" eat without scruple. There was obviously a controversy on this point between gentile and Jewish Christians.

At the time when this letter was written, therefore, the members of the church were evidently of mixed origin. It is impossible to determine which group formed the majority.

It is not hard to imagine that difficulties might arise when gentile Christians were admitted into an originally Jewish Christian community. These difficulties probably became acute because of Claudius' edict. After that time the gentile element in the Christian community, which was possibly already present, must have grown considerably. When the edict was lifted following Claudius' death in 54 and the expelled Jews returned it must have been difficult for both groups to live together in a mixed community.

3. Purpose of the Letter

At the beginning of the letter Paul announces his intention of visiting Rome. He says that he has long desired to do so but has so far been prevented (1, 8-15). At the end of the letter we discover that his desire to visit Rome is not the only reason for his intended journey. He considers his task in the East finished and now wants to go to Italy in order to travel on from there to Spain. He hopes to receive the aid necessary for his further journey from the Romans (15, 19-24).

It is thus clear that his visit to Rome is not meant as one-sided support for the church in that city, but that Paul in his turn will seek the support of the Romans. Paul speaks of mutual encouragement (1, 12) and he excuses himself for his bold manner of writing (15, 15).

The mere announcement of a visit, however, does not justify an extensive letter. Evidently Paul wishes, through this letter, to introduce himself and his preaching. For if he is to proclaim the gospel in Rome (1, 15) there must be a bond of mutual trust. Since the Romans do not know him he gives an exposition of his views on the gospel. According to him the gospel is, in the first place for Jews and then also for gentiles, a saving power of God for everyone who has faith (Rom. 1, 16). With this definition Paul situates the content of the faith in the context of the Roman church where Jews and gentiles had to live together as Christians.

And so the purpose of the letter led Paul to give a concise exposition of his ideas about the Christian faith, although these ideas are so presented as to fit the situation in Rome.

4. Time and Place of Origin

From what he says in 15, 22-28, it may be inferred that Paul considers his work in the East finished and is intending to travel to Jerusalem with a sum of money raised in Achaia and Macedonia for the church in Jerusalem. These plans agree with the account given in Acts, where we read that Paul travelled from Greece to Jerusalem (21, 5) by way of Macedonia (20, 3). The fund raised for the poor of Jerusalem is also mentioned there (Acts 24, 17). The letter was therefore doubtless written during the third missionary journey. Since Romans 16, 1 recommends a servant of the church called Phoebe, from Cenchreae the port of Corinth, the letter must have been written in Corinth. Paul was there in 56/7.

5. UNITY OF THE LETTER

With regard to the unity of the letter there are two difficulties which call for separate discussion.

a. The doxology in 16, 24 does not occur in a number of manuscripts while the one in 16, 25-27 appears in different places in the concluding part of the letter in the various manuscripts. [1]

b. Chapter 16 gives a long series of greetings to a number of people Paul is not likely to have known in Rome.[2]

The following diagram shows where the two doxologies occur in the various manuscripts:

	1, 1-14, 23	16, 25-27	15, 1-16, 23	16, 24	16, 25-27	
a.	x	x	x	x	x	L syʰ Chr
b.	x		x		x	Sin B syᵖ
c.	x	x	x	x	x	A P
d.	x		x	x		D G F
e.	x	x				Am Fuld
f.	x		x	x	x	Koine
g.	x	x	16, 1-23			p⁴⁶
	(+ 15, 1-33)					

[1] J. DUPONT, „Pour l'Histoire de la Doxologie finale de l'Epître aux Romains", in: *Rev. Bénéd.* 58 1948, p. 3-22.

[2] W. SANDAY-A. C. HEADLAM, *The Epistle to the Romans*, in: *Intern. Crit. Comm.*, Edinburgh 1902í, p. LXXXV-XCVIII, and R. SCHUHMACHER, „Die beiden letzten Kapittel des Römerbriefes", in: *Neutest. Abhandl.* XIV 4 1929.

Leaving g. out of consideration, the best way to judge the other groups is by basing ourselves on e. Origen comments on a text such as this in his *Comm. in ep. ad Rom.*, Lib x 43 (in Patr. Gr. (Migne) XIV, c. 1290 A-B). He writes:

Caput hoc (16, 25f.) *Marcion, a quo scripturae evangelicae et apostolicae interpolatae sunt, de hac epistola penitus, abstulit; et non solum hoc, sed ab eo loco, ubi scriptum est 'omne autem, quod non est ex fide, peccatum est'* (14, 23) *usque ad finem cuncta dissecuit.*

"This chapter (16, 25f.) was completely cut by Marcion, who falsified the evangelical and apostolical writings. He cut not only this, but also everything from where it is written: "anything which does not arise from faith is sin" (14, 23) right to the end."

This passage is not quite clear. For one thing we do not know for certain whether *dissecuit* means "cut out" or "cut up". Since, however, we do have manuscripts that leave out chs. 15 and 16 but none with an abbreviated text we may assume that Origen refers to a text such as is found in Am and Fuld (without the long doxology). The passage further indicates that Marcion had a short text, but it is doubtful whether Origen is correctly informed when he says that Marcion is responsible for it. Marcion may have found the text already in this form, as his reasons for shortening it are not at all clear. In this connection, however, that is not really important. As the Latin text was influenced by Marcion (see Ch. XXIV below), it is probable that Am and Fuld ultimately go back to the text Marcion knew. To this text the doxology of 16, 25-27 was added at a later date.

Next to be discussed are those manuscripts which contain the last two chapters. These may be divided into three groups:

a. and d. with the doxology of 16, 24
b. and c. with the doxology of 16, 25-27
f. with both doxologies.

Of these groups, a. and c. show the influence of the text to which Origen refers. They do have chs. 15 and 16 but the long doxology still follows after chapter 14.

In determining which is the original text, it seems that a choice will have to be made between the long doxology and the short one, because f. seems to have a combination of both.

When the two doxologies are compared, we are compelled to prefer the shorter version because it is the only one that corresponds with the conclusions of Paul's other letters. As far as its contents are concerned the long doxology may be considered Pauline in character, but such a doxology at the end of a letter is foreign to the structure of Paul's letters.

This, however, leaves the existence of the long doxology still to be explained. The most plausible assumption would appear to be that the long doxology was added when Paul's letters were first collected in one volume ending with the letter to the Romans. With these words, Paul's gospel was summed up as a mystery revealed by God to the gentiles. When the order of the letters was changed (see Ch. XV below), the long doxology went with the letter to the Romans to its present position.

The different texts may therefore be explained as follows:

1st comes the original text represented by d. (and a. omitting 16, 25-27 after ch. 14);

2nd the text that resulted when the letters were collected into one volume, as represented in f.;

3rd texts that show the results of attempts to get rid of the difficulties caused by the two doxologies, in b. and c.

The main arguments for not accepting ch. 16 as belonging to the letter to the Romans are that Aquila and Priscilla are said to be in Rome (16, 3), while we are told in Acts 18, 18 that they are living in Ephesus; that Epaenetus is referred to as the "first in Asia" (16, 5); and that it is rather unlikely Paul knew so many people in Rome. And therefore since a few names point to Asia Minor, ch. 16 has been supposed by some to represent a short letter of introduction for Phoebe addressed to the church at Ephesus.

On closer consideration these are rather weak arguments. The letter was written in the year 57, so Aquila and Priscilla might well have returned to Rome after Claudius' edict had been lifted. Epaenetus may also have gone from Asia Minor to Rome. It is not clear, moreover, why Paul should have devoted so much space to greetings in a letter of introduction, nor how such a letter could come to be attached to the letter to the Romans.

It may be argued, on the contrary, that the last chapter fits in very well with the letter. Paul wants to establish a link with Rome and what better method could he employ than to show his personal acquaintance with such a large number of Roman Christians? It is also interesting to note that in naming these Christians, Paul continually adds references to their origins. Aquila and Prisca (v. 3-4) are Jews who have risked their lives for Paul, but also for the gentile Christians. Mary is a Jewess who has done a great deal for the Romans, that is also for the gentile Christians (v. 6). The mother of Rufus, a gentile by birth, has been a mother to Paul, who was a Jew (v. 13). Paul's countrymen Lucius, Jason and Sosipater greet the Romans (v. 21). To Andronicus, Junias (v. 7) and Herodion (v. 11), who are also referred to as his countrymen, he sends greetings. This whole passage, in pointing out people's origins and their relations with persons of different origin, has an obvious intention. Paul wished to illustrate with actual examples that gentile and Jewish Christians can live together.

In view of these remarks there is not much reason to consider that P46 (g. in our list, above) supports the assumption that ch. 16 did not originally belong to the letter. The insertion of the doxology after ch. 15 should be regarded as an attempt to end the letter at a point where it is still suitable for reading to a congregation.

6. Contents of the Letter

When the composition of the church community was discussed above, we saw that in this letter Paul is addressing a group of Jewish and gentile Christians. We also noted that it is the gentiles who are addressed in the first place. Paul repeatedly seems to be trying to protect the Jewish Christians against the gentiles. In 14, 1 he says that the strong should protect the weak and in chs. 9-11 it is pointed out to the gentiles that Israel possesses a number of privileges. This shows that the gentile Christians are beginning to predominate in the Roman church. This situation gives rise to certain dangers which Paul discusses in detail.

In the first place Paul points out that both Jews and gentiles are to be saved through faith: "There is no just man, not one" (3, 10). This view evokes two questions: how can a gentile share in the promises of Abraham, and what significance does Israel still have?

In ch. 4 Paul is concerned with the significance of Abraham. Paul describes him not only as the father of the circumcised but also as the father of all who have faith, for "Abraham's faith was counted as righteousness" before he was circumcised (4, 9-12). The history of God's dealings with the world does not start with Abraham but goes right back to Adam, when "sin entered the world" (5, 12). Salvation therefore comes about through "one act of righteousness for all men" (5, 18).

Now that Paul has dissociated salvation from belonging to the people of Israel, Israel seems to have lost its significance. But they "were entrusted with the oracles of God" (3, 3); "God has not rejected his people" (11, 1). Israel remains the chosen people. "A partial blindness came upon Israel" in order that the gentiles might be saved (11, 25), but at last "the whole of Israel will be saved" (11, 26). Israel is a warning to gentile Christians: they, too, cannot leave God with impunity (11, 22).

For Jews and gentiles alike there is only one way of salvation, but Israel is God's chosen people, to whom in the past his promises were entrusted and who in the future may hope for God's salvation. At the present time, however, there is no reason for one group to feel superior to the other. The remainder of the letter (from 12, 1) contains admonitions to the members of the church telling them to live together in harmony.

From a historical point of view the letter appears at a decisive moment in the history of the church. A community which began initially as a Jewish group is in the process of detaching itself from its Jewish background. Its members wish to share in the privileges that were granted to Israel, but this is done at the expense of the Jewish people who are denied all significance. Paul in this letter attempts to keep Israel and the church together. They are branches growing from the same root (11, 13-14). The people of Israel cannot be ignored, for "it is impossible that the word of God should have proved false" (9, 6). It may be said that this is the last attempt for some time to come to give Israel a place in God's dealings with the world. The gentile church goes its own way in the world without concerning itself about Israel.

CHAPTER SEVEN

THE LETTERS TO THE CORINTHIANS

1. The City of Corinth

The city of Corinth is situated on the isthmus that connects
Northern and Southern Greece. It is at this point that the Ionian
and Aegean seas come closest to each other. This position made the
city important both politically and commercially. The Romans
completely destroyed it in 146 B.C. and it was not rebuilt until
46 B.C. Partly on account of the many foreigners that lived there,
Corinth had a bad reputation. Its way of life is reflected in Rom.
I, 24-27, a passage which was written in Corinth, and in I Cor.
5, 1-5. In Paul's time this city was the seat of the proconsul for the
province of Achaia (see Acts 18, 12).

2. The Origins of the Christian Community in Corinth

We read in Acts that Paul first visited Corinth on his second
missionary journey. Coming from Macedonia he went to Corinth by
way of Athens (18, 1). He stayed at the house of Aquila and
Priscilla, Jewish tentmakers, who had been obliged to leave Rome
because of Claudius' edict. His preaching in the synagogue met
with resistance, so Paul moved the centre of his activities to the
house of Titius Justus (18, 7). After an eighteen months' stay
(18, 11) Paul left Corinth for Ephesus, accompanied by Aquila and
Priscilla. Their departure was hastened by an incident with the
Jews, in which the proconsul Gallio played a part (18, 12-17).

3. Composition of the Congregation

The Christians of Corinth were mainly of gentile origin (I, 12, 1).
Most of them came from the poorest and humblest classes of the

population (I, 1, 26). There was, however, a Jewish element as well (I, 7, 18), and even some quite distinguished citizens belonged to the church (I, 11, 21).

The Christians did not form an isolated community in a heathen society. Outwardly they continued to lead the life of heathens (fornication: I, 6, 12-20), while they were also in continuous contact with the outside world. They went to pagan law-courts (6, 1-11), Christians married heathens (7, 12-16), they had meals with heathen friends in temples (8,10) and at those friends' homes (10, 27).

There does not appear to have been any central authority in the community. The congregation probably met at the homes of certain Christians (I, 1-11: "those who are of the house of Chloe"). Thus, different groups could easily arise and one group might tolerate fornication while the other advocated virginity (I, 7, 26-28).

4. Time and Place of Origin

a. I *Corinthians*

According to I, 16, 8 Paul was staying at Ephesus when he wrote this letter. He was planning to travel from there to Corinth by way of Macedonia (I, 16, 5). This itinerary was carried out on Paul's third missionary journey (Acts 20, 1-2).

Before Paul wrote the letter he sent Timothy to Corinth, but Timothy was not expected to reach that town until after the arrival of the letter (I, 16, 10). This journey of Timothy's may be identified as the one referred to in Acts 19, 21-22. There it is said that Paul sent his companions Erastus and Timothy to Macedonia. If the letter was sent from Ephesus directly to Corinth and Timothy went by way of Macedonia, we may indeed assume that Timothy arrived in Corinth after the letter, although he left Ephesus before it was written.

It follows that:

a. Paul was staying in Ephesus on his third missionary journey when he wrote this letter;

b. Paul had certain plans for the continuation of his journey;
c. Paul's stay in Ephesus was therefore drawing to an end. The letter may therefore be assigned to A.D. 55.

I Corinthians contains some more important data. It appears that Aquila and Priscilla were with Paul (I, 16, 19) and according to Acts 18, 26 they were indeed in Ephesus at this time.

We also read in I Corinthians that some called themselves followers of Apollos (I, 1, 12). Acts tells us that this Apollos left Ephesus for Corinth about the time Paul arrived in Ephesus (19, 1).

Finally we are told that Stephanas, Fortunatus and Achaicus came to Paul from Corinth (I, 16, 17).

b. II Corinthians

This letter is from Paul and Timothy (II, 1, 1).

Paul has travelled from Troas to Macedonia where he met Titus who brought him good news from Corinth (II, 2, 12-13 and 7, 6-7.)

The letter must, therefore, have been written during Paul's third missionary journey, at the time of his stay in Macedonia (Acts 20, 1-2) and may assigned to the year 56.

c. Other letters to the Corinthians

In I, 5, 9 Paul refers to a letter to the Corinthians about fornication. The letter in question must thus have been written before I Corinthians. Nothing else is known about such a letter, but some scholars consider II, 6, 14-7, 1 to be a fragment of it. This passage does indeed deal with fornication and may be omitted from the letter without damage to the whole (see 6, 13: ".... open wide your hearts ..." and 7, 2: "... make a place for us in your hearts ..."). These, however, are not really strong arguments.

In II, 2, 4 and 7, 8 Paul mentions a letter he wrote to Corinth "with many tears". This cannot refer to I Corinthians, which does not give the impression of having been written in sorrow. The letter referred to must have been written between I and II Corinthians. The words "with many tears" indicate that some difficulties must have arisen between Paul and the community in Corinth after the writing of I Corinthians. This is confirmed by II, 1, 23 and 2, 1, where Paul says he cancelled his intended visit to Corinth out of consideration for them. He does not want to be sorry again.

These passages show not only that there were certain difficulties but also that Paul visited Corinth "in sadness". The visit to Corinth mentioned in Acts 18, 1-17 is not marked by sorrow. We must assume, therefore, that another visit is meant. This must have taken place between the writing of I and II Corinthians. Acts does not mention this short visit to Corinth from Ephesus.

With the help of these data, the following course of events may be reconstructed:

1. A letter about fornication. Time and place of writing unknown.
2. I Corinthians from Ephesus in A.D. 55.
3. Timothy arrives in Corinth from Macedonia.
4. Unfavourable reaction to I Corinthians in Corinth.
5. Visit to Corinth does not solve the disagreement.
6. "Severe letter".
7. Paul travels to Macedonia on his way to Corinth.
8. Paul meets Titus who brings him good news from Corinth.
9. II Corinthians written in Macedonia in A.D. 56.

The "severe letter" was probably taken to Corinth by Titus, since he is the one who brings the good news from there.

The severe letter has been lost, but many scholars believe that II, chs. 10-13 represent a fragment of it. This is quite possible, for the transition from the initially kindly tone of II Cor. to the sharp outbursts of ch. 10 makes it seem likely that two different parts have here been joined together. This must have taken place in Corinth. [1]

---

[1] See for other ideas about the composition of the letters: W. SCHMITHALS, *Die Gnosis in Korinth*, in: *Forsch. z. Rel. u. Lit. des A.u.N.T.* 48 1965 and W. MARXSEN, *Einleitung in das Neue Testament*, Gütersloh 1963, p. 73-77.

5. Reasons for Writing the Letters

I Corinthians was written in reply to questions from the Corinthian community as well as in consequence of certain tidings received concerning this community. In 1, 10 Paul begins by saying that he has heard from persons of the house of Chloe that the community is divided. Some say they follow Paul, some Apollos, Peter or Christ. Other information too, has reached him: grave sins are being committed in the community (ch. 5), and jurisdiction is sought in pagan courts when members of the community cannot reach agreement among themselves (ch. 6). In 7, 1 he replies to written questions from the community. These are concerned with marriage (ch. 7), eating food consecrated to heathen deities (ch. 8), the headdress of the women (11, 2 ff.), the gifts of the Spirit (12, 1 ff.), and the resurrection of the dead (15, 1 ff.). These questions were probably brought to Paul by Stephanus, Fortunatus and Achaius (16, 17).

The "severe letter" (II, Ch. 10-13) is addressed to certain persons who have been throwing discredit on Paul. They considered Paul's behaviour weak and carnal (cf. 10, 2). According to Paul these persons are "superlative apostles" (11, 5; cf. 11, 13). They are Jews by origin (11, 22) and live at the community's expense (11, 8-9; cf. I 9, 1-14). They feel superior to Paul because of the signs they have performed through the Spirit. Paul says that his own gifts are not inferior to those of the "superlative apostles" (cf. 12, 1 ff.), but he chooses to be weak because Christ also humbled himself to weakness (cf. 12, 9-10).

II Corinthians removes the last traces of misunderstanding between Paul and the Corinthians. These relate in the first place to his promise of a visit to Corinth which he did not fulfil. He was to have travelled to Macedonia by way of Corinth and then visited that city again on his way back to Jerusalem. Some people accused him of being fickle because he did not come. Paul says that he stayed away out of consideration for them (1, 12-2, 4). It is not known when this promise was made. Paul continues his letter to speak of his office as an apostle. He considers himself a servant of the new covenant (3, 6), his knowledge of God he carries with him like a treasure in an earthenware pot (4, 6-7), he is an ambassador of Christ (5, 20). In chs. 8 and 9, finally, he speaks of the contributions he is to take to Jerusalem.

6. The Situation in the Congregation

When the letters are viewed side by side (i.e. I Cor., II Cor. and the "severe letter") there is an evident development to be noted. I Corinthians is concerned with things and the other letters with people. Did the difficulties between Paul and the Corinthians reach a personal level through certain occurrences, or did Paul at first fail to see how things really stood in Corinth?

Some arguments may in fact support the latter point of view. It appears, for instance, that Paul knew there were factions in Corinth that called themselves after certain persons, but it is not clear whether Paul knew what their objectives were. He gives no more than the names. When, later on in the letter, he mentions certain abuses with respect to the Lord's Supper, he says: "To begin with, I am told that you fall into sharply divided groups (σχίσματα ἐν ὑμῖν) and I believe there is some truth in it. For dissensions are necessary if only to show which of your members are sound" (11, 18-19). From this remark it is obvious that Paul did not know just what the various groups aimed at. In this connection Paul writes in I, 9, 1-14 about his qualifications and his rights as an apostle. The passage II, ch. 10-13, however, shows that the attacks on his person included a rejection of his apostleship.

On the basis of these considerations, the situation in the congregation may be conceived as follows:

After Paul left Corinth certain Jews (II 11, 21-22) arrived there whose message differed from that proclaimed by Paul. One of their mottoes was: "We are free to do anything" (7, 35 and 10, 23). They lived at the expense of the congregation who were impressed by their forceful manner. Part of the congregation responded to their preaching and were moved to actions which others thought doubtfully in accordance with the teachings of Paul. This caused

them to ask a number of questions about expressions of
libertinism in the congregation. Paul replied to the best of his
ability, but without touching the heart of the matter. This again
led to ever bolder conduct on the part of the false teachers, who
directed their attacks more and more against Paul personally. This
was the situation when Paul appeared in Corinth, after which he
wrote the severe letter. As a result, the congregation of Corinth
rallied round Paul once more.

7. OPPONENTS

Certain Jews, coming from outside the congregation, caused
confusion in Corinth. They boasted of the gift of the Spirit which
enabled them to act with great assurance. Because of this, they felt
committed to no one, which resulted in contempt for their fellow-
men and libertine conduct. They expressed contempt for Paul, whom
they reproached for his weakness and lack of Spirit. They possessed
the wisdom and understanding to know God (cf. I, 1, 18-2, 5).

The source of these notions is hard to determine. It will have to be
looked for in those circles of Jews that were strongly influenced by
hellenistic thought. Their preaching of freedom, however, cannot be
totally divorced from Paul's teachings. In I Corinthians especially,
Paul's plea against some expressions of libertinism is hardly based
on reasons of principle. In Paul's opinion, too, all things are lawful,
although not all things are expedient (I, 6, 12). In his reply to the
questions we notice such turns of phrase as: "if, however, they . . .
For it is better" (I. 6, 12); "it is not I who command, but
the Lord . . . But to the rest I say, as my own word, not as
the Lord's . . ." (I, 7, 10-11); "if we do not eat, we are none the
worse, and if we eat, we are none the better" (I, 8, 1-13); and
"Judge for yourselves: is it fitting for a woman to pray to God
bare-headed?" (I, 11, 13). In the same way Paul's plea against
the accusation that he is not a true apostle is hardly convincing.
He defends himself by saying that what is possible for his opponents
is possible for him also. Paul also eats consecrated food (I, 8, 4); he,
too, can use ecstatic language (I, 14, 6); Christ has appeared also

to Paul (I, 15, 8) and he, too, has been caught up to the third heaven (II, 12, 1-5) [1].

These very similarities between Paul and his opponents explain why the Corinthians may have inclined to libertinism. Yet Paul did not draw the same inferences from his preaching of freedom as his opponents. The latter had completely broken away from tradition and lived in direct communion with the Risen Lord. Paul opposed his ties with the traditions concerning the "life of Jesus" (I, 11, 23 and 15, 3). This induced him to regard the life of a Christian as an association not only with the Risen Lord, but also with the Crucified Lord (I, 2, 2). Paul is weak as Christ was weak (2, 13, 4) and his life is a life of suffering just as Christ suffered on this earth. (II, 11, 23-28). Anticipation of the future through the Spirit leads to neglect of the body which is later also to share in the renewal (I, ch. 15 and II, 4, 16-5, 10).

If the origin, significance and extent of this trend in the Pauline churches is obscure, its offshoots have come to light in the history of the church. They are to be found in those Christian sects which are collectively known by the name of "Gnosticism". In spite of their differences they have many traits in common. They usually teach a dualism of matter and spirit, a salvation on earth through "knowledge", a neglect of history expressing itself in the rejection of the Old Testament and an attitude to life characterised sometimes by asceticism and sometimes by libertinism. [2]

---

[1] See for a different approach J. C. Hurd Jr., *The Origin of I Corinthians*, London 1965, which, however, does not take into account the relation between I Cor. and II Cor. ch. 10-13.

[2] See also: E. KÄSEMANN, „Die Legitimität des Apostels. Eine Untersuchung zu II. Korinther 10-13", in: *Zeitschr. f. d. neut. Wissensch.* 41 1942, p. 33-71; R. BULTMANN, „Exegetische Probleme des zweiten Korintherbriefes", in: *Symb. Upsal.* 9 1947 and G. BORNKAMM, „Die Vorgeschichte des sog. Zweiten Korintherbriefes", in: *Sitz. ber. Heidelb. Ak. der Wissensch., phil.-hist. Kl.* 1961, 2.

CHAPTER EIGHT

THE LETTER TO THE GALATIANS

1. Galatia

In the course of the third century before Christ, a Celtic tribe wandered eastward, plundering the country it traversed. They crossed the Bosporus and settled down in Asia Minor when king Attalus of Pergamum put a stop to their further advance about 240 B.C. The region in which they settled comprised the basins of the rivers Halys and Sangarius. In 25 B.C. the Galatians, as these Celts were called, came under Roman rule. Their territory was enlarged by the addition of land to the south of their actual place of abode. The province of Galatia which was thus formed was bounded by the provinces of Asia to the west, Cappadocia to the east, Pontus and Bithynia to the north, and Pamphylia and Cilicia to the south. The capital of Galatia was Ancyra. The towns of Iconium, Lystra and Derbe, in the southern part of this province, were visited by Paul on his first missionary journey.

2. Destination and Date

As we have just seen, the real country of the Galatians and the province called Galatia were not identical. The country of the Galatians was situated in central Asia Minor whereas the province extended much further southward. We must therefore try to determine whether Paul is addressing inhabitants of the province or people living in the actual Galatian territory. This is important because Paul did visit the province on his first missionary journey (Acts 13, 50-14, 28) but did not go into the Galatian territory until his second journey (Acts 16, 6 and 18, 23). If by "Galatians" Paul means inhabitants of the Galatian territory proper, the letter must have been written during or after the second missionary journey. If he merely means inhabitants of the province, it may have been written during or after the first missionary journey. Arguments may be found to support either one of these assumptions. The most important arguments in favour of Galatia proper as destination are:

a) In Acts only the Galatian territory is mentioned. In 16, 6 we read: "They travelled through the Phrygian and Galatian region" and in 18, 23: "He made a journey through the region of Galatia and Phrygia".
b) In giving geographical indications Paul does not keep strictly to the boundaries of the provinces. In Gal. 1, 21 Syria means the country of Syria and in I Thess. 2, 14 Paul speaks of the country of Judaea.
c) The words "O, Galatians" would be expected in addressing persons who are Galatians in the strict sense rather than inhabitants of the province (cf. also 3, 1).

The main arguments in favour of the province of Galatia as destination are the following:

a) Nothing is known about the founding of congregations in Galatia proper. From Acts 16, 6 it appears that Paul was prevented from preaching in this region. In 18, 23 we are merely told that Paul brought new strength to the converts in the region of Galatia.
b) The account of his life which Paul gives in Galatians goes no further than the conference at Jerusalem (Acts 15). This is shown by a comparison of the descriptions of Paul's life as given in Acts and in Galatians:

Galatians	Acts
1, 11-16: Conversion of Paul	9, 1-19a: Conversion of Paul
1, 17: To Arabia and Damascus	9, 19b-25: In Damascus
1, 18-19: Back to Jerusalem after 3 years	9, 26-29: In Jerusalem

1, 21-24: To Syria and Cilicia (the province in which Tarsus is situated)

9, 30: To Tarsus

2, 1-10: After 14 years Paul returns to Jerusalem with Barnabas because of a revelation. He meets James, Cephas and John. They agree that Paul is to work among the heathens and will remember the poor of Jerusalem.

11, 25-30: Barnabas fetches Paul from Tarsus to Antioch. On account of a prophecy Paul goes with him to Jerusalem to bring support to the congregation there.

2, 11-14: Quarrel with Peter in Antioch

12, 24-25: Paul and Barnabas return to Antioch.

15, 2: Paul and Barnabas leave Antioch to meet the apostles and elders in Jerusalem.

A few details claim our attention. Galatians and Acts initially give different accounts. According to Acts Paul goes to Jerusalem by way of Damascus directly after his conversion. In Galatians, however, he says that three years passed before he went to Jerusalem. Possibly Acts merely combines events that took place over a somewhat longer period of time. There is, on the other hand, a striking parallel between Gal. 2, 1-10 and Acts 11, 25-30. This might be interpreted to mean that in Galatians Paul could not yet describe events connected with the conference at Jerusalem. Since Paul in giving an account of his life particularly wants to show his relations with Jerusalem, it is hard to understand why he should fail to mention the journey to Jerusalem on this occasion if the letter was indeed written after this event.

The advocates of a later date for this letter, i.e. after the conference at Jerusalem, are well aware of this difficulty. They can only solve it by supposing that the journey described in Acts, 11, 30 and 12, 25 is the same one as described in Acts 15, 2. The author of Acts, they argue, may have known two sources that gave an account of this journey but have failed to see that they described in fact one and the same journey. [1]

There are two further arguments, one supporting an early and one a late date:

a. If the letter was written after the conference at Jerusalem, it seems strange that Paul, while arguing against circumcision, does not refer to the decisions made on that occasion. This is not a conclusive argument. In the first place the apostolic decree seems to have been intended for Antioch, Syria and Cilicia (Acts 15, 23 but see Acts 16, 4). In the second place he did not refer to the decisions made in Jerusalem when he opposed those who in Corinth forbade the eating of consecrated food (I Cor. 8, 1-13).

b. In 4, 13, Paul says that he preached the gospel τὸ πρότερον. If this is translated as "the first time", it means that he has been in Galatia twice by the time he writes this letter, which would indicate that the letter wasn't written until after the second missionary journey. But this again is not a strong argument, since the words can just as well be translated as "formerly".

There are no really conclusive arguments, therefore, to support any particular date for this letter. The evidence may be slightly in favour of an early date, which would then have to be A.D. 48. In that case the letter was written in Antioch (Acts 14, 26). A later dating would give us A.D. 54, in which case it was written at Ephesus (Acts 19).

3. SITUATION IN THE CONGREGATION AND PURPOSE OF THE LETTER

The congregations of Galatia consisted mainly of gentile Christians:

4, 8: Formerly, when you did not acknowledge God . . .

5, 2: . . . . if you receive circumcision . . . . (cf. 6, 12).

During Paul's absence serious difficulties arose in the congre-

---

[1] J. R. Porter, "The 'Apostolic Decree" and Paul's second Visit to Jerusalem", in: *Journ. of Theol. St.* 47 1946, p. 169-174; L. CERFAUX, „Le Chapître XVe du Livre des Actes à la Lumière de la Litérature ancienne", in: *Studi e Testi* 121 1946, p. 107-126 and S. GIET, „Le second Voyage de S. Paul à Jérusalem", in: *Rev. des Sc. Rel.* 25 1951, p. 265-269.

gation. It is in reaction to this that Paul begins his letter with the words "I am astonished . . . . ." instead of with a prayer of thanksgiving as in the other letters. The difficulties may be reconstructed to some extent from the following remarks in the letter:

1, 6: people are turning away to follow a different gospel;
1, 7: some are distorting the gospel;
1, 10: Paul is seeking favour with men;
1, 11: Paul contests the view that his gospel is a human invention;
4, 10: people are observing special days and months, seasons and years;
5, 2 and 6, 12-13: they want to be circumcised.

It is clear, from this list, that pressure was brought to bear on these Christians from outside, to convince them that they should be circumcised. In 4, 10 we read that other Jewish customs were also going to be adopted. It is not quite clear whether it was intended that the Jewish law should be introduced. In 5, 3, Paul warns his readers that whoever is circumcised is obliged to keep the entire law. Possibly, however, this remark is meant ironically, for in 5, 13-26 we find that apparently all sorts of practices had survived from the time they still lived as heathens.

The congregation is not only turning towards Jewish practices, but Paul's apostleship is also being undermined. He is accused of being an apostle only "by human appointment" (see 1, 1 and 1, 12). The meaning of this accusation is not directly clear. Paul refutes it by stating emphatically that he has been called by Christ through a revelation (1, 1; 1, 12; 1, 16). The question arises, though, whether it is his calling by Jesus himself or his calling through revelation that constitutes the main point of his defence. If the Galatians demand a calling through revelation they may be compared to those whom Paul calls "superlative apostles" in Corinth. These persons based their claim to apostleship on their direct calling by the Risen Lord to preach the gospel. Or else, the Galatians would call apostles only those who, like the 12 disciples, were called by Jesus.

It is evident, from Paul's argumentation, that the latter assumption is correct. In 1, 15-2, 4 Paul describes his life, stressing on the one hand his independence with regard to the church in Jerusalem (not appointed by men):

a) direct revelation (1, 1; 1, 12; 1, 15-16);
b) rare contacts with Jerusalem (1, 17; 1, 18-19; cf. 1, 11 and 2, 1).

On the other hand he keeps stressing the fact that the apostles in Jerusalem are in complete agreement with him every time they meet.

a) agreement with the gospel of the apostles (1, 24; 2, 2; 2, 3-6).
b) the apostles shake hands with Paul (2, 9).

The repeated assurances that Paul and the apostles in Jerusalem are in complete agreement might lead us to conjecture that the Galatians claimed to derive their ideas from the apostles in Jerusalem and that they regarded Paul as merely an emissary of these apostles.

4. OPPONENTS AND PAUL'S GOSPEL

The trend in the early Christian church with which we are concerned in Galatians is not an isolated one. In Acts 10 and 11 and later at the conference at Jerusalem (Acts 15) the question of circumcision is extensively discussed. Many persons appear to regard circumcision as obligatory for heathens converted to Christianity. The question was, therefore, by which road men were called to God. Was it by way of Israel, or was God's call addressed directly to all mankind? In Acts we read that anyone who has received the Holy Spirit may be considered to have been called by God into His community (Acts. 11, 17). The desire of the heathen Christians to be circumcised must therefore be regarded as an attempt to be doubly sure of salvation. Through circumcision a man belongs to that people which received God's promises. It is true, then, that certain persons in Jerusalem did want the heathens to be circumcised, but it may be doubted whether the difficulties in Galatia were caused by persons from Jerusalem. There is no evidence at all to show that there were difficulties on that score between Paul and this congregation. From 6, 13 it might even be inferred that the advocates of circumcision were of heathen origin themselves (. . . οἱ περιτεμνόμενοι . . . θέλουσιν ὑμᾶς περιτέμνεσθαι . . .). However it is evident from Paul's plea that they did claim support for their views in Jerusalem. The Jewish Christians in Jerusalem continued to circumcise their children (Acts 21, 20-21). Paul knows this, but says that for this reason the territory of activities has been divided between Peter and Paul: Paul goes to the gentiles and Peter to the Jews (Gal. 2, 7-9).

Paul defends his views by calling circumcision a form of slavery. Those who are justified by faith no longer need to be guided like children (3, 24). They are free sons of God who may call God "Father" through the Spirit (4, 6). In the course of his plea Paul makes certain assertions which practically pronounce the law obsolete. Abraham was given the promise (3, 16), then came the law to keep mankind "in custody" (3, 23), but now faith has come (3, 25). A return to the law, therefore, is a return to an earlier stage in the history of God and mankind. In this way Paul even goes so far as to regard the keeping of the law by heathens as a return to paganism (4, 8-10).

The difficulties in Galatia were evidently of a temporary nature. As the Christian church began more and more to occupy a place of its own in the heathen world it also became separated from its Jewish background. Paul's later letters are no longer concerned with these matters.

CHAPTER NINE
THE LETTER TO THE EPHESIANS

I. Destination

According to most of the manuscripts the letter is addressed to the congregation at Ephesus, but some manuscripts from Egypt omit the words "at Ephesus" in 1, 1. Thus we find in B, Sin., 424 and 1739 ". . . . to the saints and believers that are . . . . ." (τοῖς ἁγίοις τοῖς οὖσιν καὶ πιστοῖς). Manuscript P⁴⁶ avoids the difficulty by writing: ". . . . that are saints and believers . . . ." (τοῖς ἁγίοις οὖσιν καὶ πιστοῖς). Origen also knew the letter without the words "at Ephesus".

Origen, *Comm. in Ep. Eph.* [1]

Ἐπὶ μόνων Ἐφεσίων εὕρομεν κείμενον τὸ τοῖς ἁγίοις τοῖς οὖσι.	"Only at the beginning of Ephesians do we find the text: to the saints that are".

It is not only in the Egyptian manuscripts, however, that the words are omitted, for Marcion did not find them either. This is evident from two passages in Tertullian.

Tertullian, *adv. Marc.* 5, 11:

Praetereo hic de alia epistola quam nos ad Ephesios praescriptam habemus, haeretici vero ad Laodicenos.	"I shall here leave out the other letter at the beginning of which we have "To the Ephesians", but the heretics "To the Laodiceans".

Tertullian *adv. Marc.* 5, 17:

Ecclesiae quidem veritate epistolam istam ad Ephesios habemus emissam, non ad Laodicenos, sed Marcion et titulum aliquando interpolare gestiit, quasi et in isto diligentissimus explorator. Nihil autem de titulis interest, cum ad omnes epistolas scripserit, dum ad quosdam.	"We consider it a truth of the church that the letter was sent to the Ephesians, not to the Laodiceans. But Marcion was eager to substitute a different title so that he might be regarded as a most diligent investigator in this matter also. Titles, however, are of no consequence to us. When he (the apostle) writes to a particular church he writes to all churches".

---

[1] J. A. F. Gregg, "The Commentary of Origen upon the Epistle to the Ephesians", in: *Journ. of Theol. St.* 3 1902, p. 233-244.

These quotations show that Marcion did not find the words "at Ephesus" in 1, 1, but that he published the letter with the heading (*titulum*) "To the Laodiceans". He probably based this heading on Col. 4, 16 which mentions a letter to Laodicea.

Both Origen and Marcion, therefore, knew the letter with no indication of its destination in the prescripts, but Origen believed that Ephesus was the destination and Marcion Laodicea. It may be inferred then, that the heading was added at a later date. Perhaps Ignatius is a witness from the time when the letter contained no precise indication of its destination.

Ignatius, *ad. Eph.* 12, 2:

. . . . Παύλου συμμύσται . . . ὃς ἐν πά-
ση ἐπιστολῇ μνημονεύει ὑμῶν ἐν Χριστῷ
Ἰησοῦ.

". . . You are fellow initiates of Paul, who mentions you (i.e. the congregation at Ephesus) in every letter in Christ Jesus".

From this passage it may be concluded that Ignatius was not yet thinking of any particular letter addressed to the Ephesians.

The development must have been as follows:
a) Letter without a title and without the words "at Ephesus" in 1,1.
b) Letter with a title which in Egypt, in any case, read "To the Ephesians" but in Marcion's copy "To the Laodiceans".
c) Letter including the words "at Ephesus" in 1, 1 under the influence of b.

If we assume the original letter to have carried no specific address, this may be explained by the fact that it was a circular letter. There are various arguments to support this view:

a) In contrast with Paul's other letters, this letter contains no references to any particular situation. The congregation addressed consists of Jews and heathens, who are urged to live together in harmony. The letter contains no greetings to particular persons. The only name mentioned is that of Tychicus, who carries the letter (6, 21). Paul does not know the readers of his letter (cf. 1, 15).

b) The omission of an address, such as we find in Ephesians, appears to serve the purpose of giving the letter a general character. In manuscript G the letter to the Romans is made suitable for a wider circle of readers in the same way by omitting the words "in Rome" in 1, 7 and 1, 15.

We do not know for certain, however, whether Paul was responsible for the omission of the address. Quite possibly the letter circulated originally with various addresses (with, for instance, "in Laodicea"). In that case the person who collected the letters into one volume may have left out the address altogether in order to show that the letter was meant for general use.

The addition of the title "To the Ephesians" at a later stage may be due to II Ti. 4, 12, where we read that Tychicus was sent to Ephesus. [1]

2. Connection with the Letter to the Colossians

In Appendix D, below, we have printed some passages from Ephesians and from Colossians that show that there is a certain amount of resemblance between the two letters. For this fact there are three possible explanations: Eph. depends on Col., Col. depends on Eph. or both are dependent on a third source. [2]

Of the four examples given, Eph. 6, 5-9 / Col. 3, 22-4, 1 show the greatest resemblance. In the other passages the resemblance goes no further than a single word or a short phrase. It is striking, too, that such similar words or phrases often occur in different contexts. Both Eph. 5, 15-20 and Col. 3, 16-17, for example, mention the singing of psalms and songs. In Ephesians this occurs in connection with the possession of the Spirit, but in Col. with admonishing each other. A rather similar case is presented by Eph. 2, 11-22 and Col. 1, 21-23. Both texts are concerned with heathens who are

[1] N. A. DAHL, „Adresse und Proömium des Epheserbriefes", in: *Theol. Zeitschr.* 7 1951, p. 241-264.

[2] E. PERCY, *Die Probleme der Kolosser- und Epheserbriefe*, in: *Skrifter Utgivna av Humanistika Vetenskapssamfundet i Lund* XXXIX, Lund 1946 and C. L. MITTON, *The Epistle to the Ephesians*, Oxford 1951, p. 280-321.

"estranged" and "hostile", but in Eph. the relations with Israel are meant and in Col. those with God.

If the parallels went no further than a word here and there we might doubt the literary connection. But in Eph. 1, 15-23 and Col. 1, 9-20 the train of thought also proves to be identical. Both passages are concerned with the raising of Christ above all the powers of the heavenly realms, making him the head of the church. In Col. 1, 15-20, however, this leads to a brief hymn about Christ as mediator of Creation, a subject which is not touched at all in Eph. In this instance, therefore, Col. proves to be fuller than Eph., but on the other hand Col. 1, 21-23 with the remark about Paul as minister of the gentiles (v. 23) is much briefer than Eph. 3, 1-13 which expands on this subject.

From this we may conclude that the often expressed assumption that Eph. is dependent on Col. is not tenable. It might seem as if Col. 1, 15-20 has been expanded into an argument and as if Eph. 2, 11-22 is a paraphrase of Col. 1, 21-23. On the other hand it is hard to see why the remark about Paul being the minister of the gentiles in Col. 1, 23 is not taken up till Eph. 3, and the differences between Eph. 6, 5-9 and Col. 3, 22-4, 1 are so great as almost to preclude any thought of direct dependence.

If we assume Col. to be dependent on Eph., Col. must be regarded as a kind of summary of the other letter. This again is subject to many objections.

For these reasons the existence of a third source must be assumed. This source has, however, had only a limited influence. The actual parallels between Col. and Eph. never consist of more than five consecutive words at the most, and even then they are often found in different contexts. We might say that the source influenced in particular the vocabulary used. The words in question are pithy expressions for Christian notions, such as "estranged", "hostile", "light", "head", "body". It is not likely, therefore, that a written source was used. Paul drew on the vocabulary of the church which did not yet express its faith in fixed formulas, but did already use stereotyped words and phrases.

3. Authenticity of the Letter

There are a number of aspects to this letter which can scarcely be reconciled with Paul's other letters. Consequently its authenticity is often doubted.

a) The connection with the letter to the Colossians is often explained as dependence of Eph. on Col. If this is true Eph. cannot be regarded as authentic. In view of the observations made above, however, it is preferable to assume one author rather than two. This connection is therefore no reason for not attributing Eph. to Paul.

b) Language and style of Eph. differ from those of the other letters. It has long sentences (cf. 1, 3-14) and numerous genitive constructions (1, 14: "to the praise of his glory", εἰς ἔπαινον τῆς δόξης; 1, 18: "the eyes of the heart" ὀφθαλμοὶ τῆς καρδίας; 1, 19: "the working of the strength of his power", ἐνέργεια τοῦ κράτους τῆς ἰσχύος; 2, 2: "children of disobedience" υἱοὶ τῆς ἀπειθείας). It also contains certain words which are not found in other letters, such as διάβολος and ἐπουράνια. Such grammatical and stylistic arguments, however, are not very significant for the determination of authorship. Especially as in letters the circumstances of both author and persons addressed play an important part in matters of style and vocabulary, and if it has been established, as it has in this case, that the letter in question has a special character of its own, being a circular letter, grammatical and stylistic deviations again afford no reason to deny its authorship to Paul.

c) The manner in which the church is referred to is more significant in this respect. According to Eph. the church is built on the foundations laid by apostles and prophets (2, 20). The word "church", moreover, is only used in the sense of "universal church" and not in that of "local congregation".

The problem here is to decide what Paul could and what he could not have written. If we take into account the fact that Matt. 16, 18 speaks of Peter as the foundation of the church, Paul's train of thought need not surprise us. This notion went back, in any case, as far as the earliest, Aramaic-speaking, church, so Paul may well have been acquainted with it. It would be hazardous, anyway, to accept this as a motive for not attributing the letter to Paul.

There remains one important consideration in favour of believing the letter to have been written by Paul: there is no reason why anyone else should have published this letter under Paul's name. It is typical of pseudepigraphic literature that someone wants to express new thoughts under the protection of the name of a well-known and respectable person. More on this subject will be found in our chapter on the pastoral letters below. There is nothing particularly revolutionary about the letter to the Ephesians. This has always been an obstacle to those who wish to prove that the letter was not written by Paul. Some of those who contest Paul's authorship have used this very lack of originality in the letter as an argument to prove its secondary character. They assume the letter to be a combination of all sorts of Pauline conceptions, a sort of compendium of Pauline theology. This letter, they suppose, was used as an introduction to the *corpus paulinum*. Its author, in that case, was the person who collected the letters of Paul into one volume. [1] This hypothesis, however, is not acceptable. In the first place there is no conclusive evidence to show that this letter ever came first in the volume and in the second place it bears too many characteristics of an actual letter to be regarded as an introduction.

4. REASONS FOR WRITING THE LETTER

The letter is edifying in character. It is intended to make its readers realize what they have received through their faith (1, 13-14). The author prays that they may have eyes to see this (1, 15-23). What has been gained becomes more obvious if one realizes what has been left behind (2, 1-10). The readers, originally heathens (2, 11), are told how great a privilege it is to be allowed to serve one God together with the Jews (2, 11-22). It is a joy to Paul that he may proclaim this to the heathens (3, 1-13). He charges them to be

---

[1] E. J. GOODSPEED, *An Introduction to the New Testament*, Chicago 1937, p. 222-239; MITTON, o.c. and J. KNOX, *Philemon among the Letters of Paul*, New York-Nashville 1959[2].

united (4, 1-16) in a new life filled with the Spirit (4, 17-32). The church is threatened from outside by false teachings (5, 1-21). For the life within the congregation so-called "Haustafeln" (household tables) are given which are intended to regulate mutual relations within the family (5, 22-6, 9). Finally an appeal is made to the readers to stay watchful (6, 10-20).

The letter bears witness to the author's solicitude for a young congregation that is finding it difficult to conquer remnants of heathenism and to live as Christians together with Jews. This is obviously the reason why Paul constantly uses specifically Christian words and expressions. By doing so he reminds his readers of the moment when they joined the church. The words he uses are not only the words with which the gospel was preached to them, but they are also the words that were spoken on the occasion of their baptism when they were admitted into the church.

5. PLACE AND TIME OF ORIGIN AND DESTINATION

A single indication of the circumstances in which this letter was written is found in 3, 1; 4, 1 and 6, 19, where we read that Paul is in prison. In addition it is said that Tychicus will carry the letter (6, 21). The connection with the letter to the Colossians and Paul's imprisonment, as well as the fact that Tychicus also carried the letter to the Colossians, lead us to suppose that Eph. and Col. were written one directly after the other and that Tychius took both letters with him. Since Col. offers more indications on the question of date and destination than are given by Eph. we may refer to the chapter on the letter to the Colossians for further details. In anticipation it may be said that the letters are dated to 53/4 and must have been written in Ephesus. Asia Minor is the destination.

It is not quite clear how a circular letter was sent to its various destinations. Tychicus may have carried a number of letters with identical contents, but he may also have travelled from one congregation to the other with one letter. In Col. 4, 16 the congregation at Colossae is told to read the letter addressed to Laodicea. Perhaps the letter was sent in the first place to Laodicea,

and was then taken by way of Colossae to other congregations as
well. Among the latter must have been the congregation at Hierapolis (Col. 4, 13).

6. THE PLACE OF THIS LETTER AMONG THE LETTERS OF PAUL

The interesting point about this letter is the fact that Paul
in this case draws on traditional material. We are thus given a
glimpse of theological usage in the hellenistic (-judaic) church.
Because of a lack of material for comparison, there is much that has
not yet been appreciated at its true significance. On the one hand
a literary similarity to the texts of the Dead Sea scrolls has been
discovered. [1] On the other hand parallels have been drawn with
mythological gnosticism. With respect to the latter the peculiar use
especially of the concept of "body" in this letter has been pointed
out (cf. 2, 16; 4, 4; 12, 16; 5, 23-30). [2] There can be no question of
direct borrowing in either case. The explanation must rather be
found in a complex of notions that were present in some Jewish and
heathen circles and which were annexed by the Christian church.

---

[1] K. G. KUHN, ,,Der Epheserbrief im Lichte der Qumrantexte'', in:
New Test. St. 7 1960/61, p. 334-346.

[2] G. SCHILLE, *Liturgisches Gut im Epheserbrief*, diss. Göttingen, 1953, cf.
Theol. Literaturz. 82 1957, c. 325-334.

CHAPTER TEN

THE LETTER TO THE PHILIPPIANS

1. The City of Philippi and the Origins of the Christian Congregation in this Place

The city of Philippi was named after Philip of Macedon, the father of Alexander the Great. When Antony defeated Brutus and Cassius in 42 B.C. he permitted his followers, who were forced to flee from Italy, to found a *colonia* in Philippi.

Paul visited Philippi on his second missionary journey (Acts, 16, 11-40). On the third missionary journey he must have visited the city twice on his way to and from Greece (Acts 20, 1-6).

There was a cordial relationship between Paul and the congregation as appears from Phil. 4, 10-20 and II Cor. 11, 9 which mention gifts received by the apostle from Philippi.

The congregation must have consisted mainly of gentile Christians. This is evident from Acts 16, 13, where we read that Paul, who is looking for a meeting-place of Jews, at last finds a "place of prayer" (προσευχή) by the river outside the city. Moreover the names that are mentioned in the letter, Euodia, Syntyche (4, 2) and Clement (4, 3) are not of Jewish origin.

The conversion of gentiles to the Christian faith in this region continually brought Paul into conflict with the Jews. The reason for this must be the fact that the Jews also regarded the gentiles as an object of missionary activity. In Acts 17, 5 it is said that the Jews were "jealous" and chased Paul from the neighbouring city of Thessalonica. Paul then went to Beroea but there again the Jews forced him to leave.

In I Thess. 2, 2 Paul mentions the "injury and outrage" he suffered at Philippi. We do not know whether his persecutors in this case were Jews or gentiles, for we read in the same letter that the Christians in this region also suffered persecution at the hands of the gentiles (I Thess. 2, 14).

From this it appears that the troubles in this congregation were mainly caused by outside factors.

2. Reasons for Writing this Letter

On behalf of the congregation Epaphroditus brought support to Paul, who is in prison (2, 25; 4, 14 and 18). During his stay with Paul Epaphroditus fell ill and now Paul is sending him back with the letter (2, 26-30).

These circumstances determine the contents of the letter, in which the following subjects are treated:

a) Gratitude for the faith of the congregation (1, 3-11);
b) Paul's own situation (1, 12-26);
c) appeal for harmony (1, 27-2, 18);
d) plans for the future (2, 19-3, 1);
e) warning against false teachings (3, 2-21);
f) admonitions (4, 1-9);
g) thanks for gifts and greetings (4, 10-23).

Evidently the situation in the congregation does not call for severe action on Paul's part. The appeal for harmony is kept in general terms and only two persons are mentioned by name, Euodia and Syntyche. Paul is hoping to receive good news from Timothy, whom he is planning to send to Philippi (2, 19). In these circumstances Paul has more opportunity than in his other letters to speak about his own situation. He writes about his troubles in prison and of his desire to die (1, 12-26).

The closeness of the relations between Paul and the congregation is manifested in the manner in which he speaks of the ties connecting him with the congregation. He does so in book-keeping terms. His account with the congregation is one of payments and receipts (4, 15: εἰς λόγον δόσεως καὶ λήμψεως). It is not the gift that counts for him, but the interest (4, 17: τὸν καρπόν). This interest is

placed to the credit of the Philippians' account (4, 17: τὸν πλεονά-
ζοντα εἰς λόγον ὑμῶν). Everything is receipted (4, 18: ἀπέχω δὲ
πάντα), everything has been paid (4, 18 πεπλήρωμαι).

3. The False Doctrine discussed in the Letter

In 1, 28 Paul speaks of opponents who frighten the congregation.
Undoubtedly these are the persons on whom he suddenly turns so
fiercely in 3, 2.

In 3, 2-3, 21 Paul warns his readers against those persons who
want to turn them away from their faith in Jesus Christ. This
passage contains a number of difficulties which have given rise to
quite different evaluations of the persons to whom it refers. The
problems arise from the fact that Paul at first speaks of "evil
workers", who insist on circumcision and the keeping of the law
(3, 2-11). Subsequently, however, he speaks of those who regard
their belly as their god (3, 19). In the intervening verses (3, 11-14)
Paul writes about those who have reached perfection. The question
now is whether these are all the same persons or whether Paul has
different groups in view, with deviating doctrines. In the latter
case we might think of judaists, perfectionists or libertinists.
Such an interpretation, however, proves to be unsatisfactory.

In judging the false teachers it is best to take as a point of
departure the beginning where Paul is clearly referring to persons
who are telling the congregation to be circumcised. Paul opposes to
this his own life which used to be characterized by a painstaking
observance of the law but which he exchanged for a life directed towards Jesus Christ. Through this life he is hoping to arrive at ressur-
rection from the dead (3, 11). The fulfilment of his faith, therefore,
lies in the future. This agrees with the sequel where it is stated once
more that he has not yet reached perfection. He is striving for it (3,
14). Paul is obviously defending himself against those who offer an
already present perfection. This idea is not foreign to judaism, which
states repeatedly that a person who has been circumcised and is
true to the law can reach perfection. [1] Finally Paul complains that

---

[1] B. Rigaux, „Révélation des Mystères et Perfection à Qumran et dans
le Nouveau Testament", in: *New Test. St.* 4 1957/58, p. 237-262.

his opponents are enemies of the cross. Their minds are set on earthly things, they are heading for destruction, their belly is their god, their glory is their shame (3, 19). This is clearly opposed to Paul's preaching of the kingdom of heaven that he expects (3, 20). The false teachers give only a promise of perfection on earth, without the prospect of transfiguration of the humbled body as the body of Christ was transfigured (3, 21).

The most acceptable solution for the problem is to assume that the persons referred to are Jews. This confronts us with the essential difference between Paul and the Jews. Paul preaches in Christ the way to perfection and the prospect of transfiguration. Those who follow Christ are placed on the trail and have to find their way onward (3, 16). The Jews believe they can offer more: immediate perfection. To this Paul sharply opposes: "For our *colonia* (πολίτευμα) is in heaven . . . . ."(3, 20). The Jews offer participation in a πολίτευμα on earth, the Christians offer a πολίτευμα in heaven. A πολίτευμα is a group of people who live surrounded by an ethnologically different population and lead a more or less independent existence. Thus the Jews in the dispersion had their own πολίτευμα in the various cities of the Greek-Roman empire, where they were permitted to live according to their own laws.

The opponents, therefore, are Jews who will not tolerate Paul in their own missionary territory. [1]

4. Unity of the Letter

The unity of this letter has been doubted by some because of the abrupt transition from 3, 1 to 3, 2, and because the thanks for the gifts are contained in a separate passage at the end of the letter. For this reason it has been thought that there were originally three letters:

---

[1] See also W. SCHMITHALS, „Die Irrlehrer des Philipperbriefes", in: *Zeitschr. f. Theol. u. Kirche* 54 1957, p. 297-341; H. KOESTER, "The Purpose of the Polemic of a Pauline Fragment (Philippians III)", in: *New Test. St.* 8 1961/62, p. 317-332, and A. F. J. Klijn, „Paul's Opponents in Philippians iii", in: *Nov. Test.* 7 1965, p. 278-284.

a) 4, 10-23 letter of thanks for the gifts
b) 1, 3-3, 1 and 4, 4-7 news about Epaphroditus
c) 3, 2-4, 3 and 4, 8-9 rejection of false doctrine(s)

The difficulty about this assumption is that it is not at all clear how the present letter to the Philippians came to be formed from these three short letters. There is no apparent reason why the editor should place the rejection of the false doctrine in the middle of the letter. The difficulty of the present letter is thus merely shifted to the editor, which scarcely makes it less of a problem.

There is little cause, therefore, to doubt the unity of the letter. [1]

5. TIME AND PLACE OF ORIGIN

Paul is in prison (1, 7 and 1, 13) and his life is in danger (1, 20). He is hoping, however, that his life will be saved (2, 14) and that he will soon be able to visit Philippi (1, 8 and 2, 24). The whole court (πραιτώριον) has seen how Paul is imprisoned for Christ's sake (1, 13). The "saints, especially those of the emperor's household" (οἱ ἐκ τῆς Καίσαρος οἰκίας) send their greetings (4, 22).

We have two points to go by, namely the fact that Paul is in prison and the mention of a πραιτώριον. The latter point, however, is of no great significance since there was a πραιτώριον in every town where a proconsul had his seat of office (cf. also Matt. 27, 27/ Mark 15, 16).

As far as Paul's imprisonment is concerned, Acts tells us of two occasions only when he was in prison: in Caesarea and in Rome. Both places are possible but are scarcely in conformity with the information supplied in the letter. Paul's life was never in danger in either, as far as we know. It is unlikely, moreover, that Paul was planning either in Caesarea or in Rome to go to

---

[1] W. MICHAELIS, „Teilungshypothesen bei Paulusbriefe", in: *Theol. Zeitschr.* 14 1958, p. 321-326 and G. BORNKAMM, „Die Philipperbriefe als Paulinische Briefsammlung", in: *Neotestamentica et Patristica O. Cullmann,* in: *Nov. Test. Suppl.* 6 1962, p. 192-202.

Macedonia. For this reason it is more plausible to assume that Paul was imprisoned elsewhere. According to I Cor. 15, 32 Paul's life was in danger during his stay at Ephesus. This must have been at the time of his third missionary journey (Acts 19). The letter dates from the same time as those to the Colossians and Ephesians and must therefore have been written in 53/54.

6. Significance of the Letter

This letter is written by a man who is able through his faith in Christ to talk of joy in the face of death. No other one of Paul's letters speaks of joy and comfort as often as this one does. Christ's power is proclaimed here through the example given by Paul.

The hymn to Christ quoted in 2, 5-11 is rather significant. He has humbled himself in order that he may receive the "name above all names". This hymn is an expression of the faith of the hellenistic church.

Finally, the letter is significant on account of the information it gives concerning the relations between Christian and Jewish preaching among gentiles. From ch. 3 it is evident that Christian preaching was difficult mainly because it did not offer immediate "perfection". Both the Jews and the preachers with a libertinist tendency (see above, the chapter on the letter to the Corinthians), on the other hand, offered a guarantee of perfection to be acquired immediately. Paul blames the former group for their earthly-mindedness and the latter for withdrawing entirely from the earth. In Paul's eyes his preaching is not consummated as long as created things, of which the human body forms a part, do not share in the renewal. Against those who anticipate the future in any manner whatsoever, this letter preaches with the words "already, but not yet".

CHAPTER ELEVEN

THE LETTER TO THE COLOSSIANS

1. THE CHRISTIAN COMMUNITY OF COLOSSAE

In Paul's time Colossae was a small town, situated in the valley of the river Lycus, about 110 miles east of Ephesus as the crow flies. Paul never visited the town but he has heard about the congregation there (1, 4 and 9; 2, 1). The origins of the congregation are not definitely known but Epaphras was probably the founder. In any case he informed Paul about the congregation (1, 7-8). Epaphras is called Paul's "fellow slave" (1, 7) and "one of yourselves" (4, 12). It may be assumed that he worked, on Paul's instructions and perhaps with Ephesus as the base of his activities, in the region east of Ephesus, visiting not only Colossae but also the nearby towns of Laodicea and Hierapolis (2, 1 and 14, 13).

The congregation consisted chiefly of gentile Christians (1, 21; 2, 13 and 3, 5-7). They gathered in so-called "house-churches", among which those at the houses of Nympha (4, 15) and Archippus (4, 17, cf. Philem. 2) are known by name.

2. CIRCUMSTANCES IN WHICH THE LETTER WAS WRITTEN

Paul wrote the letter in prison (1, 24; 4, 3.10 and 18). Epaphras visited him there (1, 7-8) and stayed with him even after the letter was sent off (4, 12). Fellow-prisoners of Paul's were Timothy (1, 1) and Aristarchus ("my fellow-captive" 4, 11). Also in his company were Mark (4, 10), Justus ("who is of the circumcision", 4, 11), Luke and Demas (4, 14). Tychicus who was also with Paul, carried the letter and was on that occasion accompanied by Onesimus (4, 7-9). Mark, too, was to go to Colossae.

3. REASONS FOR WRITING THE LETTER

The letter shows that Paul was grateful for what he heard from Epaphras concerning the congregation. He found it necessary, however, to exhort the Christians to live righteously and keep to the true faith. Righteous living was a matter typically attended by difficulties in gentile-Christian congregations which found it very hard to adjust themselves to the Christian way of life (cf. Gal. 5, 16-26; Eph. 4, 17-32; I Thess. 4, 1-8). This difficulty is touched on at the beginning of the letter (1, 10) and the whole conclusion, too, is devoted to the new way of life (3, 5-4, 6). This life is inseparably bound up with the gospel to which Paul's readers have been called (1, 21-23).

With respect to the true faith, it appears that there were certain persons who attempted to make these people change their minds. This made it necessary for Paul to expand on the subject of the false teachings propagated at Colossae.

4. THE FALSE TEACHINGS PROPAGATED AT COLOSSAE

Paul calls these false teachings "specious arguments" (πιθανολογία 2, 4) and "philosophy" (φιλοσοφία 2, 8). From this it appears that they were in some particular way concerned with divine and human existence. These speculations carried with them certain consequences for daily life. According to Paul people are being taken to task about what they "eat and drink" and about the observance of "festivals, new moon and sabbath" (2, 16). The mention of festivals would seem to point to Jewish notions, but the abstention from food appears to be connected with an ascetic attitude to life. This is confirmed by the passage which speaks of "mortification of the body" (2, 21-23). This way of life has an "air of wisdom" (2, 23). Evidently this attitude to life is based on some profound reasoning which rejected all things material.

Paul also speaks of vain deceit according to the "spirits of the world" (στοιχεῖα τοῦ κόσμου, 2, 8) and about the propagation of "voluntary humility" and "angel-worship" (2, 18). The question is whether the theological speculations referred to actually contained notions about "spirits of the world" and angels. It is quite possible that Paul merely inferred from the practices of the false teachers that their life consisted in fact of the serving of angels and "spirits of the world". We find in the letter to the Galatians that Paul identifies life under the "spirits of the world" with life under the law (Gal. 4, 3). The letter to the Colossians contains a similar notion where Paul says that his readers have passed beyond the reach of the spirits of the world. In his eyes, therefore, the false teachings constitute a relapse into heathenism. The observance of "certain days" may have been regarded by Paul as a form of angel-worship, for in these regions planets and angels were not kept strictly distinct. However this may be, Paul's reproach to the false teachers is that their way of life as Christians is not derived from their faith in Christ but from human reasoning and observation.[1]

Against this, Paul opposes the all-embracing power of Christ. In him everything was created (1, 16). There is no reason, therefore, to neglect or abstain from the material world. To show this Paul draws on Jewish notions concerning "wisdom", the mediator in creation, through whom God created everything (1, 15-20). He transfers these notions to Christ and adds to them by pointing out that Christ has also conquered the powers. He has disarmed them (2, 15).[2]

This emphasis on Christ as mediator of creation and conqueror of the powers indicates that we are indeed dealing with Jewish notions, but that these false teachings are not the same as those in Galatia and Corinth. The heart of the matter is not the importance of circumcision (in spite of 2, 11 which does not refer to any obligation to be circumcised), nor direct communion with the Risen Lord, but the question of the oneness of God. The point is whether the "completeness" of God is scattered over the universe in the form of divine beings, angels, powers and planets, or whether it is to be found in God alone, who has made his godhead to dwell in Christ

---

[1] G. BORNKAMM, „Die Häresie des Kolosserbriefes", in: *Theol. Literaturz.* 73 1948, c. 11, 20.

[2] E. KÄSEMANN, „Eine urchristliche Taufliturgie", in: *Festschr. R. Bultmann*, Stuttgart-Köln 1949, p. 133-148.

(1, 19). Paul's reply is that on the one hand God and the material world should be kept separate, but that on the other the connection between God and His creation must not be severed. The false teachings bring about a synthesis of Jewish beliefs concerning creation, and Greek thought, which considers everything to emanate from God. Paul corrects this line of thought by pointing out that there is in fact only *one* emanation, being Christ, and that this emanation does not mean any diminution of the fullness of God, but that the complete godhead is present in it.

The false teachings discussed here clearly form the origin of later gnostic systems, such as that of the Valentinians, which regard the whole of the universe as a diffusion of the supreme God fading away gradually into a corrupt creation. In this corrupt material world, man has the task of following the way back from creation to its origin.

5. TIME AND PLACE OF ORIGIN

The letter was written during Paul's imprisonment. According to Acts there are only two places to choose from, Caesarea and Rome. Certain indications, however, make such a choice a difficult one. Paul has been visited by Epaphras from Colossae and he sends Tychicus, who is accompanied by Onesimus, back to Colossae (4, 7-9). Onesimus is the person mentioned in the letter to Philemon, a slave who ran away from his master, this same Philemon. It seems unlikely that Onesimus could have fled all the way to Caesarea or Rome or that he could have found Paul there. In view of the great distance this seems very doubtful indeed. For this reason it would be more plausible to assume that this letter was written at Ephesus as was that to the Philippians. In that case, the letter should also be dated in 53/4. The only argument against this rather early date is the fact that the letter states in 1, 6 and 1, 23 that the gospel has been preached in the whole world. If we take this preaching of the gospel to refer to Paul's activities alone, the statement is a little extravagant. But if we take into account the fact that the gospel was preached at an early date both in Rome and in Egypt, though not by Paul but by Jews, there is certainly no exaggeration in Paul's remarks.

The letter was written at the same time as that to the Ephesians. This may be inferred not only from the similarities discussed in our chapter on the letter to the Ephesians but also from the fact that Tychicus carried both letters.

6. AUTHENTICITY

If the authenticity of the letter to the Ephesians is doubted, it is necessary to pronounce some judgment also concerning the letter to the Colossians. If the letter to the Ephesians is accepted as authentic, the authenticity of Colossians cannot be doubted.

7. SIGNIFICANCE OF THE LETTER

The letter is of great significance because it does not, as do the letters to the Galatians and the Romans, discuss the relations between judaism and Christianity, but those between Christianity and Greek thought. This letter does not deal with sin and righteousness through faith in Christ, but with subjection to the whims of fate and the victory of Christ. It is notably not the cross and reconciliation that are stressed here, but the resurrection and the ascension of Christ. Paul preaches that insight into man's condition is not what determines his fate, but his relationship with the Lord who was resurrected after death (2, 14-15). Especially in the Greek church, which suffered much in the early days from various gnostic sects, Paul's ideas acquired great significance. The letter to the Colossians thus represents the first confrontation of Christianity with a trend against which it was to be forced to defend itself for centuries to come.

CHAPTER TWELVE

THE LETTERS TO THE THESSALONIANS

1. THE CITY OF THESSALONICA AND THE ORIGINS OF ITS CHRISTIAN COMMUNITY

In Paul's days the city of Thessalonica, (nowadays called Salonica) was already more than three centuries old. It was a flourishing port, connected on the landward side with the Via Egnatia, a paved road leading from the Adriatic Sea to the Bosporus. There were Jews living in this town, who had their own synagogue (Acts 17, 1-4).

Paul visited Thessalonica on his second missionary journey. According to Acts he preached "three sabbaths" in the synagogue, after which the Jews forced him and his companion Silas to leave the city (17, 1-12). The picture here given may be supplemented by information from the letters. From these we gather that the majority of the congregation at Thessalonica were gentile Christians (I, 1, 9; I, 2, 14). The letter also confirms the account given in Acts which says that preaching here was attended by considerable difficulties (I, 2, 2). There appear to have been close ties between Paul and this congregation, as also between Paul and the Christians of the nearby town of Philippi (I, 2, 9; 1, 3, 6).

We may wonder whether the congregation could really have been formed, as we read in Acts, after three weeks of preaching. The time seems to be rather short to make it an "example" (I, 1, 6). The fact, moreover, that Paul apparently earned his own living seems to indicate a longer stay (I, 2, 9; II, 3, 8), as does the fact that he also appears to have received assistance several times from the congregation at Philippi (Phil. 4, 16). On the other hand it must be noted that Paul evidently did not consider his mission in the town completed (I, 3, 10).

2. CIRCUMSTANCES IN WHICH THE LETTERS WERE WRITTEN

I Thess. was sent off by Paul while he was in the company of Silas
and Timothy (I, 1, 1; cf. II, 1, 1).

Paul has sent Timothy from Athens to Thessalonica (I, 3, 1-2).

Timothy has returned (I, 3, 6).

These data may be compared with those furnished by Acts:
Paul travels from Philippi (16, 12) to Thessalonica (17, 1).

After a short stay in this city Paul is accused by the Jews (17, 5-6)
and leaves for Beroea (17, 10).

Paul has to leave Beroea because the Thessalonian Jews are
impeding his activities there. He leaves Silas and Timothy
behind (17, 10-14).

Paul goes to Athens and Corinth, where he is joined again by
Silas and Timothy (18, 5).

Timothy's arrival in I, 3, 6 may be identified with Timothy's
arrival in Corinth (Acts 18, 5). This implies that the letter was
written around 50 A.D. in Corinth.

With the help of I Thess. and Acts the travels of Timothy and
Silas may now be reconstructed. According to I Thess. 3, 1-2.
Timothy, who stayed behind in Beroea (Acts 17, 13-14), was sent
to Thessalonica from Athens. We must therefore assume that he
first went from Beroea to Athens, or that Paul called him to Athens
from there. From Athens, then, he travelled to Thessalonica. In the
meantime Paul went to Corinth where he was again joined by
Timothy. It is not possible to reconstruct Silas' activities during this
time. Possibly he went from Beroea direct to Corinth.

II Thes. gives no information about the circumstances in which
it was written. Two things, however, may help us to determine
the date. In the first place the prescripts of the two letters are
of like content, and in the second the two letters contain a number
of similar passages:

I Thess. 2, 9:
... τὸν κόπον ἡμῶν καὶ τὸν μόχθον·
νυκτὸς καὶ ἡμέρας ἐργαζόμενοι πρὸς τὸ
μὴ ἐπιβαρῆσαί τινα ὑμῶν ...

II Thess. 3, 8:
... ἀλλ' ἐν κόπῳ καὶ μόχθῳ νυκτὸς καὶ
ἡμέρας ἐργαζόμενοι πρὸς τὸ μὴ ἐπιβαρῆσαί τινα ὑμῶν

I 3, 4:   II 3, 10:
καὶ γὰρ ὅτε πρὸς ὑμᾶς ἦμεν   καὶ γὰρ ὅτε πρὸς ὑμᾶς
I 5, 12:   II 2, 1:
Ἐρωτῶμεν δὲ ὑμᾶς, ἀδελφοί   Ἐρωτῶμεν δὲ ὑμᾶς, ἀδελφοί
I 2, 1:   II 3, 7:
Αὐτοὶ γὰρ οἴδατε . . .   αὐτοὶ γὰρ οἴδατε . . .

In addition there are many similarities in the contents of the
two letters. For these reasons we may assume that they were written
within a short time of each other.

3. Reasons for Writing the Letters

Timothy's return from Thessalonica with news about the congregation in that city is the immediate cause of the writing of
I Thess. Apparently Paul had been worried about the life of this
congregation which he had been forced to leave prematurely. He
would have liked to pay another visit to "mend your faith where it
falls short" (I, 3, 10).

It might be inferred from the letter that Paul heard from Timothy
that the Thessalonians were rather disappointed because he had
not come personally, only sending them one of his fellow-workers.
This may be why he keeps stressing that he had wanted to come
(I 2, 17-18; 3, 6), that Satan himself prevented him (2, 18) and that
it had even been a sacrifice for him to send Timothy (3, 2). By
writing extensively about the affection he feels for the congregation
he shows that his failure to visit them was not the consequence of
any estrangement between them and himself (2, 1-12).

It is evident, moreover, that Timothy brought Paul good tidings
about the congregation. This reassured him, for he had been afraid
they would give way under "oppression". They suffered this
oppression at the hands of heathens (2, 14). This prompts him to a
sharp outburst against the Jews (2, 15-16). This outburst is not easy
to explain. It may be that Paul has had some unpleasant experiences
with Jews in Corinth where he wrote the letter (cf. Acts 18, 5-6),
but possibly he remembers how the Jews in Thessalonica stirred the
heathens up against him when he was there (Acts 17, 5-9).

Only two things Timothy told him oblige Paul to go into details on concrete points. This is in the first place the way of life of the Christians which still stands in need of correction (4, 1-12). In the second place certain questions had been asked about "those who sleep in death" (4, 13-18). The precise nature of these questions is no longer clear. Paul replies, however, that there will be no discrimination against the dead as compared with those who are still alive at the time of the Second Coming. First the dead will rise, then "we who are left alive" will be "caught up in the clouds" together with them "to meet the Lord" (4, 17). It seems as if the Thessalonians believed that only those who are alive when the Messiah comes will share in eternal salvation.

II Thessalonians is a short letter and the reason why it was written is immediately clear: certain questions concerning the Second Coming (2, 1). Paul is worried about the congregation which has been thrown into confusion by "some oracular utterance, or pronouncement, or some letter purporting to come from us" (2, 2). It would be interesting to know what Paul means by a "letter purporting to come from us". We cannot be sure that this is the right translation. If ὡς δι' ἡμῶν is translated "as (if) from us" Paul may be referring to the possibility or even the actual presence of such a forged letter. In that case the conclusion (3, 17) is intended to prevent their believing in such forged letters. On the other hand we might translate "as (the one) from us". This might then refer to I Thess., which has caused confusion among the Thessalonians.

The main point to be noted about this letter, however, is the fact that Paul no longer speaks of "those who sleep in death" but of "the Day of the Lord". Apparently some have alleged that this day "is already there" (ἐνέστηκεν ἡ ἡμέρα τοῦ κυρίου, 2, 2). Most likely this should be interpreted to mean that some people say full salvation is now already given on earth. Ideas of this sort were current in certain circles where a disproportionate stress was laid on the possession of the Spirit (I Cor. 15) as well as in some Jewish groups (Phil. 3). The remark about the "oracular utterance" might point to the former possibility, but the nearness of Philippi makes the latter more likely. Whichever assumption is true, though, Paul points out in this connection that the Day of the Lord certainly hasn't come, since the "lawless one" has not yet been revealed (cf. 2, 7-12). The apostasy is still to come.

If according to current ideas in Thessalonica salvation had already been realized, this does throw light, not only on the problem of "those who sleep in death" but it also explains why this second letter was written so soon after the first. The dying of Christians, about which the Thessalonians had evidently asked Paul, through Timothy, for information, presented a problem if they had already received full salvation. For how is death to be reconciled with the life received in Christ, that no longer needs to wait for completion? In I Thess. Paul replies to this as best he can, not knowing that the question arises from certain notions about the "Day of the Lord" which the Thessalonians had not learned from him (II, 2, 15). In some way or other, however, he finds out that the difficulties about the dead are caused by in his opinion erroneous views about the Day of the Lord. In the second letter, then, he can do no better than repeat what he has always said: the Day of the Lord is still to come and it will complete whatever is still lacking for the full salvation of mankind. What Paul said in I Thess. retains its significance: this completion concerns both those who are still living at that time and those who have already died.

4. AUTHENTICITY OF II THESSALONIANS

The authenticity of II Thess. has been doubted on account of the statement that opens the passage about the Second Coming, namely that what follows is in accordance with what Paul "frequently" told them when he was still with them. This has been thought incompatible with I, 4, 13-18 where Paul, in speaking about the Second Coming, is evidently saying things that are new to the Thessalonians. For this reason some have thought that II Thess. was written after the time of the apostles when the church had to be prepared for a long wait before the Lord was to return.

Some have sought to solve this discrepancy by assuming that the two letters were addressed to different groups within the congregation (II Thess. to Jewish Christians, I Thess. to gentile Christians).[1] Others supposed that II Thess. preceded I Thess. in time.[2] These assumptions, however, find little factual support, since there is nothing to show that the letters were sent to different groups, and since II, 2, 15 presupposes a previous letter from Paul to the Thessalonians.

The difficulty is eliminated, however, if we take note of the fact that I Thess. does not so much discuss the question of the Second Coming as, rather, the dying of Christians *before* the Second Coming. They are deeply concerned about the fate of the individual Christian. In discussing this subject, Paul may well be telling them things he did not mention in his preaching. Later, when Paul learns more details, he realizes that the difficulties concerning the dead were caused by certain notions about the Day of the Lord, which was believed to be already there. Now he can repeat what he has often said before: the Day of the Lord is still to come. He proves this by saying that before that Day the "lawless one" first has to be revealed.

There is therefore no need to doubt the authenticity of II Thess. The two letters supplement each other. The second letter is evidently based on more detailed information concerning certain difficulties for which the first letter could not yet provide an explicit answer.

---

[1] A. v. HARNACK, „Das Problem des zweiten Thessalonischerbriefes", in: *Sitz. ber. der kgl. Preus. Akad. der Wissensch.* 1910, p. 560-578.

[2] As early as HUGO GROTIUS, cf. B. RIGAUX, *Saint Paul. Les Épîtres aux Thessaloniciens*, in: *Études Bibl.*, Paris-Gembloux 1956, p. 69.

CHAPTER THIRTEEN

THE LETTERS TO TIMOTHY AND TITUS

There is such a great similarity between these letters both in contents and from a literary point of view that they may treated together. From the 18th century onwards it has been customary to call these letters "the pastoral letters", referring to the fact that they are mainly devoted to pastoral directives concerning the internal life of the Christian communities.

1. PERSONS ADDRESSED

Timothy and Titus were Paul's most faithful companions on his travels.

Timothy was living in Lystra or Iconium (Acts 16, 1) when Paul visited these parts on his second missionary journey. He had a Greek father and a Jewish mother. His mother's name was Eunice and his grandmother's Lois (II Tim. 1, 5). From here on he accompanied Paul, who had him circumcised so that he might be accepted by the Jewish communities of the Greek world which were frequented by Paul (Acts 16, 3). From Asia Minor Paul travelled with Timothy to Thessalonica and Beroea, where Timothy and Silas stayed behind (Acts 17, 14). When Paul was in Athens, Timothy joined him again (I Thess. 3, 1-2) after which he left once more for Thessalonica. He came to Corinth to report to Paul on this visit (Acts 18, 5) which report led to the writing of Paul's first letter to the congregation at Thessalonica. When Paul was in Ephesus on his third missionary journey, Timothy was in his company (Acts 19, 22). Paul sent him by way of Macedonia to Corinth, which he reached after the arrival of the first letter to the Corinthians (I Cor. 16, 10). After this we lose sight of Timothy. His name is mentioned only once more, when we read in Acts that Paul met him in Troas. He had travelled ahead to Troas from Greece (Acts 20, 4).

The following letters of Paul were written while Timothy was in his company: Romans (see 16, 21 at Corinth in 56/57); II Corinthians (see 1, 1 in Macedonia in 56); Philippians (see 1, 1 at Ephesus in 53/54); Colossians (see 1, 1 at Ephesus 53/54); I and II Thessalonians (I, 1, 1 and II, 1, 1 at Corinth in 50) and Philemon (see 1, at Ephesus in 53/54).

It appears from all this that Timothy occupied himself especially with the various congregations in Macedonia. This is confirmed by Phil. 2, 19 where Paul says he will send Timothy to Philippi.

Titus is only mentioned in the letters to the Galatians and the Corinthians. From Gal. 2, 1 and 3 it appears that he accompanied Paul on the latter's journey from Antioch to Jerusalem. This journey is described in Acts 11, 25-30. Titus was a Greek, but he was not "compelled to be circumcised" (Gal. 2, 3). It was he who carried the "severe letter" to Corinth, after which he met Paul in Macedonia where he was able to give Paul good news about the congregation at Corinth (II, 7, 6, 13 and 14). II Cor. 8 tells us, furthermore, that Titus was to make preparations for a collection of money for Jerusalem in Corinth before Paul's visit to that city.

Thus we may infer that Titus occupied himself especially with the congregation at Corinth.

2. CIRCUMSTANCES IN WHICH THE LETTERS WERE WRITTEN

a. I *Timothy*

Paul has instructed Timothy to stay in Ephesus while he himself goes to Macedonia (I, 1, 3). He is planning to visit Timothy (I, 3, 14 and 4, 13).

b. II *Timothy*

Paul is in prison (II, 1, 8) in Rome (II, 1, 17). His case has been heard, but his defence seems to have been successful (II, 4, 16-17). In spite of this he is expecting to die (II, 4 ,18 and 4, 6-8). He requests Timothy to come to him (II, 4, 9 and 21).

The letter contains a great deal of information, particularly about a number of persons who are unknown to us:

In Asia many people have fallen away from the church (II, 1, 15);

Paul suffered persecution in Antioch, Iconium and Lystra (II, 3, 11);

Paul left his cloak behind with Carpus at Troas (II, 4, 13);

Erastus stayed behind at Corinth (II, 4, 20);

Paul left Trophimus ill at Miletus (II, 4, 20);

In Asia Phygelus and Hermogenes deserted Paul (II, 1, 15);

Onesiphorus helped him at Ephesus (II, 1, 16 and 4, 19);

Demas deserted him and went to Thessalonica (II, 4, 10);

Crescens went to Galatia (II, 4, 10);

Titus went to Dalmatia (II, 4, 10);

Luke is with Paul (II, 4, 11);

Tychicus was sent to Ephesus (II, 4, 12);

Paul is hoping that Mark will come with Timothy (II, 4, 11);

Alexander the copper-smith has done Paul much harm (II, 4, 14);

Greetings are sent to Aquila and Priscilla (II, 4, 19);

Greetings are sent from Eubulus, Pudens, Linus, Claudia and others (II, 4, 21).

c. *Titus*

Paul has left Titus behind in Crete (1, 5). He himself is at Nicopolis (3, 12) where he is planning to spend the winter. He is going to send Artemas and Tychicus to Crete and hopes that Titus will come to him from there (3, 12). Zenas, the lawyer, and Apollos are commended (3, 13).

3. REASONS FOR WRITING THE LETTERS

a. I *Timothy*

The letter is intended to supplement the instructions Paul gave to Timothy before he left Ephesus. Timothy is warned against erroneous doctrines (I, 1, 3-11). This is a task with which Paul, who was himself called by Christ, can trust Timothy (I, 1, 12-20). A passage containing instructions concerning prayer, women, bishops and deacons (I, 2, 1-3, 16) is followed by another warning against false teachings (I, 4, 1-16). Next come instructions about widows, elders and slaves (I, 5, 1-6, 2). The letter concludes with a warning against riches (I, 6, 20-21.)

b. II *Timothy*

The admonitions in this letter are mainly addressed to Timothy himself. He is told to be firm (II, 1, 3-18), to take his share of hardship (II, 2, 1-13), to adhere to the true doctrine (II, 2, 14-3, 13), and to continue teaching (II, 3, 14-4, 8).

c. *Titus*

Titus is instructed to appoint elders to keep discipline (1, 5-6). This is followed by admonitions concerning old men, young men and slaves (2, 1-15). The letter is concluded with an appeal for a life of good works (3, 1-11).

These letters are intended as directives for a new congregation on matters of controlling, guiding, keeping and teaching its members. The congregation is threatened from outside by all sorts of false teachings which attempt to throw the members into confusion. These influences are combated by appointing officials whose way of living is known to be above reproach, and by an appeal to adhere to the true doctrine.

4. AUTHENTICITY OF THE LETTERS

Paul's authorship is contested on the following five grounds:

a) The situation as described in the letters is not in conformity with the data supplied by Acts.
b) The literary usage of the letters is not in conformity with Paul's other letters.
c) The church is described in a manner not found in Paul's other letters.
d) The definition of the Christian faith differs from that found in other letters of Paul.
e) The false teachings do not fit into the Pauline period.

A discussion of these points yields the following result:

a. *Situation*

According to I Timothy Paul has set out for Macedon from Ephesus, leaving Timothy behind. He is hoping to visit him later on.

On his third missionary journey Paul did go from Ephesus to Macedonia (20, 1), but there is nothing to show that Timothy stayed behind. On the contrary, Timothy very likely did accompany him on this journey, since we read (Acts 20, 4) that Timothy travelled on ahead from Macedonia.

The imprisonment in Rome of which we read in II Tim. could only be that of Acts 28, 11-23. But the facts of the two texts are incompatible. Paul's third missionary journey did take him to Troas (Acts 20, 6) and Miletus (Acts 20, 13-38), but this must have taken place three or four years before his imprisonment in Rome. The remarks in II Tim. about a cloak left behind in Troas and about Trophimus who was kept in Miletus by an illness would seem to indicate that Paul's visits to those places were of quite recent date.

The letter to Titus was written in Nicopolis. Paul may have visited this town on his travels through Macedonia (Acts 20, 3) but he certainly did not have the opportunity of founding a congregation in Crete where Titus was left behind. Acts 27, 8 des describe a visit of Paul to Crete, but he came there as a prisonoer and was no able to develop any missionary activity.

On account of these facts it is generally believed that the situation as described in the pastoral letter cannot be fitted into the travel narrative furnished by Acts. One possibility remains, namely that Paul was set free after the imprisonment of Acts 28 and that he travelled to the east once more. There are more data to support the former assumption than the latter. The following texts from early Christian literature are important in this connection:

I Clement 5, 7:	After he had taught the whole
δικαιοσύνην διδάξας ὅλον τὸν κόσμον,	world righteousness and had come
καὶ ἐπὶ τὸ τέρμα τῆς δύσεως ἐλθὼν καὶ	to the extreme west and testified
μαρτυρήσας ἐπὶ τῶν ἡγουμένων, οὕτως	before the rulers he was taken away
ἀπηλλάγη τοῦ κόσμου, καὶ εἰς τὸν ἅγιον	from this world in this way and
τόπον ἀνελήμφθη, ὑπομονῆς γενόμενος	brought to the sacred place, the
μέγιστος ὑπογραμμός.	greatest example of patience.

Actus Petri cum Simone I
Et ieiunans triduo Paulus et petens a domino quod aptum sibi esset, vidit itaque visionem, dicentem sibi dominum: Paule surge et qui in Spania sunt corpore tuo medicus esto.

And Paul fasted for three days and asked the Lord what was best for him and he had a vision and the Lord said to him: Paul, stand up and become a physician to those who are in Spain by going there yourself.

Fragmentum Muratori 34-39
... Acta autem omnium apostolorum sub uno libro scripta sunt. Lucas optimo Theophilo comprendit quae sub praesentia eius singula gerebantur sicuti et semota passione Petri evidenter declarat sed et profectione Pauli ab urbe ad Spaniam proficiscentis ...

The Acts of all the Apostles have been written down in one book. Luke sums up for the excellent Theophilus all the various events that took place in his presence, as he makes clear by his omission of Peter's martyrdom and also of Paul's departure from the city for Spain.

Eusebius, *Hist. Eccl.* II, 22, 2
τότε μὲν οὖν ἀπολογησάμενον, αὖθις ἐπὶ τὴν τοῦ κηρύγματος διακονίαν λόγος ἔχει στείλασθαι τὸν ἀπόστολον, δεύτερον δ' ἐπιβάντα τῇ αὐτῇ πόλει τῷ κατ' αὐτὸν τελειωθῆναι μαρτυρίῳ· ἐν ᾧ δεσμοῖς ἐχόμενος τὴν πρὸς Τιμόθεον δευτέραν ἐπιστολὴν συντάττει ...

After he (Paul) had defended himself he went away again, so it is said, in the service of preaching but when the apostle came to the same city (Rome) a second time, his life ended in martyrdom. During his imprisonment on this occasion he wrote the second letter to Timothy ...

Evidently there were very old traditions according to which Paul went to Spain. We can't be certain, however, that these traditions were not based on the letter to the Romans, in which Paul unfolds his plan to go to Spain (Rom. 15, 23 and 28). Only Eusebius mentions a new trip to the east. Very likely, however, Eusebius derived his information only from II Timothy. Many colophons of later manuscripts repeat what Eusebius says.

It may concluded, therefore, that the situation described in the pastoral letters argues against Paul's authorship.

b. *Literary usage*

In comparison with other letters of Paul the pastoral letters contain many words, that are not found elsewhere in Paul's writings. Examples are: σώφρων, σωφρόνως, σωφρονίζειν, σωφρονισμός, σωφροσύνη, εὐσεβεῖν, εὐσεβῶς, εὐσέβεια, λογομαχεῖν, λογομαχία, συνείδησις ἀγαθή and καθαρά, λόγος ὑγιής. Instead of κύριοι the pastoral letters use δεσπόται for the masters of slaves.

Other words, which do occur in Paul's other letters, are not found here: ἀκροβυστία, ἀποκάλυψις, διαθήκη, δικαιοσύνη θεοῦ, ἐλευθεροῦν, ἐνεργεῖν, καυχᾶσθαι, ἄρα, διό, ἔπειτα, μήπως, ὅπως and πάλιν.

In the style of the pastoral letters we miss the anacolutha that occur so frequently in the other letters. The subject-matter of the pastoral letters is also differently disposed. In the other letters similar subjects are always placed together, while here the author returns to the same subject in different places.

Style and usage cannot be taken as positive proof in questions of authorship. In this connection the subject treated is very important. Since the question of the relations between gentile Christians and Jews or Jewish Christians is not treated here, it is not surprising if such words as circumcision, covenant and "righteousness" do not occur.

c. *The church*

The church is a "pillar and bulwark of the truth" (στῦλος καὶ ἑδραίωμα τῆς ἀληθείας; I, 3, 15). It is not only the repository but also the guardian of the truth. For this reason it is necessary that its members should adhere to the traditional faith and the right doctrine (I, 4, 6). This demands close ties with appointed leaders. A person may "aspire to leadership" (I, 3, 1), but this important office requires a life above reproach. This is true of "bishops" (I, 3, 1-7; Tit. 1, 7-9) and deacons (I, 3, 8-13) as well as elders (I, 5, 17-19; Tit. 1, 3-6). They must be appointed in a regular manner by the laying on of hands as Paul (II, 1, 6) and the elders (I, 4, 14) did to Timothy. Timothy in his turn must lay his hands on the leaders of the congregation (I, 5, 22) and Titus must appoint elders (Tit. 1, 5).

The church is thus strictly organized, but the offices of elders and bishops are not yet kept distinct (cf. I, 3, 1-7; and Tit. 1, 5-9). This agrees with Acts 20, 17 and 28 but it differs from the way the later church was organized. There does seem to have been only one bishop where there were a group of elders (cf. I, 3, 2 and Tit. 1, 7).

It is not easy to evaluate these data. Compared with II Cor. 12-14 the offices appear to have gained a practical aspect which does not seem likely in Paul's time. We cannot be sure, however, that the congregation of Corinth may be taken as an example of Paul's ideas about offices. Phil. 1, 1, for instance, does mention bishops and deacons. It should be noted, furthermore, that we cannot conclude from the pastoral letters that the notions in them are generally accepted. They seem to be directives, rather, for people who still have to be instructed in these matters.

If we wish to defend Paul's authorship, however, we must assume that Paul's own views have developed. The same author who previously talked in rather general terms about leaders of the congregations (προϊστάμενος; cf. I Thess. 5, 12-13 and Rom. 12, 8) has now arrived at a conception of office which is not only divorced from the "gift of the Spirit" (Cor.) but which has also developed into a strict system based purely on common moral virtues.

d. *The Christian faith*

The Christian faith is a treasure which has been entrusted to the believers (I, 6, 20 and II, 1, 14). The believer has been taught to know it as the truth (I, 4, 3; II, 2, 25; II, 3, 7). That is why the faith is a doctrine (I, 4, 13; Tit. 2, 10).

Certain adjectives constantly and conspicuously accompany both faith and doctrine: wholesome teaching (I, 1, 10; II, 4, 3; Tit. 1, 9; 2, 1), the good profession (I, 6, 12) and unfeigned faith (I, 1, 5). All these should proceed from a clean heart (I, 1, 5; II, 2, 22), a good conscience (I, 1, 5; 1, 19) or a clear conscience (I, 3, 9; II, 1, 3).

It naturally follows that it is possible to "know" the faith. It is possible to have knowledge of the truth (II, 2, 25; 3, 7). The believers possess this knowledge (I, 4, 3).

This way of speaking about the faith arises from the danger of false doctrines (I, 1, 3 and 6, 3). For this reason the faith must be defined and adhered to and defended as a creed or doctrine. This is an obvious development as compared with the letters of Paul, in which the faith consists in the first place of communion with the Risen Lord.

This development that may be inferred from the pastoral letters is no conclusive proof against Paul's authorship. The danger of false doctrines may well have led even Paul to a more objective definition of the faith. Nevertheless it is rather striking that this development took place at the expense of the expression "in Christ" which occurs so frequently in the other letters.

e. *The false doctrines*

The remarks about false doctrines may be summed up as fol'ows:

a) They occupy themselves with "myths" and "interminable genealogies" (γενεαλογία: I, 1, 4; cf. Tit. 3, 9).
b) Marriage (I, 4, 3) and certain foods are forbidden (I, 4, 3; cf. Tit. 1, 15).
c) Their proponents have a weakness for "arguments" and "disputes about words" (ζήτησις : I, 6, 4, cf. Titus 2, 23 and λογομαχία: I, 6, 4, cf. II, 2, 14).
d) The false teachers are "of the circumcision" (i.e. Jews: Titus 1, 10). They are concerned with "Jewish myths" (μῦθος) and "commandments of men" (Tit. 1, 14).
e) The resurrection of the dead has already taken place (II, 2, 18).
f) The doctrine is summed up as "the contradictions of so-called knowledge" (ἀντιθέσεις τοῦ ψευδωνύμου γνώσεως; I, 6, 20).

From a few remarks it is evident that the persons in question were conspicuous for their ascetic attitude to life. The aversion for created and transient things which such an attitude entails, expressed itself in a denial of the resurrection of the dead. It is not quite clear what is meant by "arguments", "disputes about words" and "myths", words which remind us of the "philosophy" and the "hollow speculations" of the false teachers at Colossae (Col. 2, 8). Evidently the doctrine is unfolded in profound reasoning. The "genealogies" mentioned in the letter may refer to Jewish adaptations of Old Testament genealogies, such as are found in the Jubilees, or else to the division of humanity into two groups, one controlled by good and the other by wicked angels, as in the "Dead Sea Scrolls". In any case they are originally Jewish notions of a syncretic nature. Such notions claimed to give the knowledge which opens the way to perfection.

The false doctrines definitely need not be of post-Pauline origin. It has sometimes been thought that the letters contain references to the "Antitheses" (cf. I, 6, 20), a book written by Marcion, but this possibility must be excluded on account of the Jewish origin of the false teachings.

As for Paul's authorship of these letters: we cannot say with absolute certainty that Paul did not write them. Their description of the situation, the church and the faith, however, suggest that this work dates from the post-Pauline period.[1]

5. TIME AND PLACE OF ORIGIN

If the letters were not written by Paul, they must have originated in Asia Minor. This is indicated by their similarity to the letter to the Colossians, with respect to the nature of the false doctrines discussed. Moreover it was especially in Asia Minor that Paul's memory was kept alive. Here too the Acts of Paul were written around the middle of the second century, describing a journey Paul made from Jerusalem to Rome (Tertullian, *De Baptismo* 17, c. 190 A.D.).

What were the circumstances in which these letters were written? As a concession to their alleged Pauline authorship the letters have been supposed by some scholars to have been composed around fragments of authentic letters of Paul.[1] Others have thought them the work of a secretary who wrote them on the basis of oral communications from Paul. Both assumptions are unacceptable since there is no trace of proof for either.

If the letters are to be placed in the earliest church we must take them to be the work of a Paulinist, someone who preserved and expanded the Pauline heritage. In doing so, this author made use not only of Pauline theology but also of traditions concerning Paul's travels and his companions. Evidently he did not make use of

---

[1] See E. E. ELLIS, *Paul and his recent Interpreters*, Grand Rapids 1961, p. 49-57.

[2] See P. N. HARRISON, *The Problem of the Pastoral Letters*, Oxford 1921.

Acts but rather of vague traditions about Paul's life. Similar traditions are found in the Acts of Paul, which mention a large number of places Paul visited and people with whom he associated. The same is true of the pastoral letters, which mention Iconium, Lystra, Derbe, Ephesus, Miletus, Troas and other places, and Timothy, Titus, Luke, Mark and other persons.

These letters must be dated to the end of the first century. They are of the utmost importance for an understanding of the manner in which Paul's preaching was developed. There is no further need to point out that the liveliness of Paul's preaching has for the greater part been lost and that a process of systematization has started. It should be noted, though, that the letters testify to the same aversion towards Jewish-gnostic tendencies as is found in Paul's writings. Even though the church offices are surrounded with common ideals of morality as we know them from the Hellenistic world, the author still adheres to certain originally Jewish conceptions such as the resurrection from the dead and the importance of the flesh, that were stubbornly defended by Paul. In their external appearance the Pauline congregations may resemble the societies of the Greek world, their internal nature remains unchanged.

CHAPTER FOURTEEN

THE LETTER TO PHILEMON

1. CIRCUMSTANCES IN WHICH THE LETTER WAS WRITTEN

Paul is in prison and in Timothy's company. He addresses
Philemon, Apphia and Archippus (1-3) and conveys to them greet-
ings from Epaphras, Mark, Aristarchus, Demas and Luke (21-24).
Paul's company is thus the same as when he wrote the letter to the
Colossians. Only Jesus Justus is not mentioned (Col. 4, 11). As in
Col. 4, 17 the name of Archippus appears among the persons ad-
dressed.

2. REASONS FOR WRITING THE LETTER

The letter is addressed to Philemon, whose slave Onesimus has run
away and come to Paul (10-11). Paul sends the slave with a letter
back to his master, hoping the latter will give him a kindly re-
ception (17).

3. TIME AND PLACE OF ORIGIN

In Col. 4, 7-9 Paul writes that he is sending the letter to Colossae
through Tychicus "together with Onesimus". This information,
added to the fact that Paul's company is the same as when he wrote
his letter to Colossae while the persons addressed are also largely
the same indicates that the letter was written about the same time
as the letter to the Colossians, that is at Ephesus in A.D. 53/54.

CHAPTER FIFTEEN

THE COLLECTING OF PAUL'S LETTERS

From the letters of Paul that are found in the New Testament it is clear that at least two of his letters have been lost: the letter that preceded I Cor. and the so-called "severe letter". If the letter to the Laodiceans is not the same as the letter to the Ephesians, three letters of Paul are not known to us. Possibly even more letters were lost, but early Christian literature contains no quotations at all that are not found in the letters of Paul included in the New Testament. Ever since the earliest times, therefore, only those letters of Paul were known that we still have. Evidently there was a fixed body of Pauline letters quite soon after Paul's death.

The collecting of Paul's letters goes back at least partly to Paul himself. In Col. 4, 16 he asks the congregation of Colossae to exchange letters with the Laodiceans. As early as II Pet. 3, 15-16 we find a reference to "all the letters" of Paul. It is not clear how many letters are meant, but it is evident that the letters could already be designated as a body.

In the collecting of Paul's letters two periods may be distinguished; a period before A.D. 150, and a period after that date. For the former period we depend on the apostolic fathers. In their time the New Testament did not as yet have the function of an authoritative book, since the church was still relying on oral traditions. What might be called quotations from the New Testament are usually allusions of which the source is not clear. Paul is quoted in the same manner.

Polycarp mentions Paul's name (3, 2-3 and 11, 2) and quotes from his letters in a way which shows that his readers knew their contents (see 1, 3; 4, 1 and 5, 1). We cannot tell from these quotations exactly which letters Polycarp knew. He does not quote from I Thess., Titus or Philemon, but this may be mere coincidence.

With Ignatius the situation is the same. He shows no evidence of being acquainted with II Thess., Philippians, II Cor., II Tim. or Philemon.[1]

It is obvious, at any rate, that the letters had a wide circulation even before 150. We might suppose that all the letters were directly collected into one volume or that this volume was composed from a number of smaller collections. But it seems that the procedure was rather different. A passage from Polycarp shows how such collections came into existence. In Polycarp's letter to the Philippians we read that in addition to his own letter he is sending to Philippi the letters that Ignatius sent to "us" (that is to Polycarp and to Smyrna, where Polycarp was a bishop) and all the others (Polyc., *ad. Phil.* 13). Thus we see how a small number of letters is supplemented with others. Paul's letters that were already present at some central point were probably supplemented with others in the same way. Where this took place may possibly be inferred from the order of the letters. On this matter, however, we have no information dating from before 150.

After 150 we have Marcion who, according to Tertullian (*adv. Marc. V*) knew the following letters of Paul: Gal., Cor., Rom., Thess., Eph. (Laodiceans), Col., Phil., and Philem. Epiphanius confirms this order (*adv.Haer.*XLII), though Philemon with him precedes Philippians. In *Canon Muratori* we find the order: I and II Cor., Eph., Phil., Col., Gal., I and II Thess., Rom., Philem., Tit. and I and II Tim. This is more or less in accordance with Tertullian (*adv. Marc.* V 21) who has: I and II Cor., Gal., Phil., I and II Thess., Eph., (Col.? is not mentioned) and Rom. We find that I and II Cor. come first both for *Canon Muratori* and for Tertullian. The different order recorded for Marcion may be due to Marcion's preference for Galatians. Romans always occurs in last position before the pastoral letters, whenever these are actually mentioned. Tertullian (*adv. Marc.* V 21) believes that Marcion deliberately omitted the pastoral letters, but there seems to be no reason for this.

---

[1] See A Committee of the Oxford of Historical Theology, *The New Testament in the Apostolic Fathers*, Oxford 1905.

A more likely assumption is that these letters were not included in the oldest collection.

There is no point in mentioning Irenaeus, Clement of Alexandria and Origen, who were acquainted with all of Paul's letters.

On the basis of these data we may assume that the letters were collected at Corinth. In the oldest lists the letters to this congregation occupy the first place. This may perhaps be confirmed by the prescript of I Cor. 1, 2 which reads "to the congregation of God's people at Corinth. . . along with all men everywhere who invoke the name of our Lord Jesus Christ". The words "along with all men everywhere" seem to be an addition which fits in better with a situation where the letters were presented as a body to the church than with the situation in which this letter was written. Now that we know that Romans was probably for some time the last letter of the collection we can also explain the addition of the long doxology of 16, 25-27 (see ch. VI 5 above).[1]

---

[1] See A. v. HARNACK, *Die Briefsammlung des Apostels Paulus*, Leipzig 1926; C. L. MITTON, *The Formation of the Pauline Corpus of Letters*, London 1955; W. SCHMITHALS, ,,Zur Abfassung und ältesten Sammlung der paulinischen Hauptbriefe", in: *Zeitschr. f. d. neut. Wissensch.* 51 1960, p. 225-245.

CHAPTER SIXTEEN

THE LETTER TO THE HEBREWS

1. NATURE AND CONTENTS

This letter is addressed to a particular group of Christians (cf. 13, 24: "Greet your leaders. . ."), but it is not a real letter since it does not have a prescript. The author himself calls it a "word of exhortation" (λόγος τῆς παρακλήσεως, 13, 22). To this he adds a few personal words in the form of a conclusion to a letter (13, 22-25).

Among the other writings of the New Testament this "word of exhortation" has a character of its own. It may be regarded as a written sermon. This means that the personality of the author retires to the background to allow full light to fall on his message (cf. the introduction in 1, 1-2). Information of a personal kind is only included at the very end. This tells us that the author and his readers know each other and are parted for some reason unknown to us. He is hoping to return to them soon (13, 19). He has written down here what he really wanted to tell them personally and that is why now and again he naturally uses a style more suited to speech than to writing (11, 32: ἐπιλείψει με γὰρ διηγούμενον ὁ χρόνος. . .).

The designation "word of exhortation" is in conformity with the contents of the work which treats the following subjects:

Christ has taken his seat at the right hand of God (1, 1-4) and therefore he is mightier than the angels (1, 5-2, 14) and his glory is greater than that of Moses (3, 1-6).
Appeal to avoid sin (3, 7-19) and to be serious about the sabbath rest (4, 1-10).
Christ is the great high priest (4, 14-5, 10).
Appeal to adhere to the teachings concerning Christ and to keep up hope (4, 11-6, 20).

Christ is a high priest after the order of Melchizedek (7, 1-28) and ministers in heaven (8, 1-2) as mediator of the New Covenant (8, 3-13) having brought redemption through his own blood (9, 1-10, 18).

Appeal to adhere to the creed as did the witnesses to faith (11, 1-12, 4).

God disciplines as a Father disciplines his son (12, 4-17), for God is a God of judgment (12, 18-29).

Last admonitions (13, 1-25).

Unlike the letters of Paul, where the admonitions always occur in the second part of the letter, this letter has them scattered over its whole length. These admonitions consist of an appeal to the readers to stand firm because they are in danger of drifting from their course (2, 1), deserting the living God (3, 12), missing their chance (4, 1), falling (4, 11), growing dull of hearing (5, 11), no longer runing the race (12, 1), or letting their hands drop down (12, 12). The exhortative aspect of this letter dominates to such an extent that the descriptive passages are also adapted to it: 2, 1: "Thus we are bound to pay all the more heed"; 3, 1: "Therefore consider"; 3, 7: "Therefore. . . do not harden your hearts"; 4, 1: "Let us therefore fear"; 4, 14: "Since therefore we have . . . let us. . ."; 12, 28: "Let us therefore".

2. AUTHOR AND ADDRESSEES

The letter contains no mention at all of either the author's name or of the names of those he addresses. The title "To the Hebrews" was added at a later date.

There are ancient traditions, but apparently these were confined to Egypt, which ascribe the letter to Paul. Clement of Alexandria, who in his lost work *Hypotyposes* mentions Pantaenus as his teacher, was already writing about this question *c.* A.D. 200 (Eusebius, *H.E.* VI 13 2 and 14 2):

καὶ τὴν πρὸς Ἑβραίους δὲ ἐπιστολὴν Παύλου μὲν εἶναι φησι, γεγράφθαι δὲ Ἑβραίοις Ἑβραικῇ φωνῇ, Λουκᾶν δὲ

Of the letter to the Hebrews he (Clement) says that it was indeed written by Paul but in Hebrew for

φιλοτίμως αὐτὴν μεθερμηνεύσαντα ἐκ-
δοῦναι τοῖς "Ελλησιν . . . μὴ προ-
γεγράφθαι δὲ τὸ Παῦλος ἀπόστολος
εἰκότως.

the Hebrews. Luke, however, gave it to the Greeks in a faithful translation. But he says that it rightly does not bear the title "Paul, the apostle"

Origen goes even further (Eusebius, *H.E.* VI 25 13):

ἐγὼ δὲ ἀποφαινόμενος εἴποιμ' ἂν ὅτι τὰ
μὲν νοήματα τοῦ ἀποστόλου ἐστιν, ἡ δὲ
φράσις καὶ ἡ σύνθεσις ἀπομνημονεύ-
σαντός τινος τὰ ἀποστολικὰ καὶ ὥσπερ
σχολιογραφήσαντός τινος τὰ εἰρημένα
ὑπὸ τοῦ διδασκάλου . . . τίς δὲ ὁ γράψας
τὴν ἐπιστολήν, τὸ μὲν ἀληθὲς θεὸς οἶδεν.

I should like to say frankly that the ideas are the apostle's but style and composition seem like those of a person who remembers the words of the apostle or who summarizes briefly what the teacher said . . . Who wrote the letter, then, only God truly knows.

Origen suggests that perhaps Clement of Rome was the author.

From the third century onwards, however, in spite of these considerations, the whole of the Greek and Syrian church accepted Paul's authorship (cf. for instance the oldest manuscript of the Pauline letters, P[46], which places Hebrews between Romans and Corinthians).

In the western church the letter was not known until late (it is not found in the *Canon Muratori* of *c.* 200), and when it was known, Paul's authorship was rejected. According to Eusebius, *H.E.* VI 20 3, Gaius († 243) did not count the letter among those of Paul, and Tertullian, *de Pudic.* 20, believed that is was written by Barnabas. As a result of eastern influence the letter was regarded as Pauline in the western church also after the fourth century, and was included in the canon.

At present Paul's authorship is universally rejected. It is not only that Paul's name is not mentioned, but the style (excellent Greek), the composition of the letter (exhortations scattered over its whole length), its theology (Christ as high priest), theological argumentation (the ceremonial law being cancelled by the sacrifice of Christ), the lack of Pauline terms and of those subjects which keep reappearing in Paul's letters ("in Christ", the contrast between flesh and Spirit, relations between Jews and gentiles, justification through faith)—all these show that Paul can not be the author.

Since Paul can not have been the author, there have been all sorts of speculations about who was. We have already seen that Clement thought of Luke's influence in this connection, that Origen suspected that Clement of Rome was the author and that Tertullian believed it was written by Barnabas. An interesting suggestion was put forward by Luther, who assumed Apollos to have been the author. For none of these various possibilities, however, is there any real proof.

Even though we do not know the author's name, it is obvious that he must have belonged to circles which had connections with Paul. As early as Origen we find talk of Pauline ideas in connection with this letter. The notion of Christ as mediator of creation (Hebr. 1, 2; cf. Col. 1, 16), who has brought about reconciliation and put the new Covenant into operation is one which Paul and the author of Hebrews have in common. If the Timothy mentioned in Hebr. 13, 23 is the Timothy who was Paul's companion, the connection between Paul and the author would be established. In any case the latter is a Christian of the second generation, who has received the gospel from those who "faithfully" passed it on (2, 3).

At some later date the letter was given the title "To the Hebrews". The meaning of this is not quite certain. The word Hebrews may refer to Jewish Christians in general (see II Cor. 11, 22), or in a narrower sense to Hebrew-speaking Jewish Christians (Acts 6, 1), or even Jews. In any case it is evident that the letter is addressed to Christians (3, 1-4; 6, 4-9; 10, 23-26). But were these Christians of Jewish descent? The reference to instruction and faith in God in 6, 1 seems rather to point to gentile origins (cf. also 2, 12 and 11, 6). Perhaps the choice of title was suggested by the numerous quotations from the Old Testament contained in this letter. These quotations, however, in no way prove that either the author or his readers were of Jewish descent. The second generation of Christians had already completely appropriated the Old Testament. Moreover the passage in 7, 27 that assumes that the high priest offers sacrifices daily, indicates a defective knowledge of the contents of the Old Testament that is not to be expected in the case of Jews.[1]

---

[1] See H. WINDISCH, *Der Hebräerbrief*, in: *Handb. z. N. T.*, 14, Tübingen 1931, p. 68-69.

3. Place and Date of Origin

The author does not comment on concrete happenings, and thus gives us little to go by in establishing the date of the letter. The passage about sacrificial rites in 5, 1-5 is in the present tense, but since it refers to the Old Testament this is no indication that the temple at Jerusalem still existed. In any case 2, 3 points to the second generation of Christians. The references to oppression (12, 4) and persecution (10, 32-24) would also seem to point to the period towards the end of the first century. Since I Clement (written before A.D. 96) knew the letter, somewhere around 85 seems to be the most acceptable date.

The words "greetings from our Italian friends" in 13, 25 may mean that the letter was written in Italy, but they may also mean that it was sent to Italy. In the latter case persons who originally lived in Italy are sending greetings to their fellow-countrymen.

The fact that the author of I Clement knew the letter might be an argument in favour of Italy as destination. If this is so, it is rather odd, on the other hand, that the Western church did not accept the letter until quite late.

4. Purpose of the Letter

We have already seen that the purpose of the letter is exhortation. People are in danger of deserting the church on account of persecutions. These, however, seem to have grown less by the time the letter was written (10, 32-34). False teachings are an additional danger, but the letter does not expand on this subject (13, 9). The author supports his appeal for firmness by pointing out the sublimity and victorious strength of Christ. He has made the perfect sacrifice and has entered the heavenly sanctuary (9, 24), thus opening the way to his people. A characteristic expression used time and again in this connection is the word τελειοῦν with its derivatives (τέλειος in 5, 14; 9, 11; τελειότης in 6, 1; τελειοῦν in 2, 10; 7, 19; 7, 28; 9, 9; 10, 1; 10, 14; 11, 40; 12, 23; τελείωσις in 7, 11; τελειωτής in 12, 2; τέλος in 3, 6; 3, 14; 6, 8; 6, 11; 7, 3). The church is on its way, leaving the past behind and turning to face the future (cf. the "witnesses of the faith" of ch. 11).[1]

The sacrificial rites of the Old Testament, in particular, are considered a thing of the past. They are regarded as a mere shadow (8, 5 and 10, 1) of what has come to pass. Passages from the Old Testament are continually cited by the author to show the relativity of the First Covenant (9, 15) and its laws. His manner of interpretation in doing so is Jewish. Take for example 10, 1-13 where Psalm 40, 7-9 is cited. The Psalm says that God does not delight in sacrifice. The quotation continues with the words "Then I said, look I come. . . to do the will of God". The author contrasts the beginning of the quotation with the second part, and says that the second part annuls the first. The second part, he says, refers to the coming of Christ who, therefore, put an end to offerings. The author makes frequent use of allegory (the bodies of sacrificial animals are taken outside the camp; thus Christ died outside the gate, 13, 11-13) and typology (Melchizedek and Christ, ch 7). This manner of interpretation is certainly not strictly confined to Alexandria, where the Jew Philo is notable for his allegorical interpretation of the law, but it may be called characteristic of hellenistic Judaism.[2]

As a result of this exegesis, God's dealings with the world and the history of salvation, fall into the background. The First Covenant is obsolete (8, 13: πεπαλαίωκεν). In this respect this letter bears more resemblance to pseudo-Barnabas than to Paul's letters, which firmly adhere to the historic line connecting Abraham through Israel with Christ and the church (cf. Gal. 3, 15-29; Rom. 4, 1-12).

---

[1] See E. KÄSEMANN, Das wandernde Gottesvolk, in: Forsch. z. Rel. u. Lit. des A.u.N.T. 37 1938, 1961⁴.

[2] See J. COPPENS, ,,Les Affinités qumrâniennes de l'Épître aux Hébreux'', in: Nouv. Rev. Théol. 94 1962, p. 128-141 and 257-282.

CHAPTER SEVENTEEN

INTRODUCTION TO THE CATHOLIC LETTERS

Since the eighteenth century the letters of James, I and II Peter, I, II and III John and Jude have been designated as the "Catholic letters". What this name is intended to convey is that these letters are not addressed in the first place to a certain Christian congregation or to a certain person, as is the case with Paul's letters, but to the church as a whole.

The designation "catholic" for one or more of these letters, however, is quite ancient. Apollonius, who opposed the montanist Themison (196/7), called I John "catholic" (see Eusebius, *H.E. V* 28 5):

ἔτι δὲ καὶ Θεμίσων . . . ἐτόλμησεν, μιμούμενος τὸν ἀπόστολον, καθολικήν τινα συνταξάμενος ἐπιστολήν . . .	Themison furthermore ventured, in imitation of the apostle, to write a catholic letter. . .

The designation "Catholic letter" for I John appears to have been in general use, for it is also found in Dionysius of Alexandria (265/5), according to Eusebius, *H.E. VII* 25 7:

. . . Ἰωάννην . . . τὸν ἀπόστολον τὸν υἱὸν Ζεβεδαίου, τὸν ἀδελφὸν Ἰακώβου, οὗ τὸ εὐαγγέλιον τὸ κατὰ Ἰωάννην ἐπιγραμμένον καὶ ἡ ἐπιστολὴ ἡ καθολική.	. . .John . . . the apostle, the son of Zebedee, the brother of James, who wrote the gospel according to John and the Catholic letter.

Eusebius is the first to call all seven letters "catholic" (*H.E. II* 23 25):

τοιαῦτα καὶ τὰ κατὰ Ἰάκωβον, οὗ ἡ πρώτη τῶν ὀνομαζομένων καθολικῶν ἐπιστολῶν εἶναι λέγεται.	This about James, to whom the first of the so-called Catholic letters is attributed.

These letters may indeed justifiably be called "Universal", although II and III John are clearly meant for a very limited group of people.

In the old Greek manuscripts these letters often follow Acts, preceding the letters of Paul. This was because these letters were attributed to a disciple of the Lord. All the same a few of them (II and III John, II Pet.) were not regarded as authorative until quite late.

CHAPTER EIGHTEEN

JAMES

1. NATURE AND CONTENTS

This letter begins with the usual Greek prescript containing the names of the writer and the addressees as well as the single hellenistic χαίρειν. It ends, however, without any greetings or wishes. As a matter of fact it is not a letter in the usual sense, since it also lacks any personal communications. Since it contains nothing but exhortations it might be called a written sermon.

One exhortation follows the other without any real connection. For that reason it is hardly possible to give a summary of the contents. The following list shows that a new subject is broached each time:

The joy of being tempted (1, 2-18).
Listening to God's word and living in accordance with it (1, 19-27).
Avoid snobbery (2, 1-13).
Faith should be accompanied by action (2, 14-26).
The danger of talking too much (3, 1-12).
Seek the heavenly wisdom (3, 13-18).
Avoid envious desires and submit to God (4, 1-10).
Do not speak evil of one another (4, 11-12).
Make plans, but only with proper reserve (4, 13-17).
Beware of riches (5, 1-6).
Be patient (5, 7-11).
Pray for and look after one another (5, 12-20).

Attempts have been made to construct some sort of order for these disconnected topics by assuming the letter goes back to an original Jewish work that gave an explanation in allegorical

terms of the names, characteristics and adventures of the sons
of Jacob. The κύριος τῆς δόξης of 2, 1 would then refer to Judah,
and the ἀπαρχή of 1, 18 to Ruben. This rather artificial hypothesis is
far from being generally accepted.[1]

Even if there is no well-defined line of thought to be discerned
in this work (which, however, is not unususal for Jewish exhortative
literature; think of the book of Proverbs!) there is certainly one
theme that keeps returning: the necessity of submitting to God.
This attitude to life is endangered by the desire for riches and by
speaking and making plans unthinkingly.

In form and contents the work is related to Jewish literature
of an exhortative nature. This is not surprising if we remember
that early Christian ethics was based on and developed from
Jewish ethics (the Sermon on the Mount!). All sorts of parallels
have been found for James in Jewish as well as Christian parenetical literature. Such parallels are found in Proverbs (cf. 4, 6
and Prov. 3, 34), the Testaments of the 12 Patriarchs (cf. 5, 11 and
Test. Benj. 4, 1; 3, 9-10 and Test. Benj. 6. 5; 2, 13 and Test Zeb.
8, 3), and the Sermon on the Mount (cf. 1, 5 and Matt. 7, 7; 1, 22
and Matt. 7, 21 and 5, 12 and Matt. 5, 34-37). This clearly shows
the author drew on traditional material.[2] This is also confirmed
by the lack of any personal note in the letter and by the slight
evidence of Christian influence in its contents. The name of Christ
occurs only twice (1, 1 and 2, 1). In 5, 7 the coming of Christ is
mentioned and in 2, 7 it is said the readers have been called by
an honourable name. God is referred to in the Jewish style: He is the
creator (2, 19 and 3, 9); holy (1, 13); the source of everything good
(1, 17); merciful (5, 11); he hears prayers (1, 5-7); forgives sins
(5, 15 and 20); and judges (2, 12; 4, 12 and 5, 9).

The remarkable thing is that this Jewish material has been
moulded into a Greek form. The whole work is written in the
"diatribe" style that was very popular among the Greeks. Examples

---

[1] See A. MEYER, *Das Rätsel des Jakobusbriefes*, in: *Beih. Zeitschr. neut.
Wissen.* 10 1933.

[2] See G. KITTEL, „Der Jakobusbrief und die Apostolischen Väter", in:
Zeitschr. f. d. Neut. Wissensch. 43 1950/51, p. 54-112.

of this style are to be found in 5, 13, where the author asks questions and gives the reply himself; in 2, 14, with the rhetorical question; in 2, 18, where an imaginary partner in discourse is introduced; and 2, 22 where it is left to the readers to draw the proper conclusions. Virtues and vices are represented as persons (1, 15; 2, 13; 4, 1; 5, 3) and pericopes are concluded in a sharply antithetical manner (1, 26; 2, 13; 2, 26; 3, 15-18; 4, 12).

Evidently the Jewish material was edited in a Greek environment or by a person who spoke Greek as his native language.

2. AUTHOR AND ADDRESSEES

In the New Testament seven persons by the name of James are mentioned:

a) The son of Zebedee, brother of John and disciple of the Lord. This James was put to death by Herod Agrippa *circa* A.D. 44 (Acts 12, 2).

b) James, son of Alphaeus, disciple of the Lord (Matt. 10, 3; Mark 3, 18; Luke 6, 51; Acts 1, 15).

c) James, the brother of the Lord (Gal. 1, 19; I Cor. 15, 7; cf. also Acts 12, 17; 15, 13; 21, 18; Mark 6,3 and Matt. 13, 55).

d) James the younger, the son of Mary (not the mother of the Lord), the brother of Joseph (Mark 15, 40; Matt. 27, 56; Mark 16, 1 and Luke 24, 10).

e) James the father of Judas (Luke 6, 16 and Acts 1, 13).

f) James, the author of the present letter.

g) James, brother of Jude (Jude 1).

Of these seven, c., f. and g. are identical. About b., d and e. we have no further information at all. Only the brother of the Lord is a possible author of this letter. No other James is ever mentioned in this connection in church traditions. But could he be the author? The arguments against his authorship may be summed up as follows:

a. The language of the letter is so typically Greek that it may be doubted whether James, who always lived in Jerusalem, could be responsible for it.

b. The interpretation of the law as the perfect law of freedom (1, 25) is scarcely to be expected of James, who lived in close association with judaism.

c. No allusion at all is made to the person of Jesus, with whom the brother of the Lord had been closely connected.

d. The passage about faith and works (2, 14-19) seems possible only after Paul's time.

e. The church did not accept the letter until quite late.

On closer examination, however, none of these arguments are conclusive evidence against James' authorship. To begin with, c. and e. are of little significance. The contents of the letter do not call for any references to the "life of Jesus". And it is easy to understand that the church was so little impressed by these contents that it could afford to neglect the letter.

The argument given under a. is rather more significant, since the form bears so little resemblance to what one would expect from James. On the other hand the very lack of originality of the letter takes the weight out of this consideration. The letter seems to be addressed to Christians outside Palestine, for which reason the author was obliged to use the Greek language. If his Greek was inadequate it is not surprising, under the circumstances, that he employed someone who was well-versed in that language.

The connections with judaism (b.) must have been very close, as is shown by Eusebius, who bases himself on Hegesippus (*H.E. II 23 6*):

καὶ μόνος εἰσήρχετο εἰς τὸν ναὸν ηὑρίσκετο τε κείμενος ἐπὶ τοῖς γόνασιν καὶ αἰτούμενος ὑπὲρ τοῦ λαοῦ ἄφεσιν, ὡς ἀπεσκληκέναι τὰ γόνατα αὐτοῦ δίκην καμήλου, διὰ τὸ ἀεὶ κάμπτειν ἐπὶ γόνυ προσκυνοῦντα τῷ θεῷ καὶ αἰτεῖσθαι ἄφεσιν τῷ λαῷ.	He entered the temple alone and on his knees he prayed for forgiveness for the people, so that his knees became calloused like a camel's, for he kept falling on his knees to pray to God and to ask forgiveness for the people.

On the other hand we know that James was stoned by the Jews in the year 62 on account of transgression of the law (Josephus, *Ant.* XX 9 1):

ὁ Ἄνανος . . . καθίζει συνέδριον κριτῶν καὶ παραγαγὼν εἰς αὐτὸ τὸν ἀδελφὸν Ἰησοῦ τοῦ λεγομένου Χριστοῦ, Ἰάκωβος ὄνομα αὐτῷ, καὶ τινας ἑτέρους, ὡς παρανομησάντων κατηγορίαν ποιησάμενος, παρέδωκε λευσθησομένους.

. . . Ananus . . . instituted a trial and brought before it the brother of Jesus who was called Christ—James was his name—and some others and on the accusation of transgressing the law they were handed over to be stoned.

The last remaining point to be discussed is the relation of this letter to Paul (d.). The letter seems to oppose ideas such as are found in Rom. 3, 28. But it is not necessarily a direct attack on Romans, since Rom. 6, 1 already knows of misunderstandings of this sort. Such misunderstandings concerning Paul's preaching may well have been present *circa* A.D. 50 and need not have arisen only after Paul's death.

There is thus no conclusive evidence to show that James did not write the letter.

The persons addressed are called "the twelve tribes dispersed throughout the world". This does not refer to Jews since there is no doubt the addressees were Christians (2, 7). These Christians then, were evidently scattered throughout the world. This gives us no indication of exactly where they lived. From the passage 2, 1-15 it might be inferred that the members of the congregation were poor. Some among them were rich though (2, 2 and 5, 1-6). It is a small congregation, for the members know each other so well that they speak disparagingly of one another (4, 11-12). It is not certain that 5, 7, a proverb about the farmer and the rain, points to a rural population, since the proverb in question was undoubtedly generally known. There are thus few data about the dwelling-place of the persons addressed. Because the letter is first quoted in a work called *de Virginitate* (dating from the third century) written in Palestine, we might suppose the addressees to have lived in the region of Palestine and Syria.

Since James was stoned in 62 the letter must have been written between 50 and 60.

3. SIGNIFICANCE OF THE LETTER

In the course of the centuries the letter has found little recognition. The western church accepted it at the synods of Rome (328) and Carthage (397). Eusebius counts it among the *antilegomena* (*H.E.* II 23 25 and III 25 3). The eastern church accepted the letter at the council of Laodicea (360). Luther's unfavourable opinion is generally known.

It is not surprising, in view of its contents, that the church was not much interested in the letter. There is nothing specifically Christian about it. For the same reason it is hard to fit it into the life of the church during the first century. Nevertheless this meets with less serious difficulties than any attempt to place the letter at the end of the first century, as is necessary if James' authorship is denied. It now appears as an interesting document of a community within the church that was still in the process of adapting its Jewish background to the new faith. This process was an especially difficult one in Palestine and Syria. This is also clear from such works as the Testaments of the 12 Patriarchs, where a Christian author, like the author of the letter of James, makes extensive use of Jewish material.

This means that the letter broadens our view of the church in the first century; in a geographical sense, because it provides some insight into communities outside the actual Greek and Roman world; and in a theological sense because it shows us that the Christian church of Syria and Palestine developed into a community where the system of ethics was better thought out than the Christology.

CHAPTER NINETEEN

I PETER

1. NATURE AND CONTENTS

This work bears a great deal of formal resemblance to the letters of Paul. The prescript 1, 1-2, for instance, and the concluding wish of 5, 14 (Εἰρήνη ὑμῖν πᾶσιν τοῖς ἐν χριστῷ) are similar in content to passages in Paul's writings.

The letter is intended as an exhortation and to testify that "this is the true grace of God" (5, 12). This is evident from the contents which may be summarized as follows:

The hope in Jesus Christ outweighs all temptations (1, 3-12).
Be holy, for your freedom has been bought with the blood of Christ (1, 13-25).
The church is a "holy priesthood" (2, 1-10).
Exhortations concerning such subjects as worldly authorities, slaves, women and men, ending with the words "be ye all of one mind" (2, 11-3, 12).
Do not fear suffering (3, 13-4, 19).
Brief exhortations (5, 1-14).

From this summary of contents it is clear that the purpose of the letter is to strengthen Christians in times of suffering. Trials are imposed on the Christians by the pagans, who slander them as criminals (2, 12). The author believes that this is because the Christians no longer live in licence as they did before their conversion (4, 3-4). If they continue in their good conduct, however, the pagans will be put to silence (2, 15). Suffering on account of well-doing is moreover an expression of God's grace (2, 20 and 3, 17).

These remarks do not give the impression that systematic

persecution took place at the hands of the authorities. There is a reference in 4, 14-15 to suffering ὡς χριστιανός but that certainly does not mean that people could be condemned merely "for the name of Christ". Evidently the new way of life that the Christians have chosen keeps provoking the pagans to aggressive action.

The author does not confine his remarks to the sufferings of the congregation but he points out that suffering is characteristic for all Christians (5, 9). It proves that the end of all things is imminent (4, 7), for the judgment begins with God's household (4, 17). It will only last a short time, for the end of all things is near (4, 7).

Some scholars have thought they saw a difference in the way the subject of suffering is treated before and after 4, 12. The trials mentioned, they believe, refer to actual suffering only from 4, 12 onwards. It is undoubtedly true that 1, 6; 2, 20; 3, 14 and 17 only speak of the possibility of suffering. We might say, however, that in this first part the connection between suffering and being a Christian is treated in general terms, to show the readers that there is nothing extraordinary in it. When the author starts in 4, 12 to discuss the "fiery ordeal" (πύρωσις) that serves as a trial, then he is speaking about the situation in which the readers find themselves and about which he can now give his opinion in a theologically well-founded manner. It is a trial of the devil, who "prowls around like a roaring lion looking for someone to devour" (5, 8). The division which some wish to introduce at 4, 12 has sometimes been combined with the view that the author has used passages of baptismal liturgy in the first section. This theory is based on the passages which say that "now" the gospel has been proclaimed (1, 12) and that the readers live like "new-born infants" (2, 2). More allusions to baptism might be the statements that the readers have "now" been converted (2, 25), reborn (1, 3 and 23), and saved through baptism (3, 21).[1]

There can be no doubt that all these passages do refer to baptism,

---

[1] See W. BORNEMANN, „Der eerste Petrusbrief — eine Taufrede des Silvanus?", in: *Zeitschr. f. d. neut. Wissensch.* 19 1919/20, p. 143-165 and H. WINDISCH-H. PREISKER, *Die Katholischen Briefe*, in: *Handb. z. N.T.* 15, Tübingen 1951[3], p. 82.

but should we therefore regard this whole section of the letter as a part of baptismal liturgy? It seems more plausible to assume that in his argument the author makes use of various notions that were usually mentioned on the occasion of baptism. In this respect I Peter may be compared with the letter to the Ephesians, which also draws on the usage of the congregation. Moreover there is a striking resemblace between 1, 3-12 and Eph. 1, 3-14, and the "household tables" of 2, 18-3, 7 and Eph. 5, 22-6, 9 (Col. 3, 18-4, 1).

In conclusion it may therefore be said that the letter is addressed to a first generation of gentile Christians who have forsaken their former way of life. In doing so, they have also withdrawn from the community to which they used to belong, for which reason they have to suffer the slander of their countrymen. In these circumstances the author points out to his readers that they took an important step by being baptized. He assures them that suffering was inherent in this change, but that this very suffering indicates that salvation is near.

2. AUTHOR AND ADDRESSEES

In 1, 1-2 Peter is named as the author (cf. 5, 1). Those he addresses are "strangers", living scattered in Pontus, Galatia, Cappadocia, Asia and Bithynia. Later, in 2, 11 the readers are called "aliens in a foreign land".

Various arguments have been brought forward against Peter's authorship of this letter:

a) The letter is closely related to the letters of Paul.
b) The language of the letter is correct Greek, which is not to be expected of a Galilean fisherman.
c) The author betrays no acquaintance with the "life of Jesus".
d) The nature of the persecutions points to a time after Peter's death.

The following observations may be made:

a. The relationship with Paul is unmistakable. This is clear from parallel passages in I Peter and the letter to the Ephesians (1, 3 =

Eph. 1, 3; 1, 19-20 = Eph. 3, 5-6; 1, 14 = Eph. 2, 2-3; 2, 9 = Eph. 5, 8; 2, 18 = Eph. 6, 5; 3, 1 = Eph. 5, 22; 3, 7 = Eph. 5, 25; 3, 8 = Eph. 4, 32). We also find in 3, 16; 5, 10 and 5, 14 the typical Pauline expression "in Christ".

It is not easy to evaluate these parallels, since both letters make use of liturgical material. There is no question of direct dependence, so we must assume that the author of I Peter had access to the liturgical usage of a community with which Paul also was acquainted.

b. The correct Greek may be explained by the fact that the letter was written διὰ Σιλουανοῦ (5, 12). This undoubtedly means that Silvanus did the actual writing. This circumstance is of great importance also for the similarities between this letter and Paul's. These may to a large extent be explained by Silvanus' part in the composition of this work. Silvanus' connections with Peter and Paul can be accounted for. Silvanus met Peter in Jerusalem, where he was staying at the time of, and probably even before, the Conference. Silas accompanied Paul, Barsabbas and Barnabas to Antioch and surroundings to convey the decisions of this conference. From that time onwards we find him in Paul's company (cf. Acts 16, 19. 25. 29; 17, 4. 10. 15; II Cor. 1, 19; I Thess. 1, 1 and II Thess. 1, 1). For a right understanding of both form and contents of this letter, Silvanus is therefore of inestimable importance.

c. The argument that Peter does not refer to the "life of Jesus" is of little significance. The nature of the letter offered little opportunity to touch on this subject.

d. It has already been noted that the persecutions were of an individual kind. There is no reason to assume that systematic persecutions of Christians were carried out by the authorities.

From all this it follows that there is no conclusive evidence against Peter's authorship.

The addressees are to be found in the northern part of Asia Minor, at least if by Galatia the territory and not the province is meant. In the latter case the region to which the letter is addressed included a large part of southern Asia Minor as well.

The inhabitants of these regions are pagans and the Christians who live there were also originally of pagan descent (1, 14; 1, 18; 2, 9 and 4, 3).

It is not quite clear why the addressees are called παρεπιδήμοι διασπορᾶς. The most obvious translation is "sojourners in the dispersion". The word "sojourn" includes a notion of "being strange", which is also to be found in the words πάροικοι καὶ παρεπι-δήμοι of 2, 11. The notion of "alienism" (παροικία in 1, 17) is particularly emphasized in this letter, which explains the use of these expressions. The persons referred to are scattered foreigners. The word "foreigner" is given the profound sense of "being foreign to the world and the pagans around one".[1]

3. Time and Place of Origin

If Peter wrote the letter, he must have done so towards the end of his life, since it is unlikely that Peter would write to congregations in Asia Minor during the period of Paul's activity in that region. If Peter was put to death by Nero in 64 the letter must date from the early sixties.

The place is harder to determine. The letter ends with the words "Greetings from her who dwells in Babylon, chosen by God like you, and from my son Mark" (5, 13). This Babylon may be one of three places:

Babylon in Mesopotamia, in those times a Roman *colonia*;

Babylon in Egypt;

Babylon meaning Rome, as in Rev. 14, 8 and 18, 2.

Babylon in Mesopotamia must be discarded since there is no evidence to show that Peter ever visited this region. If Babylon means Rome, we may wonder why this abusive name is used. This presents no problem, of course, to those who believe that the letter refers to persecutions organized by the authorities. Since we have rejected this theory, Babylon in Egypt is to be preferred. This

---

[1] Cf. W. C. van Unnik, *De Verlossing I Petrus* 1: 18-19 *en het Probleem van den eersten Petrusbrief*, in: *Meded. Nederl. Akad. v. Wetensch., afd. Letterk.* 1942.

assumption is perhaps supported by a tradition according to which Mark, who was Peter's companion when this letter was written, is regarded as the first bishop of Alexandria (Eus., *H.E.* IV 21 6). Even if this is not true, it shows that certain traditions linked Mark with Egypt.

4. Significance of the Letter

If Peter's authorship is accepted, the letter becomes an important document of the life of the primitive church in general and more specifically of the relationship between Peter and Paul. For it appears, then, that these two apostles drew on the same traditions, which indicates a oneness in their preaching that has often been denied.

The letter further testifies anew to the difficulties that faced the members of a gentile-Christian congregation when they wished to profess their faith while living among pagans.

Finally the letter is important because of the evidence it gives of the notions that were current in the primitive church on the subject of the conversion that was confirmed by baptism.

CHAPTER TWENTY

JUDE AND II PETER

1. Nature and Contents of the Letters

a. *Jude*

In the prescript the author calls himself Jude, servant of Jesus Christ and brother of James. He is addressing "those whom God has called". The letter is thus "catholic" in the true sense of the word. Its purpose is exhortation (3), because certain persons who have entered the congregation are leading a licentious life (4). The author warns his readers that God can inflict punishment as is shown by the history of Israel, the fall of the angels, and Sodom and Gomorrah (5-8). They resist every authority, which even Michael dared not do. They have gone the way of Cain and Balaam (8-11). They are a blot on the love-feasts and they will be heavily punished (12-13). Enoch has predicted their downfall (14-16). These men have to come towards the end of all time, but the congregation should be on its guard against them (17-23). The letter concludes with a long doxology.

b. *II Peter*

In the prescript the author introduces himself as Peter, apostle of Jesus Christ, and he addresses all those who have "an equally precious faith" as he has himself. The readers' attention is drawn to their privileges and their duty (1, 3-11). The author points out that the testimony is true, not only because he was an eyewitness himself but also because the testimony of the prophets was inspired by God (1, 12-21). He warns his readers against false teachers who preach freedom and who with "big, empty words" tempt the congregation to sin (2, 1-22). This passage bears a close resemblance to Jude 4-16. The author then warns his readers against those who say that the day of the Lord will not come. It will come and until it does one should live a life above reproach (3, 1-16). The letter ends with a last warning and a doxology (3, 17-18).

The purpose of both these letters is to admonish the Christians to adhere to the true faith and not to be tempted to libertinism. In addition II Peter addresses those who doubt the coming of the day of the Lord.

There is a striking difference between the way in which Jude combats the false doctrine and the way II Peter does so. While II Peter uses only examples from the Old Testament, Jude also makes use of apocryphal literature. In verse 9 the latter refers to the struggle between Michael and the devil for the possession of Moses' body, a story taken from the book of "The Assumption of Moses" (see Clement of Alexandria, *Adumbrationes in Epistolas Canonicas* II ed. O. STÄHLIN, in: Die Griech. Christl. Schriftst. 17, S. 207). In v. 14 Jude quotes from the book of Enoch 1, 9. Balaam, finally, is found used as a pernicious example only in the Jewish literature written after the Old Testament.

There is no attempt in either letter, as there is in Paul's writings, to make the false teachers desist from their wickedness. They are now threatened with heavy punishment. A sharp distinction is made between the false doctrine and the true faith, which has assumed a definite form as the "entrusted faith" (Jude 3), word of the apostles (Jude 17), command of the apostles (II, 3, 2), message of the prophets (II, 1, 19), and testimony of the eyewitnesses (II, 1, 16). The church now falls back on the testimony of the apostles.

A final difference to be noted is that Jude assumes the false teachers are present in the congregation (v. 4) but that II Peter only reckons with the possibility of their coming (II, 2, 1 and 3, 2).

2. AUTHORS AND ADDRESSEES

a. *Jude*

There can be no doubt that the James whose brother this Jude claims to be is James, "the brother of the Lord". The author believes that the name of Jude does not carry enough authority in itself and wishes to increase this authority by presenting himself as the brother of James. And in fact we have no other information at all about this Jude. Eusebius, *H.E.* III 20 tells us that some grandsons of Jude's who lived in Palestine, were accused before the emperor Domitian. When the emperor found out, however, that these were only artisans, he let them go. Jude, therefore, belonged to the Christian church in Palestine. In the letter he invokes the authority of the faith "that was once entrusted to the saints" (3) and the "words that were spoken before by the apostles of our Lord Jesus Christ" (17).

There is little objection to accepting Jude's authorship. It is not very likely that an unknown writer would try to derive the authority he lacked from the name of an equally unknown Jude who in turn had to take his authority from his brother James. The strikingly early recognition of this letter also argues in favour of its authenticity. It was quoted from as early as II Peter (see below) and was known to the *Canon Muratori*, Tertullian and Clement of Alexandria. The use of Jewish apocryphal writings such as the Assumption of Moses and Enoch's Apocalypse seems to indicate that it originated in Palestine.

About the addressees nothing is known. Libertines were found everywhere in the church. They were encountered both in Corinth and in Asia Minor, as is evident from II Cor. and Rev. 2, 14 and 20.

b. *II Peter*

The writer introduces himself emphatically as an apostle (1, 1) and eyewitness of the life of Jesus (1, 16), and he also refers to a previous letter written by him (3, 1).[1] He calls Paul his "beloved brother" (3, 15). Even so there are a number of arguments against Peter's authorship:

1. II Peter bears a close resemblance to Jude. Similarities are found especially in II, 2, 4 and Jude 6 (the fallen angels); II, 2, 6 and Jude 7 (Sodom and Gomorrah); II, 2, 15 and Jude 11 (the way of Balaam); II, 2, 13 and Jude 12 (blot on the feasts); II, 2, 17 and

---

[1] See G. H. BOOBYER, "The Indebtness of 2 Peter to 1 Peter", in: *New Testament Essays . . . in mem. of T. W. Manson*, Manchester 1959, p. 34-53.

Jude 12 (clouds carried away by the wind). These similarities indicate an indebtedness of II Peter to Jude, for II Peter omits the
examples from apocryphal literature and gives examples of salvation
in addition to examples of judgement (II, 2, 7: Lot and 2, 5: Noah).

2. II Peter uses words of hellenistic origin which do not occur
in I Peter and therefore betray a different background. These are
such expressions as "divine power" (θεία δύναμις: 1, 3), "godliness"
(εὐσέβεια: 1, 3) and "divine nature" (θειά φύσις: 1, 4).

3. Whereas I Peter speaks as a matter of course about a day of
judgment that is soon to come, (I, 4, 7 and 17; 5, 4) this question has
become a problem by the time II Peter is written. This points to a
development that is not to be expected before the end of the first
century.

4. The letter invokes the authority of Paul, whose letters have
already been collected, at least in part, and are being interpreted
(3, 15-16). This also points to the end of the first century.

5. The letter is first mentioned at quite a late date, namely by
Origen who adds that its authenticity is disputed.

These arguments lead us to regard the letter as a pseudepigraph.
It is not hard to see why it was written. The writer of the letter
obviously knew the letter of Jude and thought he could lend this
letter greater authority by publishing it anew under the name of
Peter. To this purpose he rewrote the letter adding a passage that
was important for the circumstances of his time.

3. TIME AND PLACE OF ORIGIN

Time and place of origin cannot be exactly determined for either
letter. If Jude is the author of the letter that is known under his
name, the letter must have been written in Palestine. We might
venture to date it between 60 and 70 but this is no more than a
rough guess.

II Peter must have been written after Jude. The contents indicate
some time towards the end of the first century. It was obviously
written in an environment where Peter was held in high esteem.
This may have been either Rome or Antioch. Antioch is to be pre-

ferred since it is not very distant from Palestine, which means that Jude may easily have been known there.

4. SIGNIFICANCE OF THE LETTERS

Both letters contribute to our knowledge about the libertine tendencies that must have been widespread in the primitive church. For our knowledge of the development of this primitive church they are even more important. Remarkable in this connection is the appeal to the authority of the apostle in II Peter. The contents of the letters, which are based on the apostolic testimony and the traditional faith, point in the same direction. A sharp distinction between orthodoxy and heresy arises. The question of how an orthodox faith developed out of the early stages when "orthodoxy" and "heresy" were not yet separated, is still a disputed one, though it is partly answered by these letters. Note also that II Peter 1, 20 warns against private interpretation of the Scriptures. This is a further indication that the church was adhering more strictly to existing norms. It is remarkable, on the other hand, that church offices seem to have little significance as yet (in contrast to the pastoral letters). In any case the letters are of the greatest significance for a right understanding of the post-apostolic church.

CHAPTER TWENTY-ONE

I, II AND III JOHN

Of these three letters numbers I and II are similar in content. II and III are both in the form of a letter written by the same person. The language and style of these three letters point to a common author.

1. Contents and Nature of the Letters

a. *I John*

This is not a real letter, for the customary beginning and ending are lacking. It begins with some solemn sentences (reminiscent of the first verses of Hebrews), which speak of the revelation of Life. It ends with the words: "My children, be on the watch against false gods". The author is evidently addressing a particular group of Christians whom he knows. This is clear from his repeated "children" and "my children" (cf. 2, 1; 2, 12; 2, 18). For a sermon the contents are not topical enough and the terms in which they are expressed too general. For that reason this work may be better described as an encyclical letter.

The work consists mainly of exhortations and continually repeated assurances that the readers have received life. There is no systematic division of contents, as is clear from the following summary:

We have felt the word of life with our own hands (1, 1-4).
God is light and He forgives us our sins (1, 5-2, 2).
He who knows God keeps his commandments and stays in the light (2, 3-11).
Do not set your hearts on the world (2, 12-17).
The antichrist appears and denies the Father and the Son, but the Christians have received the anointing through which they know them (2, 18-27).

You are God's children and keep his commands (2, 28-3, 10).
The most important commandment is to love each other (3, 11-24)
Test the spirits to see whether they acknowledge that Jesus has
  come in the flesh (4, 1-6).
God loves us and therefore you love your brothers (4, 7-21).
God gives us eternal life with water, Spirit and blood (5, 1-12).
Appeal to pray for sinful brothers (5, 13-21).

The Christians are called on to live in strict isolation from what
is called "the world": "Do not set your hearts on the world or
anything in it" (2, 15); "We know that . . . the whole world lies in
wickedness" (5, 19). In the world lives the antichrist who wants to
make the congregation forsake its creed. There are men who say that
Jesus did not come in the flesh (4, 2). Christians, on the other hand,
know God because they are anointed (2, 27).

It is quite clear what sort of false doctrine is opposed here. The
people referred to neglect "the flesh", but this does not, as in
Corinth, lead to libertinism, but to conclusions which are important
for their christology. They fall victims to the heresy called docetism,
which implies total denial of the "flesh" of Jesus (cf. 2, 22; 4, 2
and 5, 1). To this the author opposes his testimony that he has
"felt" the life with his hands (1, 1-4). His teaching is thus the same
as that of the gospel of John, which speaks of the Word that became
flesh (1, 14).

On account of strongly exhortative character of the letter, the
author has drawn on church traditions particularly in as far as these
were of a paranetical nature. This is evident from certain parallels
with passages from the gospels:

I John 4, 21 and Matt. 22, 37-40 about loving God and one's
  neighbour.
I John 2, 17 and Matt. 7, 21 about doing God's will.
I John 3, 1-3 and Matt. 5, 9b about being God's children.
I John 4, 1 and Matt. 24, 11 and 24 about false prophets.
I John 4, 17 and Matt. 10, 25 about the fate of Christ and his
  followers.

I John 5, 3 and Matt. 11, 30 about commands that are not burdensome.

I John 3, 22 and Matt. 7, 8 about praying and receiving.

I John 3, 7 and Mark 13, 5 about being misled.

I John 5, 15 and Mark 11, 24 about receiving what one asks for.

I John 3, 13 and Luke 6, 22 about the hate of the world.

Short statements are repeatedly introduced with the words "If" or "Whoever" (1, 6; 2, 3; 2, 9 and 10-11; 2, 4-6; 2, 22-23 etc.), indicating a form of teaching which goes back, in structure, to a form known from judaism. Some scholars have attempted to separate the exhortative passages from the more descriptive parts (2, 18-21 and others). It is doubtful, however, whether these literary differences are sufficient grounds for the assumption that the author made use of sources, especially since the whole letter is uniform in style. This does not mean, though, that the author did not draw on certain traditional material known to both him and his readers. He used it, however, according to his personal tastes and discretion.[1]

A noteworthy feature, from the point of view of textual criticism, is the so-called *comma Johanneum* (5, 7-8), with an explicit trinitarian formula. This text is found in only a few very late manuscripts, dating from the 14th to 16th centuries. This passage was included in the third edition of the Greek New Testament published by Erasmus. Thus it found a place in Elzevier's printed text and in the modern translations based on it.

b. II John

This is in the form of an actual letter, written by "the elder" and addressed to "the elect lady and her children". Greetings are sent by "the children of your elect sister". Obviously the letter was from one congregation to another. The contents may be described as a very brief summary of I John. The readers are charged to love one another and watch out for those who do not believe that Christ came in the flesh.

---

[1] Cf. W. NAUCK, *Die Tradition und Charakter des ersten Johannesbriefes*, in: *Wissensch. Unters. z. N.T.* 3 1957.

c. III John

This again is a real letter, written by "the elder" and addressed to Gaius. At the end greetings are sent to "friends". The purpose of this letter is not quite clear. Apparently certain strangers go out "for the name's sake" (3, 7). These people must be received. The letter then continues with a remark about Diotrephes who does not receive "us". He even refuses to receive "the brothers" and expels from the congregation those who do receive them (3, 9, 10). Demetrius, on the other hand, does get a good testimony.

Apparently Diotrephes is opposing the "elder" and in doing so he even goes so far as to expel from the church those who will receive the brothers of the elder. Gaius and Demetrius appear to be supporting the elder. Evidently there is no central authority in this congregation, so that certain of its members can assume the right to excommunicate others.[1]

2. AUTHOR AND ADDRESSEES

None of the three letters mention the name of the author. Only in II and III John the author calls himself "elder". This may be a title of office, as in the pastoral letters, but it may also indicate a person's status in the community. Thus Peter calls himself "elder" in I Pet. 5, 1.

We can only arrive at a closer determination of the author's identity by observing that I and II John are so closely related in language, style and contents that they must have a common author. We may further observe that these two letters show so much resemblance to the gospel of John that we may conclude all three of these works to have been written by one person. As a result, the question of the authorship of I and II John merely takes us back to the same question concerning the gospel.

Some, however, have disputed the assertion that I John and the gospel of John were written by one and the same author. In this

---

[1] Cf. E. KÄSEMANN, „Ketzer und Zeuge", in: *Zeitschr. f. d. neut. Wissensch.* 47 1951, p. 292-311 and R. SCHNACKENBURG, „Der Streit zwischen dem Verfasser von 3. Joh. und Diotrephes", in: *Münch. Theol. Zeitschr.* 4 1953, p. 18-26.

connection it has been pointed out, for instance, that the words οὖν and γάρ which occur so frequently in the gospel hardly appear at all in I John (γάρ only three times in I John). The two works also differ in contents, for the gospel contains few references to the Second Coming whereas I John pays a good deal of attention to this subject (I, 2, 28; 3, 2 and 4, 17). It is doubtful, however, whether these differences are sufficient to warrant the assumption of two authors. The views expressed in these works on the "world" and the significance of Jesus' death (reconciliation in the gospel of John 1, 29; 3, 14 and 12, 24) are in any case so much alike that both works must derive from the same circle.[1] The identity of the person who ultimately wrote them down can perhaps no longer be determined, but it is certain that there is a forceful personality at the back of them who is responsible for style, language and contents. It can scarcely be doubted that this person was the apostle John. This means that these writings date from the end of the first century.

The addressees belong to the circles of John, for which the gospel was also written. This means that the persons to whom the letters were written lived in Asia Minor or in Syria. The heresy of docetism points to Asia Minor, since it is also mentioned in the letters of Ignatius. The three witnesses, Spirit, water and blood, of I, 5, 8 may point to Syria. A distinctive feature of the Syrian church was the fact that when a person was admitted to the congregation a prayer for the gift of the Spirit preceded the actual baptism. In the western church the request for the Spirit was not made until baptism had been administered.[2]

3. SIGNIFICANCE OF THE LETTERS

Together with the gospel of John these three letters introduce the reader to a sector of the church that differs from the Pauline

---

[1] Cf. C. H. DODD, *The Johannine Epistles*, in: *Moffatt N.T. Commentaries*, London 1947², p. XLVII-LVI and W. G. WILSON, ,,An Examination of the Linguistic Evidence adduced against the Unity of the Authorship of the First Epistle of John and the Fourth Gospel", in: *Journ. Theol. St.* 49 1948, p. 147-156.

[2] See J. A. T. ROBINSON, "The Destination and Purpose of the Johannine Epistles", in: *New Test. Stud.* 7 1960/61, p. 56 ff.

congregations and from those where the synoptic gospels originated. This group was characterized by a strong antithesis with regard to the surrounding world. Its members led rather introvert lives with a strong emphasis on mutual understanding.

The most salient characteristic of this group, however, is the forceful personality that must have dominated it. This person expressed the Christian faith in a language of his own, using, of course, a mode of expression familiar to his environment, but differing greatly from the language found in the other writings of the New Testament.

With this central authority there must have been little need for well-defined offices. There are no references to such offices in the Johannine writings.

For similar reasons these rather late writings contain no appeal at all to tradition or apostolic testimony. Their testimony is based completely on the authority of the writer.

CHAPTER TWENTY-TWO

THE REVELATION OF JOHN

1. CONTENTS

The book is introduced as a revelation of Jesus Christ telling his servants what must shortly happen. The author is told to write down what is and what will shortly occur (1, 19). The passage from 1, 1 to 3, 22 tells of "what is" and the remainder is concerned with the future (cf. 4, 1: ". . . and I will show you what must happen hereafter"). The contents may be summarized as follows:

Calling of John 1, 1-20.

Letters to the congregations at Ephesus, Smyrna, Pergamum, Thyatira, Sardis, Philadelphia and Laodicea 2, 1-3, 22.

The throne with the 24 elders, seven spirits, the crystal sea and the four beasts 4, 1-11.

The One sitting on the throne gives a scroll with seven seals to the Lamb 5, 1-11.

After the breaking of the first four seals four horses appear, after the fifth the souls are seen underneath the altar and after the sixth there is an earthquake 6, 1-17.

The sealing of the 144,000 from the tribes of Israel 7, 1-8.

A throng of martyrs which no one can count 7, 9-17.

The opening of the seventh seal and a silence for half an hour 8, 1.

Seven trumpets are given to seven angels who blow them to announce six disasters 8, 2-9, 21.

An angel descends from heaven with a book which the author has to eat. He is told to measure the temple. Two witnesses appear 10, 1-11, 14.

The seventh trumpet announces God's sovereignty over the world 11, 15-19.

The woman and the dragon 12, 1-18.

2. NATURE

This book is an example of apocalyptic literature, which speaks of the end of the world and the last judgement. The oldest apocalyptic passages we know occur in the prophetic literature of the Old Testament, such as Isa. 24-27, Zech. 9-14 and Joel 2, 28-3, 8. In the Old Testament the genre comes to a climax, and to an end, with Daniel. Around the beginning of the Christian era, apocalypticism was very much alive in certain Jewish circles, as is evident from such books as Baruch, Enoch and IV Ezra.

It is a marked feature of the New Testament that the apocalyptic element falls right into the background. In the gospels Mark 13 and parallels contain an apocalypse. Apocalyptic passages are also found in I Thess. 4, 15-17; II Thess. 2, 1-12; I Cor. 15, 20-28 and II Cor. 5, 1-5. As the early Christians were convinced that they shared in life and that the Second Coming was to take place very soon, they were not fertile in apocalyptic speculations. Note that it is in the very letters where he had to comment on deviating notions concerning the Second Coming that Paul reverts to apocalypticism.

The Jewish tradition from which the book of Revelation stems has put a clear stamp on its contents: the throne of God (4, 2), the sealed ones from the tribes of Israel (7, 4), Michael and his angels (12, 7) and the new Jerusalem (21, 10). Certain images which are found in other "revelations" also occur in the Revelation of John: four angels at the four corners of the earth (7, 1 and Zech. 6, 5), a scroll containing God's plans (5, 1 and 10, 8-11 and Ezech. 2, 9-3, 3), a trumpet as a warning of the coming judgement (8, 6ff and Ezek. 33, 4-5), the fight with the dragon (12, 7-9 and Isa. 27, 1) and "one like a son of man" (14, 14 and Dan. 7, 13).

The apocalypse of this book, however, bears the mark of Christianity. In the first place the revelation is granted not to some personage of the Old Testament such as Enoch or Baruch, but to a person, John, whom the readers know (1, 1; 1, 4; 1, 9 and 22, 8). In the second place the book has the letter-like character typical of the writings of the early Christian church. Not only does it contain seven letters (chs 2 and 3), it also concludes with a well-known formula that is often found at the end of letters: "The grace of the Lord Jesus be with you all" (22, 21). In the third place the book is intended for reading to the congregation (1, 3 and 4; 22, 18), thus resembling such works as Hebrews and I John. And, finally, it was not written to satisfy any curiosity about the realms of heaven and hell. On the contrary, it is concerned with concrete historical situations regarding the Roman empire and the cult of the emperor.

Numbers play an important part in apocalyptic literature. The reason for this is plain. Since it is concerned with the end of all things and the events that are to precede this end, the question of a time-limit is necessarily brought up. Thus Daniel 9, 24 speaks of seventy weeks that will pass before the transgression is finished. The number seven to indicate completeness keeps recurring as a motif in Revelation also: the book is addressed to seven churches, seven spirits stand before the throne of God (1, 4), the Lamb has seven horns and seven eyes (5, 6), seven trumpets are sounded, the book in God's hand is sealed up with seven seals, there are seven bowls full of God's anger and seven plagues strike the world. The number four also has a special significance, for it indicates totality in space: the earth has four corners. Four beasts surround

God's throne (4, 6), four angels are stationed at the four corners of heaven (7, 1), four horses go forth over the earth (6, 1-8). The number twelve, derived from the twelve tribes of Israel, indicates the totality of mankind. The 144,000 at the foot of God's throne are a multiple of this number (7, 1-8). The wall of the new Jerusalem is 144 cubits high and the city is built on 12 foundation stones (21, 14). The only number which presents a mystery is that of the "beast" indicated as 666 or 616 according to P[47], 046, 1 and other manuscripts. Whether this refers to a particular emperor we do not know.

A characteristic feature of the book are the numerous hymns included in it (5, 9-10. 12 and 13; 11, 15. 17-18; 12, 10-12; 15, 3-4; 19, 1-2. 5. 6-8). These hymns are of a liturgical nature, but they probably derive from the author himself. The singing of hymns is an activity that takes place through the Spirit (Luke 1, 67; Eph. 5, 18-19) and therefore belongs to the heavenly world.

Another remarkable aspect of the book is the unusual language in which it is written. Nothing like it is found in any other work. It shows an even stronger Hebrew influence than the Septuagint, yet it is not a translation from the Hebrew. The person who wrote this either thought in Hebrew and wrote in Greek or else he deliberately hebraized his Greek. The latter was probably the case. The peculiar nature of the book is thus expressed in its form as well as in its contents.

In conclusion it may be stated that, although the author follows a Jewish tradition, the book is fully determined by the Christian faith. God's victory over Satan cannot be divorced from the victory gained by Christ. Christ is seated on God's throne (3, 21); Jesus has gained the victory and thereby the right to open the scroll (5, 5); the Lamb will be victorious in the end (17, 14). There is great longing for the coming of Christ (22, 17) who has freed from their sins all who follow him (1, 5) and cleansed them through His blood (7, 14). Thus the author is not only able to comfort his readers by pointing out what is to come but also to support his message by showing what has been: "who is, who was and who is to come" (1, 4; cf. 2, 8).

3. Sources and Structure

In our summary of the contents, above, we pointed out that the book may be divided into two parts: what is, and what is to come hereafter. The second part begins with 4, 1. The structure of this second part is not always quite transparent. Starting with 6, 1 we read about the breaking of the seven seals on the scroll. This section is interrupted after the breaking of the sixth seal by the passage (7, 1-17) about the sealed from Israel and the throng which no one can count. After the breaking of the seventh seal (8, 1) the angels with the seven trumpets appear. This is again interrupted by the instruction to eat the opened book and the passage about the two witnesses (10, 1-11, 14). If we view the whole in relation to the number of seven we see how chs. 12, 13, 14, 15, 1-4 are placed between the passages about the seven trumpets and the seven bowls. Chapters 10 and 11 seem to speak of a new calling of the prophet. Should the chapters 10,1 to 15, 4 therefore be regarded as a separate section? Was this passage taken from some source or does it tell of a new calling? It is doubtful whether in literature of this type such irregularities may be smoothed out by the assumption of sources. Obviously the book owes its origin to a person of visionary capacity. There is no doubt, furthermore, that the visions did not all come to him in direct succession. The author must have done some editorial work in placing the different visions one after the other to arrive at a climax. Such a climax is evident in the description of the seven seals, the seven trumpets and the seven bowls. The trials grow more and more severe. From chapter 17 onwards there is a clear succession of events: the downfall of Babylon, the millennium, a new heaven and earth and a new Jerusalem. Instead of looking for sources, therefore, it is better to look for the view-points according to which the author edited his work. Once we realize that the climax comes each time with God's victory we can also see that the author is justified, from a structural point of view, in placing 10, 1-11, 14 (since this passage preaches judgement) between the sixth and the seventh trumpets. For the seventh trumpet, unlike the other six, does not announce judgement but victory (11, 15-19).

Although it is possible to recognize certain passages within this book which are complete in themselves and which each touch on a particular theme, it is necessary for purposes of exegesis to keep an eye on the whole. Right from the beginning the author kept the ending in view and it is on the basis of this ending that the preceding passages should be interpreted.[1]

4. AUTHOR

The author refers to himself as John four times (1, 1.4.9; 22, 8). He is known to his readers, to whom he presents himself as a "companion in suffering" (1, 9).

At quite an early date the apostle John was assumed to be the author. Thus Justin writes, *Dial. c. Tryphone* 81, 4:

Καὶ ἔπειτα καὶ παρ' ἡμῖν ἀνήρ τις, ᾧ ὄνομα Ἰωάννης εἷς τῶν ἀποστόλων τοῦ Χριστοῦ ἐν ἀποκαλύψει ... προεφήτευσε ...

And furthermore, a man from among us called John, one of the apostles of Christ, prophesied in a revelation ...

Clement of Alexandria, *Quis. div. salv.* 24, also believed this book was written by the apostle John. The situation changes with the growing opposition to ideas about the millennium. Eusebius records Origen's acceptance of the book (*H.E.* VI 25 9) but personally he classes it with the *antilegomena* (*H.E.* III 25 2). Dionysius of Alexandria in particular, bishop and head of the school of catechumens in that city (264/5), opposed the apostle's authorship (Eusebius, *H.E.* VII 25 7-8).

καλεῖσθαι μὲν οὖν αὐτὸν Ἰωάννην καὶ εἶναι τὴν γραφὴν Ἰωάννου ταύτην οὐκ ἀντερῶ, ἁγίου μὲν γὰρ εἶναί τινος καὶ θεοπνεύστου συναινῶ· οὐ μὴν ῥᾳδίως ἂν συνθείμην τοῦτον εἶναι τὸν ἀπόστολον, τὸν υἱὸν Ζεβεδαίου, τὸν ἀδελφὸν Ἰακώβου, οὗ τὸ εὐαγγέλιον τὸ κατὰ Ἰωάννην ἐπιγεγραμμένον καὶ ἡ ἐπιστολὴ ἡ καθολική. τεκμαίρομαι γὰρ ἔκ τε τοῦ ἤθους ἑκατέρων καὶ τοῦ τῶν λόγων εἴδους καὶ τῆς τοῦ βιβλίου διεξαγωγῆς λεγομένης, μὴ τὸν αὐτὸν εἶναι.

I shall not deny that he calls himself John and that this book was written by some John, and I concede that it was written by a holy man who was inspired by God, but I find it hard to admit that this is the apostle, the son of Zebedee, the brother of James, who wrote the gospel according to John and the Catholic letter. For, from the usage of both authors and the literary form and from what may be called the argumentation of the book I conclude that it is not the same person.

---

[1] Cf. M.-E. BOISMARD, „' L'Apocalypse' ou 'les Apocalypses' de S. Jean", in: *Rev. Bibl.* 56 1949, p. 507-541 and 59 1952, p. 172-181.

Dionysius here brings forward an argument in favour of a different authorship which still has force. The language and style of Revelation are indeed different from those found in the gospel and letters of John. The fact that the gospel pays practically no attention to the future of God's kingdom while Revelation devotes very much attention to this subject is rather less significant as an argument against a common author. The authorship of the apostle John can only be maintained if the differences in language and style are attributed to the nature of the book. On the other hand it strikes us as strange that the author should speak of twelve foundation stones bearing the names of the twelve apostles if he himself were one of these apostles (21, 14).

If John's authorship is rejected, no other known person can be pointed out as the author. Dionysius of Alexandria thought that John, the elder from Ephesus (see Chapter III on the gospel of John) might be the author (Eusebius, *H.E.* VII 25 16), but there is no trace of evidence for this. The only remaining possibility is to assume that the author came from the western part of Asia Minor where he was a prominent member of the Christian church.

5. Time and Place of Origin

The author says that he was granted his visions on the island of Patmos, off the coast of Asia Minor. Evidently he came from the western part of Asia Minor, perhaps from Ephesus to which the first of the seven letters is addressed. The book was not necessarily written on the island.

Irenaeus knows when the visions occurred (Ir. *adv. Haer.* V 30 3, quoted by Eusebius *H.E.* III 18 3):

οὐδὲ γὰρ πρὸ πολλοῦ χρόνου ἐωράθη, ἀλλὰ σχεδὸν ἐπὶ τῆς ἡμετέρας γενεᾶς, πρὸς τῷ τέλει τῆς Δομετιανοῦ ἀρχῆς.

For he saw it (the Revelaticn) not so long ago, but almost during our own generation, towards the end of Domitian's reign.

This date during the reign of Domitian (81-96) is practically universally accepted. The conflict between church and emperor, referred to in the Revelation, fits in well with the situation of his time. According to Suetonius, *Domitianus* 13, he called himself *Dominus ac deus noster* ("our lord and god").

Attempts have been made to determine a date on the basis of 17, 10 which speaks of seven kings, of whom five are fallen, one still is and one is yet to come. The trouble is no one knows with which Roman emperor to start counting.

For those who accept the interpretation according to which chapter 10 describes a second calling, a single date will not suffice. Some have supposed, therefore, that one part of the book dates from Nero's time and another from Domitian's.

6. INTERPRETATION

In the course of the centuries many attempts have been made to provide a significant interpretation for the book. Many have believed it to contain a prophecy of the historical future. Special attention was paid in this connection to the references to the millennium. This leads to forced interpretations which do not do justice either to the book or to church history. An allegorical method has also been used in an attempt to throw some light on certain sections. This method, however, makes the book timeless, so that the number 666 or 616, for instance, may be applied to any person at all. Actually, however, the book is not timeless. It must be interpreted in the light of the times in which the author lived. He is evidently very anxious for the fate of the congregations that he knows. But he allows the light of the victory that Christ has gained and shall complete to shine over their situation. Beside, inside and above the situation of the church he places the reality of God, which makes his own time only relative on the one hand, but most significant on the other, since it is the time in which victory breaks through. In this way the book gives meaning to the history of his time and thereby to the history of all times.

CHAPTER TWENTY-THREE

THE CANON OF THE NEW TESTAMENT

The significance of the 27 books of the New Testament consists in the fact that these have been accepted as "divine scriptures" by the whole church. This acceptance is the result of a process that covered about four centuries. The historical study of this process is the study of the history of the New Testament canon.

1. The Meaning of the Word Canon

In modern usage the word *canon*, Greek κανών, means the authoritative list of books accepted as holy scripture, and it is in this meaning that we use it in this chapter. It did not acquire this meaning, however, until a fairly late date. The basic meaning is "cane", "rod" and then "measuring rod". That is how it came to mean "norm".

Looking specifically at Christian usage we find that the word occurs only in Gal. 6, 16 where it appears to mean "rule" and in II Cor. 10, 13-16 where it refers to "the commission given us by God". Evidently the word carried no special significance.

In post-apostolic times the word is used specifically in the meaning of "norm", a meaning which the Greeks already knew. There is a "canon" of truth (Irenaeus I 9 4) and a "canon" of faith. This "canon" was determined by the church and thus the word "canonical" acquired a very special meaning. Church and canon are inseparably bound together.

It is not until the middle of the fourth century, however, that Athanasius uses "canon" in the special meaning of "list of scriptures accepted by the church". He says that the Pastor of Hermas stands "outside the canon" (ἐκ τοῦ κανόνος). In 394 Amphilochus of Iconium writes a catalogue of the bible in iambics in which he says:

οὗτος ἀψευδέστατος κανών ἂν εἴη θεο-πνεύστων γραφῶν.	This may be considered the most truthful canon of the divinely inspired scriptures.

The council of Laodicea, A.D. 360, states in can. 59:

ὅτι οὐ δεῖ ἰδιωτικοὺς ψαλμοὺς λέγεσθαι ἐν τῇ ἐκκλησίᾳ οὐδὲ ἀκονόνιστα βιβλια ἀλλὰ μόνα τὰ κανονικὰ τῆς καινῆς καὶ παλαιᾶς διαθήκης.	that home-made psalms should not be read in church, nor the non-canonical books, but only the cano-nical books of the New and Old Testament.

From this time onwards the word "canon" has been used in this special meaning in Greek, Latin and the various Western European languages.[1]

2. The Transition from Oral to written Tradition

The faith of the early church was founded on the person of Jesus. It was on his words and works that the church was built. Jesus Christ was the example that the church tried to follow.

Jesus served as a model in many things, and also in the reading and interpretation of the Old Testament. In Him the Scriptures have been fulfilled (Matthew) and it was his Spirit that spoke through the prophets (I Peter 1, 11). Because Christ was the norm used in the interpretation of the Old Testament all discussion between Jews and Christians on this point had become impossible. The numerous mis-understandings between the two parties in Justin's "Dialogue with Trypho" bear witness to this.

But Jesus did not only speak through the Scriptures, he had also spoken in Galilee and Jerusalem and was still speaking through the prophets (cf. John 16, 13 and Acts 21, 10-11). His words were a criterion for the life and preachings of the church. An appeal to Jesus' words put an end to every dispute (cf. I Cor. 7, 10; 9, 14; Acts 20, 25). When any of these words were written down, the resulting books derived their authority not from whoever wrote them but from the fact that it was Christ who had spoken these words.

---

[1] See H. W. Beyer, „κανών", in: Theol. Wörterbuch z. N.T. III 1938, p. 600-606.

It was the conviction of the church that Christ handed his words over to the apostles: to them it has been granted to know the secrets of heaven (Matt. 13, 11; Mark 10, 40; Luke 10, 17). According to Eph. 2, 19-20 the church is built on the foundation laid by the apostles and the prophets. The letter of Clement says that the apostles preached the gospel and that Jesus Christ was sent by God (I Clem. 42, 1; cf. Ignatius *ad Magn.* 7, 1 and 13, 1).

The authority of the apostles is no less, therefore, than that of Christ himself, except that theirs is a derived authority. This attitude is illustrated by a quotation given by Eusebius (*H.E.* III 39 4) who cites Papias, bishop of Hierapolis (c. 130):

οὐ γὰρ τὰ ἐκ τῶν βιβλίων τοσοῦτόν με ὠφελεῖν ὑπελάμβανον ὅσον τὰ παρὰ ζώσης φωνῆς καὶ μενούσης.

For I considered that what was contained in the books could not profit me as much as the living word that endures.

Here we see a preference for the *viva vox*, the direct words of Christ, instead of the written words of the apostles.

The same attitude is found in the writings of the so-called apostolic fathers. We find them invoking both the authority of the Lord (Barnabas, 6, 16; 7, 11; Polycarp 7, 2; Didache 9, 5) and that of the Old Testament and the Christian scriptures (Barnabas 4, 14 cites Matt. 22, 14; II Clement 2, 4 quoting Isa. and Matt. 9, 13 side by side; Didache 15, 4). It is not the names of the authors but the words they have written that are considered important. For this reason it is not thought necessary to name the writings from which the quotations are derived. It is characteristic therefore that all the gospels were written anonymously. Equally noteworthy, however, is the fact that, in John 21 the editors point out the reliability of this book on the grounds that it was written by "the apostle whom Jesus loved". Papias tells us that the gospel of Mark is based on the testimony of Peter and the *Canon Muratori* stresses the fact that the gospel of Luke was written by a companion of Paul's. Anonymity has been replaced by apostolic authority. In this connection it is also significant that the letter of Jude was republished under Peter's name.[1]

---

[1] Cf. H. Köster, *Synoptische Überlieferung bei den apostolischen Vätern,* in: *Texte u. Unters.* 65 1957.

Tradition thus develops in the direction of an authority that is based on the words of the apostles. Undoubtedly Paul had an important part in this development. When his words and authority were called in question he was forced to plead his apostleship (Galatians and the letters to the Corinthians). It is no accident that I and II Thessalonians lack the characteristic "Paul, apostle of Jesus Christ" of all the other letters. Already at an early date the legitimacy of a person who speaks by the authority of Christ is of great significance in the defence and propagation of the truth.

The period in which the authority of the words of Christ, in oral or written form, and the authority of the apostles were of equal significance comes abruptly to an end when Marcion, around A.D. 160, invokes the testimony of Luke and Paul exclusively. He is merely completing a development that had been taking place for many years before his time. He restricts the testimony, however, to that of one apostle and his companion.

3. The Development towards the Fixing of the Canon

Marcion put an end to the confusion that reigned with regard to the authority on which the church was founded.[1] The church could not follow him, since it desired a broader apostolic foundation. But this meant drawing a line somewhere. Since the limits were differently placed in different parts of the church, a number of centuries were yet to pass before one canon was generally accepted.

The first ecclesiastical author to rely solely on the written and apostolic word was *Justin Martyr* (c. 150). On Sundays, according to him, the ἀπομνημονεύματα ἃ καλεῖται εὐαγγέλια (gospels) were read (*Apol.* 66, 3). These were written ὑπὸ τῶν ἀποστόλων αὐτοῦ καὶ τῶν ἐκείνοις παρακολουθησάντων (*Dial.* 103, 8). He cites the Revelation of John as a book in which the Lord speaks (*Dial.* 81, 4).

The eastern half of the Christian world had not yet reached this stage. When Tatian arrived in Syria it was not clear on what author-

---

[1] H. von Campenhausen, *Die Entstehung der christlichen Bibel*, in: *Beitr. z. hist. Theol.* 39, Tübingen 1968, assumes that Marcion's work was the main reason for the rapid development of a christian canon of Scriptures.

ity the church in these parts based itself. As the Christians there were
of Jewish origin it is possible that the gospel of the Hebrews was
read, but it is equally possible that only oral tradition was adhered
to. In any case there was, in A.D. 170, no question of any recognized
authority of the four gospels, for Tatian was able to combine these
books into one. His *Diatessaron* was accepted.

After Justin things develop quickly in the Western church.
Irenaeus accepts four gospels, no more and no less. He speaks of a
εὐαγγέλιον τετράμορφον (*adv. Haer.* III 11, 11). He knows 13 letters
of Paul, the Revelation, I John and I Peter. According to Eusebius
he not only knows but accepts the Pastor of Hermas (*H.E.* V 8 7).
According to the same source he also mentions the letter to the
Hebrews (*H.E.* V 26). From his quotations we know that he also
knew Jude and II John. He did not know James, III John and II
Peter. An important piece of evidence for the state of affairs in Rome
is the *Canon Muratori* which dates from c. 200 (see Appendix E).
Here we find the four gospels, 13 letters of Paul, Jude, I and II John
and Revelation. The author of this catalogue knows the Revelation
of Peter and the Pastor of Hermas which, however, he does not
accept as authoritative writings.

Cyprian and *Tertullian* in North Africa are understandably
unanimous on the subject of authoritative books. Neither of these
two authors mention Hebrews, James, II Peter or II and III John.
On the other hand Tertullian does know Jude, but Cyprian does not.

Evidently a number of books were already generally accepted in
the Western church around A.D. 200: the four gospels, 13 Pauline
letters, Acts, I Peter, I John and Revelation. Jude and II John are
known, in any case, the Pastor of Hermas has a certain amount of
authority but is suspected in some quarters, and Hebrews, James,
III John and II Peter are not known.

A rather broader foundation was accepted in Egypt. Besides the
four gospels, *Clement of Alexandria* knows 14 Pauline letters (which
means that Hebrews is included). In addition he accepts Acts and
the Revelation of John. If Eusebius is to be believed, Clement
discussed all the books in his *Hypotyposes* "not neglecting the
disputed books (τὰς ἀντιλεγομένας)". These disputed writings are

the letter of Jude "and the other Catholic letters and that of Barnabas and the Revelation of Peter" (*H.E.* VI 14, 1-2). Books he does not, at any rate, quote are III John, II Peter and James. On the other hand he does accept I Clement, the Didache and the Pastor of Hermas. This shows that the Egyptian church preferred a broad foundation instead of drawing narrow limits.

A change in this situation is ushered in by *Origen*. He classifies the various writings according to their acceptance in the church. The four gospels, he says, are accepted "without contradiction" (ἀναντίρρητά). Peter has left us one "generally accepted letter" (ἐπιστολὴν ὁμολογουμένην) and perhaps another one; this is still a subject of dispute (ἀμφιβάλλεται). The Revelation was written by John, as well as one letter, and "if you like" (ἔστω δὲ καί) a second and a third. He also classes as "disputed writings" (ἀμφιβαλλόμενα): James, and Jude (cf. Eusebius, *H.E.* VI 25 3-10). Origen, evidently, judges the various writings according as they are or are not generally accepted in the church.

Eusebius follows in Origen's footsteps (*H.E.* III 25). According to him the following writings are authentic (ἐν ὁμολογουμένοις): the four gospels, Acts, the Pauline letters, I John, I Peter and "for those who think it right" (εἴ γε φανείη) the Revelation. As disputed (τῶν δὲ ἀντιλεγομένων) he lists James, Jude, II Peter and II and III John, though many people regard these writings as authentic. Unauthentic (ἐν τοῖς νόθοις), according to him, are the Acts of Paul, the Pastor of Hermas, the Revelation of Peter, Barnabas, the Didache, the Revelation of John "if you like" (εἴ φανείη) and the Gospel of the Hebrews. Heretical writings are the gospels of Peter, Thomas and Matthias and other books such as the Acts of Andrew, John or other apostles. Thus we find that Eusebius regards all the books that were eventually included in the canon as authentic and generally accepted, apart from the Revelation on which opinions still differed.

After 200, therefore, the determination of the canon progressed more rapidly in the East than in the West. The question of the Revelation remains unsolved in the East for a long time. *Chrysostom* (354-407), *Theodoretus* (died c. 460), *Basil* (d. 379), *Gregory of Nyssa*

(d. 394) and *Gregory of Nazianze* (d. 390) all rejected the Revelation.

In view of Eusebius' opinions it is not surprising that *Athanasius*, in his Paschal letter of 367, regarded all 27 books of the New Testament, as we know it, as canonical. This really marks the final definition of the canon in this area.

The eastern example was followed by the western church at the synods of Hippo Regius (393) and Carthage (397 and 419). Some hesitation was still felt here, however, on the subject of Hebrews, which was not expressly recognized as Pauline.

The Syrian church followed only very reluctantly. Of the Catholic letters the *Peshitta* included only I John, I Peter and James. Revelation was also left out. Even in Ephraim's time it was still customary to include III Corinthians among the Pauline letters. It was not until *Philoxenus* that a canon similar to that accepted in the remainder of the church was introduced into the Syrian church.

In the history of the canon all sorts of factors played a part. Apostolicity was a significant criterium in the Western church, which meant that Hebrews and some of the Catholic letters could not be accepted at first. Right from the start the eastern church, particularly in Egypt, accepted a much broader foundation. Origen then gave the impulse to arrive at an acceptance of those writings which were in general use. On this basis non-apostolic writings could also be accepted. It was especially due to the influence of Athanasius on the western church that the eastern canon was also accepted in Rome.

CHAPTER TWENTY-FOUR

THE TEXT OF THE NEW TESTAMENT

The autograph manuscripts of all the New Testament books have been lost. Some fragments of New Testament texts are known from the second and third centuries, but all our other manuscripts date from later centuries. In studying the text of the New Testament, scholars try to restore the original text with the help of the various manuscripts and to trace the history of its development.

1. THE MAKING OF MANUSCRIPTS

The materials on which manuscripts were written were papyrus and parchment. Papyrus, a fairly cheap material, was made from the pith of the papyrus plant. The sappy pith was cut in strips which were pressed together in crosswise layers and dried. Parchment, which was much more expensive, was made of the prepared skins of cows, sheep or goats. The oldest texts of the New Testament, from the second and third centuries, are on papyrus; manuscripts written on parchment are not found until the fourth century and later.

At first the sheets of papyrus or parchment were pasted together to form rolls up to thirty feet long. Soon, however, *codices* took the place of rolls. One or more sheets were folded into a quire and these quires were combined to form books.

As the church gained in significance the use of papyrus was discontinued and parchment, which was rather more durable, was used instead. We know that in 331 Constantine the Great ordered fifty parchment manuscripts from Eusebius of Caesarea for the churches of Constantinople. These were to be easily legible, handy in size and written by professional scribes (Eusebius, *Vita Constantini* IV 36).

Originally the manuscripts were written in *scriptio continua*, which means that the words followed each other without a break. No accents or punctuation marks were used. Capitals were used until the ninth century when a cursive script developed.

For purposes of textual criticism the manuscripts are distinguished according to the material on which they are written and the script used. Manuscripts on papyrus are indicated by a P followed by a number and parchment manuscripts by a capital letter (A, B, C, D, etc, also ℵ) if they are written in capitals (majuscules), or by Arabic numerals (1, 2, 3, etc) when written in cursive script (minuscules).

The *scriptio continua* made it rather difficult to find a required place quickly, for which reason the text was often divided into short columns (*stichoi*). In the codex Vaticanus (B), however, we already find a system of chapters, κεφάλαια. Each such chapter was provided with a τίτλος, giving a summary of its contents. Eusebius developed an ingenious method of dividing the four gospels into pericopes which he numbered. The numbers were combined into a list with the help of which similar passages in the different gospels might be easily found. Further simplifications that made for easier reading were short summaries for each book of the New Testament, marks at the beginning and end of liturgical lections and a system of punctuation. A division into verses does not occur until a printed text of 1551.

A typical feature of the Christian writings is the contraction of the so-called *nomina sacra*. θεός thus becomes θ̄ς, κύριος becomes κ̄ς, Ἰησοῦς becomes ῑς, πνεῦμα becomes π̄ν̄α, Ἰσραήλ becomes ῑη̄λ, οὐρανός becomes ο̄ῡνος.

At the end of a manuscript a colophon is often added. Such colophons may be important when they give an indication of when and where the manuscript was written. Usually, however, the scribe merely asks the reader to give him a kind reading and to pray for him. Others indicate where and when the original was supposed to have been written.

In these manuscripts we are further concerned with numerous

correctors. Here we may distinguish between the first correction of copyist's mistakes by comparison with the text from which the copy was made, and later corrections which try to make a manuscript up to date by comparison with some later manuscript. Sometimes these corrections are restricted to one book or even part of a book and are then adopted in manuscripts copied from such corrected copies. As a result all the various manuscripts show a great mixture of texts. One manuscript may contain a combination of all sorts of different texts.

2. EXISTING MANUSCRIPTS

We have already seen that the manuscripts are divided into papyri, majuscules and minuscules. At present we have about 90 papyri, only a few of which contain more than two or three verses. The majuscules number 270 and the minuscules more than 2700. Lectionaries, which contain only those pericopes that were used in liturgy are indicated by the letter *l*, followed by a numeral. Translations are indicated by abbreviations: lat(in), sy(riac), bo(hairic), got(hic), etc. and sometimes, as we shall see, with some further indication of the manuscript referred to. The numerous old Latin manuscripts are distinguished by the letters of the alphabet: a, b, c, d, etc.

The manuscripts include palimpsests. These are biblical manuscripts which have been erased and used again for the writing of some other work. By chemical means or infra-red rays the original writing may be made reasonably legible again.

In the following list the date of writing is included among other information. This tells us something about the manuscripts in question but by no means everything. A twelfth century manuscript may offer an earlier text than, for instance, a seventh century one, if the former was copied from a fifth century and the latter from a sixth century copy.

The following is a list of a number of important manuscripts: *Papyri*:

P^{38}, Acts 18, 27-19, 6 and 12-16, western text, c. 300.

P⁴¹, Acts 17, 28-18, 2. 24-25; 19, 1-4. 6-8. 13-16. 18-19; 20, 9-13, 15-16. 22-24. 26-28. 35-38; 21, 1-3; 22, 12-14. 17, western text, 8th century.

P⁴⁵, large parts of Matt., Mark, Luke, John, and Acts, 3rd century.

P⁴⁶, parts of Rom., Hebr., I and II Cor., Eph., Gal., Phil., Col., I Thess., mixed text, c. 200.

P⁵², John 18, 31-34. 37-38, Egyptian, early 2nd century (oldest known fragment of the New Testament).

P⁶⁶, John, mixed text, c. 200.

P⁷², Jude, I and II Peter, Egyptian, 3rd/4th century.

P⁷⁴, Acts, James, I and II Peter, I, II and III John, Jude, as A, 7th century.

P⁷⁵, parts of Luke and John, Egyptian, early 3rd century.

Majuscules:

א, Codex Sinaiticus, acquired by Tischendorf in the convent of St. Catharine on Mt. Sinai for the Russian czar and published in 1862, bought by the British Museum in 1933 for £ 100,000, the whole bible, 4th century.

A, Codex Alexandrinus, from the 14th century in the library of the patriarch of Alexandria, sold in 1621 by the patriarch of Constantinople to Charles I of England, in British Museum, whole bible, 5th century.

B, Codex Vaticanus, already in the Bibliotheca Vaticana before 1475, whole bible, 4th century.

C, Codex Ephraemi rescriptus, erased during the 12th century in order to write on it a treatise by the Syrian ecclesiastical author Ephraim, fragments of the New Testament (not including II Thess. and II John), 5th century.

D, Codex Bezae Cantabrigiensis, presented by Beza to the Cambridge University Library, Latin and Greek text side by side in columns, most important Greek sample of the western text, gospels and Acts, 5th/6th centuries.

D, Codex Claromontanus, Latin and Greek, Paul, 6th century.

E, Codex Basiliensis, gospels, 8th century.

F, Codex Boreelianus, since 1830 in Utrecht University Library, gospels, 9th century.

H, Codex Wolfii B, gospels, 10th century.

K, Codex Cyprii, gospels, 10th century.

E[a], Codex Laudianus 35, some resemblance to D, Acts, 6th/7th centuries.

E[p], Codex Sangermanensis, Latin and Greek, Paul, 9th/10th centuries.

F[p], Codex Augiensis, Latin and Greek, Paul, 9th century.

G[p], Codex Boernerianus, Latin and Greek (in alternate lines), Paul, 9th century.

H[p], Codex Coislinianus, colophon after Titus which states that the text has been corrected after a copy in the library of Caesarea written by Pamphilus.

I, Washington, parts of Paul, 5th/6th centuries.

W, a very mixed text of the four gospels (cf. Mark 16. 14), 4th/5th centuries.

Θ, Codex Koridethi, four gospels, in Mark Caesarea text, 9th century.

Minuscules:

fam. 1, K. Lake discovered that the mss. 1, 118, 131 and 209 go back to one common archetype. Many similarities to Θ, 12th-14th centuries.

fam. 13, W. H. Ferrar discovered that the mss. 13, 59, 124, 346 go back to a common archetype. The group is even more extensive and includes 230, 543, 788 and 826 among others. Caesarea text, 11th-15th centuries.

28, gospels, in Mark Caesarea text, 11th century.

33, whole New Testament except Revelation, Egyptian text, 9th/10th centuries.

Other texts, significant because they deviate from the Byzantine text are:

157, gospels, according to the colophon copied and corrected after the old manuscripts in Jerusalem; 565, in Mark Caesarea text, 9th/10th centuries; 700 with in the Lord's Prayer the text:

"May thy holy Spirit come over us and cleanse us" (Luke 11, 2), 11th/12th centuries; 1241, whole New Testament except Revelation, Egyptian text, 12th/13th centuries; 1739, Acts and Paul, Egyptian text, goes back to a manuscript from the 4th century.

The study of the lectionaries has long been neglected but recent research has shown that these texts sometimes contain old readings. The text of these is only very sporadically printed in the critical apparatus of the various editions of the Greek New Testament.

Translations

For purposes of restoring the original text the early translations have only a limited significance. The oldest translations, the Latin and the Syriac, go back to a Greek text that was used during the second century. These early translations, however, are careless, inexpert and rather free. The manuscripts in which they are found, moreover, date from at least two centuries later. For these reasons it is often hardly possible to determine what the Greek text from which these translations were made was really like.

The Syriac translations

At first the Syrian church used a combination of the four gospels into one book, the *Diatessaron*, compiled c. 170 by Tatian. The original Syriac text of this book has been lost but it still exists in all sorts of translations, such as the Arabic, Persian and Latin. From the Latin, translations were made into Middle Dutch, Tuscan, Venetian and German. Ephraim wrote a commentary on the Diatessaron which has been found in Syriac and of which an Armenian translation also exists. All the translations show a high degree of adaptation to later standard texts, so that the original Diatessaron cannot be reconstructed in detail. In quite a number of places, however, especially where eastern and western translations are in agreement, we may recognize the original text.

After the Diatessaron the separate gospels were translated into Syriac. From this early translation only two manuscripts have come down to us: the *syrus curetonianus* (sy^c) and *syrus sinaiticus* (sy^s), both dating from the 4th or 5th centuries.

Towards the end of the 4th century a standard text was produced, showing far less influence of the Diatessaron than sy^s and sy^c: the *Peshitta* (sy^p), which does not contain II Peter, II and III John, Jude and the Revelation. Over 350 mss. of sy^p are known.

The complete New Testament is found in the translation of *Philoxenus* and *Thomas Harclensis*. Apparently the translation of bishop Philoxenus, made by Polycarp in 508, was republished by Thomas Harclensis in 616. We do not know for certain whether Thomas only added the marginal notes in these manuscripts or whether he also altered Philoxenus' text. This text is called sy^{ph} and when only the marginalia are referred to, sy^h.

The so-called *Palestine lectionary*, which dates from the fifth century, does not strictly belong to the Syriac area. It contains parts of the gospels, Acts and a few Pauline letters. This lectionary was compiled for the Christians of Palestine and is interesting not only for its text (often a Caesarea text) but also from a linguistic point of view.

The Latin translations

Many old Latin manuscripts have been preserved. Jerome complained about the state of this text: . . . *tot enim sunt exemplaria paene quot codices* ("there are almost as many different forms of the text as there are codices" *Ep. ad. Damasum*). It is customary to divide these manuscripts into an African (or Afra-) and a European (or Itala-) group. The former, with which the quotations of Cyprian and Tertullian agree most closely includes:

e, Codex Palatinus, parts of the gospels, 4th century.

h, Fleury-palimpsest, parts of Acts, Catholic Letters and Revelation, 6th century.

k, Codex Bobbiensis, parts of Mark and Matthew, c. 400.

Some mss. of the European group are:

a, Codex Vercellensis, gospels, 4th century.

b, Codex Veronensis, gospels, 5th century.

c, Codex Colbertinus, gospels, 12th century.

d, Codex Bezae, the Latin columns of D.

gig, Codex Gigas (circa 35″ long and 20″ wide!), 13th century. Many of these manuscripts show Vulgate readings.

The standard Latin text is the *Vulgate*, which was compiled by Jerome on Pope Damasus' orders after 382. Jerome based his version on an old Latin text which he corrected with reference to a Greek manuscript. The manuscripts of the Vulgate are indicated by the letters A, Codex Amiatinus; C, Codex Cavensis; D, Codex Dublensis, etc. During the middle ages several revisions of the Vulgate took place.

The Coptic translation

There are translations in various Coptic dialects, the best-known of which are the Sahidic and the Bohairic versions (sa and bo). These go back to the third and fourth centuries and have an Egyptian text.

The Gothic translation

This was made by Ulfila in the middle of the fourth century. The text is Byzantine.

The Armenian translation

This dates from the fifth century. At first an Armenian Diatessaron was probably used, going back to a Syriac version of the book. This text was later replaced by the separate gospels, based on a manuscript of the Caesarea type. The standard text agrees most closely with the Byzantine text.

The Georgian translation

It is not known when the text was translated into this language. It probably goes back to an Armenian version of the New Testament and therefore also shows the influence of the Caesarea text.

The Ethiopian translation

The date of the translation of the New Testament into Ethiopian is unknown. The text is mixed, being partly Egyptian and partly Byzantine.

The texts of the Armenian, Georgian and Ethiopian versions have not yet been closely studied. No less than 1244 mss. of the Armenian New Testament text are known, but there is only one printed text, that of Zohrab (1789) which is based on only a few manuscripts. With regard to the Georgian and Ethiopian versions the situation is no better.

Quotations found in ecclesiastical authors.

For a reconstruction of the original text these quotations have little significance. In the first place we can never be sure that an author is quoting exactly, and in the second place the texts of early Christian authors have been badly preserved. It is always possible that quotations were altered to agree with later standard versions.

Nevertheless these quotations are important for the history of the text in another way, for it is usually possible to determine which text was used by a particular author. This gives an indication of which texts were current at a particular time in a particular place. From the quotations found in Irenaeus and Justin, for instance, we can tell that c. 200 a western text (as in D, lat. sy) was used in Rome and Gaul. Origen's quotations show that c. 200 in Alexandria the Caesarea text (Θ, fam. 1 and fam. 13) was used as well as the Egyptian text (אB). Cyril and Athanasius of Alexandria prove to have used a text such as found in א and B.

The lack of manuscripts from the first few centuries enhances the importance of such authors as *Marcion* and *Tatian* in particular. Both these authors occupied themselves intensively with the text. For the former was setting up a "canon" of books: the *evangelikon* and *apostolikon* (Luke and the letters of Paul) while the latter compiled a harmony of the four gospels: the Diatessaron. Both their books have been lost, but Marcion's text may be reconstructed to some extent from Tertullian's *adv. Marcionem* and the Diatessaron is known from later translations. The text of these books is largely western (D, lat, sy). The question to what extent these authors based themselves on Greek manuscripts of a western type will be discussed below. It is also possible that their versions influenced the so-called western text.

3. History of Textual Criticism

The history of textual criticism is usually considered to have started with the first printed text. This was an important event, for the printing of a text meant that a choice had to be made from the manuscripts. Before the invention of printing the differences between the manuscripts had already been noticed, however, and several authors had compared variant readings. This is particularly true of Origen and Jerome. The arguments on which these authors based their choice, however, cannot stand the test of present-day criticism.

The first edited printed edition of a New Testament text was by *Erasmus* in 1516. He compiled his text from six manuscripts. But because none of these manuscripts gave the Greek text after Revelation 22, 16, Erasmus translated Rev. 22, 16-21 into Greek from the Latin. He worked in great haste to get his edition finished before that of the *Complutensian Polyglot*, which appeared in 1522.

The editions of *Robert Estienne* acquired great authority. His editions of 1546 and 1549 were based on the text of Erasmus and the Complutensian Polyglot, that of 1550 on the fourth and fifth impressions of Erasmus' text. In the edition of 1551 the text was divided into verses.

For the protestant churches the text printed by Elzevier became the standard one. In 1633 Elzevier wrote in a preface: *textum ergo habes nunc omnibus receptum in quo nihil immutatum aut corruptum damus* ("thus you now have a text accepted by everyone in which we offer you no alteration or corruption"). This text, thus recommended, was regarded as inspired by many people until the end of the 19th century.

In the eighteenth century a start was made with the collecting of variants. Important scholars were *Mill* (1645-1707), *Bengel* (1687-1752), and *Wettstein* (1693-1754) who used Roman letters to indicate the manuscripts as is still done today, instead of names referring to the place where they were to be found (e.g. Codex Bezae Cantabrigiensis) as had been customary until then.

In the nineteenth century the manuscripts were divided into

groups, and rules for the judging of variants were formulated. Important work was done by *Griesbach* (1745-1812), who divided the manuscripts into the groups that are still used today: Alexandrian (Origen, C, L, 1, 13 and others), Western (D, Latin, Peshitta, Arabic), Byzantine (A and the minuscules). *Lachmann* (1793-1851) attempted to reconstruct the text of A.D. 380, with help of the Greek text which Jerome was said to have used for his Vulgate. This led him to doubt the infallibility of the textus receptus.

Tischendorf (1815-1874) continued Lachmann's work and published various editions of the Greek New Testament. This culminated in the *editio octava maior* of 1869 and 1872, containing a text strongly influenced by the Codex Sinaiticus which he had discovered. These editions were provided with an extensive critical apparatus which is still in general use today.

This development was brought to a conclusion in the work of *B. F. Westcott* (1825-1901) and *F. J. A. Hort* (1828-1892), who published the text in "original Greek" in 1881-1882. In the introduction to this text they said that they had preferred what they called the "neutral text" (אB). They based this choice on a comparison with the Western (D, Latin), the Alexandrian (C, L 33 copt) and the Syrian text (Byzantine, minuscules). They considered these three texts were dependent on the neutral text.

The text of Westcott and Hort quickly became popular and was accepted by all serious scholars. Perhaps some hesitation was felt regarding the "originality" of this text, but when *B. Weiss* (1827-1918) investigated the variants one by one he repeatedly found that א B was preferable to other texts.

Between 1902 and 1910 *H. von Soden* published a monumental work in three volumes, the first two consisting of studies and the third containing a text with variants. He divided the manuscripts into three types, a K(oine) text, an H(esychius) text and an I(erusalem) text. These three types correspond with the better known Byzantine, Egyptian and Western texts. From these three texts he chose the original on a basis of two versus one. In doing so, however, he consistently rejected Tatian's readings (Diatessaron). He invented an ingenious method of quoting the tremendous number of witnesses mentioned in the critical apparatus. He cited groups (K, H or I) and sub-groups. But often he mentioned of a certain group only those manuscripts that did not support a particular reading, the result being rather confusing. The apparatus cannot be used, therefore, without a special "key". This, in addition to the large number of inaccuracies, caused the work never to become popular.

After Von Soden other editions of the Greek New Testament have been published, but these are only variations of previous editions. The best known is that of Nestle (now Nestle-Aland). Originally this text was based upon the editions of Weiss, Hort and Tischendorf, the choice being made upon the basis of the majority. This principle has been abandoned in the 26th edition of 1979. The text is identical with the third edition of *The Greek New Testament* published by the United Bible Societies. The wording of this Greek text is the result of deliberations of a small group of experts. They had the disposal of a wealth of textual material mainly provided by the *Institut für neutestamentliche Textforschung* in Münster. The critical apparatus of the two editions widely deviate. The edition of the Bible Societies generally goes into variant readings which are important for the translation of the bible, cf. B. M. Metzger, *A Textual Commentary on the Greek New Testament*, United Bible Societies 1971.

4. RECENT INVESTIGATIONS INTO THE HISTORY OF THE TEXT AND THE RESTORATION OF THE ORIGINAL TEXT

Modern research begins with Westcott and Hort. Their preference for the neutral text and rejection of other texts led to a closer study of these texts. How could a text only found in quotations by Cyril and Athanasius be the original one? The question became acute when it was discovered that the Western text, scorned by Westcott and Hort, occurred not only in D and the old Latin text, but also in the old Syriac text. The papyri found in Egypt, moreover, showed that the Western text was also used in Egypt before a neutral text ever existed (P[5], 3rd century; P[19], 4th/5th century;

P[38], c. 300; P[41], 7th century; P[48], late 3rd century). The Western text, therefore, proved to be older than all other texts.

The intensive study that was subsequently devoted to the various texts led, in the first place, to the discovery of a new text, the *Caesarea text*, that was used by Origen (besides the neutral text) and Eusebius and is found in Θ, fam. 1 and fam. 13 and other manuscripts. This text stands between the Egyptian text—the designation "neutral text" beside *Egyptian text* has been dropped—and the Western text. Further research led to the division of this text into a *Caesarea text* (Θ, 565, 700, arm, georg) and a *pre-Caesarea text* (P[45], W (in Mark), fam. 1, fam. 13 and 28).

The wide distribution of the Western text, especially, invited further investigation. A partial answer to the problem was sought in assuming the text to have been influenced by Marcion and Tatian. Marcion was thought to have influenced the Latin text in particular. This, however, explains only a small portion of this text, for Marcion confined himself to Luke. Tatian undoubtedly influenced the old Syriac versions through his Diatessaron. If the Diatessaron was translated into Latin at an early date, this may explain why old Latin and old Syriac manuscripts show so many instances of agreement. But none of these assumptions can explain the typical character of the Western text in Acts.

Nevertheless it cannot be denied that both Marcion and Tatian may have had an incidental influence. As research progressed, however, it became clear that these are only two of the sources of textual corruption. We may be certain that oral traditions concerning the words of the Lord have also influenced the text. In short, it appears that the so-called *Western text* is not uniform but a "wild" text, not yet influenced by any thorough recension. It was from this "text" that various types developed in Egypt, Caesarea and in the Byzantine Empire. They are the result of a deliberate interference of the text during the process of a longer or shorter period of time. It is obvious that in all types of text original readings can have been from the beginning until the time the type was subjected to its final corrections. To restore the original text it is thus necessary to compare, not one entire manuscript with another or one entire type with another, but one variant readings with another.

The method looks for the interval evidence for a particular reading. The style and choice of words of a certain author, context, the influence of one gospel on another (harmonizations), the Aramaic background of the gospels, the influence of Attic Greek on the Koine, all these factors must be taken into account when we try to reestablish the original text. The results of this method, however, are not wholly satisfactory. The subjective element plays an important part here and especially in the case of conflicting possibilities: a Hebraistic form that is at the same time a harmonization with another gospel, or a phrase showing the influence of the Christian community and evidence of Koine Greek at the same time. In such cases it is very difficult to make a choice. Often the scholar will resort to the "good" manuscripts א and B to settle the matter. But it looks as if the establishing of the New Testament text in Greek and in modern translations in the next few years will bring to light many differences.[1]

---

[1] See B. M. METZGER, *The Text of the New Testament*, Oxford 1964.

APPENDICES

A. PAPIAS ON MARK AND MATTHEW

Eusebius quotes Papias in *H.E.* III 39 15-16:

καὶ τοῦθ' ὁ πρεσβύτερος ἔλεγεν· Μάρκος μὲν ἑρμηνευτὴς Πέτρου γενόμενος, ὅσα ἐμνημόνευσεν, ἀκριβῶς ἔγραψεν, οὐ μέντοι τάξει τὰ ὑπὸ τοῦ κυρίου ἢ λεχθέντα ἢ πραχθέντα· οὔτε γὰρ ἤκουσεν τοῦ κυρίου οὔτε παρηκολούθησεν αὐτῷ, ὕστερον δέ, ὡς ἔφην, Πέτρῳ· ὃς πρὸς τὰς χρείας ἐποιεῖτο τὰς διδασκαλίας, ἀλλ' οὐχ ὥσπερ σύνταξιν τῶν κυριακῶν ποιούμενος λογίων, ὥστε οὐδὲν ἥμαρτεν Μάρκος οὕτως ἔνια γράψας ὡς ἀπεμνημόνευσεν. ἑνὸς γὰρ ἐποιήσατο πρόνοιαν, τοῦ μηδὲν ὧν ἤκουσεν παραλιπεῖν ἢ ψεύσασθαί τι ἐν αὐτοῖς. ταῦτα μὲν οὖν ἱστόρηται τῷ Παπίᾳ περὶ τοῦ Μάρκου· περὶ δὲ τοῦ Ματθαίου ταῦτ' εἴρηται· Ματθαῖος μὲν οὖν Ἑβραΐδι διαλέκτῳ τὰ λόγια συνετάξατο, ἡρμήνευσεν δ' αὐτὰ ὡς ἦν δυνατὸς ἕκαστος.

The elder (John) also said this: Mark, who was Peter's interpreter, wrote down exactly, but not in the right order, what he remembered of what the Lord had said and done. For he had not heard the Lord and had not followed Him, but Peter, later, as I said. The latter gave his instructions according to need, but not in such a way that he made a connected whole of the words of the Lord, so that Mark did not act wrongly in writing some things down as he remembered them. For he had only one object: to leave nothing out of what he had heard and to say nothing untrue. This Papias related about Mark. But about Matthew he says this: Matthew put together the words in the Hebrew language and each one translated these as best he could.

Papias, bishop of Hierapolis around A.D. 130, is here reported quoting the elder (presbyter) John. In *H.E.* III 39 4 this John is mentioned, in another quotation from Papias, together with Aristion. Evidently they are regarded as keepers of the tradition they received from the apostles.

Of Mark it is said that he was Peter's "interpreter". The word ἑρμηνευτής can have different meanings: a person who hands on someone's words or a person who translates these words.

Next we read that Mark did not write down the incidents in the order they occurred. The reason is that Peter gave his instruction

according to need. This means that he did not give a continuous
chronological narrative about what the Lord said and did, but
selected in each case those things that were important for his
audience in some particular situation. Mark, however, deliberately
left the order of his narrative unchanged because he did not want
to omit or add anything.

Matthew wrote the λόγια in Hebrew. "Each one" rendered or
translated these to the best of his ability. Here again it is not clear
what is meant by ἡρμήνευσεν. Since, however, the reference is to a
foreign language, Hebrew, "translate" seems to be preferable. The
word λόγια means "utterances". But since it is said in the preceding
passage that Mark had "not made a connected whole τῶν λογίων of
the Lord", we shall have to suppose that these words refer to "what
the Lord has said and done" in general. For this reason, it may be
assumed that in the case of Matthew also the whole gospel is referred to. This view was also held by early Christian authors who state
that the gospel of Matthew was originally written in Hebrew
(Irenaeus, *adv. Haer* III I; Origen in: Eusebius, *H.E.* VI 23;
Eusebius, *H.E.* III 24 6-7; Augustine, *De consensu evangelistarum* I).

The most plausible interpretation of this quotation would therefore seem to be: Mark translated Peter's teachings, which were not
given in chronological order, and wrote them down as he had heard
them; Matthew wrote his gospel in Hebrew and everyone translated
this as best he could.

With respect to the gospel of Mark there are no great difficulties
attached to this quotation. The only thing is that it is not quite clear
why and against whom this gospel has to be defended. Was some
other gospel thought to give a better order? And which gospel would
that be: Matthew or John? [1]

With respect to Matthew the quotation is incomprehensible. The
language of the gospel of Matthew as we know it contains nothing
that might lead us to suppose it was originally written in Hebrew
(or Aramaic). Nor is it clear who the "each one" was who translated
the gospel.

---

[1] *Canon Muratori*, see Apend. E, writes that John *per ordinem profitetur.*

All sorts of attempts have been made to solve these problems. Some have thought, for instance, that the λόγια which Matthew wrote, might have been a "word-source", perhaps identical with the common source used by Matthew and Luke, also called Q. This would mean, however, that the word λόγια is used in two different meanings in the quotation. In that case we could assume that the reference is to a "proto-Matthew". But then it is still not clear to whom "each one" refers. As it stands, it is not possible to supply an adequate interpretation for this passage.

There remains the possibility of assuming that Papias (or John, the presbyter) was misinformed. He may have known various Jewish-Christian gospels, in Hebrew or Aramaic, and have supposed them all to go back to an original Hebrew (or Aramaic) version of Matthew. The quotation would then be founded on a faulty assumption and therefore lose all significance.

A recent attempt to explain the quotation is based on the assumption that it refers to the style of the gospels of Mark and Matthew. The words οὐ μέντοι τάξει would then mean that Mark has a disconnected style and Ἑβραΐδι διαλέκτῳ that Matthew has a Hebraic style. The concluding sentence should then be translated: "Each (Matthew and Mark) rendered them (the gospels) according to his ability". This interpretation does away with the problem of an original Hebrew or Aramaic gospel of Matthew.[1]

The obscurity of the quotation thus greatly detracts from the significance of its contents. The passage about the way in which Peter taught may be regarded as confirming the hypothesis, based on the gospels themselves, that traditions concerning Jesus' life were handed down in pericopes. In addition the passage indicates that the early Christians were already seeking an explantion for the differences between the gospels. Finally, this quotation shows us that in those times great importance was attached to the apostolic origin of the gospels.

---

[1] Cf. J. KÜRZINGER, „Das Papiaszeugnis und die Erstgestalt des Matthäusevangelium", in *Bibl. Zeitschr.*, n. F. 4 1960, p. 29-38.

B. SUMMARY OF PAUL'S LIFE

presumed date	places visited	indications of time	source	companions	letters	notes
30/31	conversion on the road to Damascus		Acts 9, 3-9 Gal. 1, 15			not mentioned in Acts
	Damascus	a few days	Acts 9, 19-25 Gal 1, 17			
	Arabia and Damascus	three years (Gal. 1, 18)				
	Jerusalem	15 days	Acts, 9, 26-29 Gal. 1, 18	visited by Barnabas (Acts 11, 25)		
32/33	Syria and Cilicia (Tarsus)	14 years (Gal. 2, 1)	Acts 9, 30 Gal. 1, 21-24			
45	Antioch		Acts 11, 25-26	with Barnabas		
	Jerusalem		Acts 11, 30 Gal. 2, 1-2	with Barnabas and Titus (Gal. 2, 1)		
	Antioch		Acts 12, 24-25 Gal. 2, 11	with Barnabas and John Mark		
46	Seleucia					beginning of 1st missionary journey
	Cyprus		Acts 13, 4-5	with Barnabas and John Mark		
	Perga		Acts 13, 13	John Mark to Jerusalem		
	Antioch		Acts 13, 14			
	Iconium		Acts 13, 51			
	Lystra					
	Derbe		Acts 14, 6			
	Lystra					

presumed date	places visited	indications of time	source	companions	letters	notes
	Iconium		Acts 14, 21			
	Antioch		Acts 14, 25			
	Perga		Acts 14, 26			
48	Antioch		Acts 15, 1-2	with Barnabas	Galatians	conference at Jerusalem
	Jerusalem					
	Antioch		Acts 15, 22	with Barnabas, Judas, Barsabbas and Silas		
	Syria and Cilicia		Acts 15, 41	with Silas (15, 40) Barnabas with John Mark to Cyprus (15, 39)		beginning 2nd missionary journey
	Derbe					
	Lystra					
	Iconium		Acts 16, 1-2	with Timothy		
	Phrygia and Galatia		Acts 16, 6			
	Troas		Acts 16, 8			Acts 16, 9-18 "we-passage" by Luke
	Philippi		Acts 16, 12	with Silas (Acts 16, 19, 25 and 29)		
	Thessalonica		Acts 17, 1 / I Thess. 2, 2			
	Beroea		Acts 17, 10	Timothy and Silas stay behind (17, 14)		

presumed date	places visited	indications of time	source	companions	letters	notes
	Athens		Acts 17, 15	Timothy to Athens and then to Thessalonica (I Thess. 3, 1-2)		
50	Corinth	18 months (Acts 18, 11) Gallio (Acts 18, 12)	Acts 18, 5	Timothy and Silas back (Acts 18, 5)	I and II Thessalonians	
end 51	Ephesus		Acts 18, 19	with Aquila and Priscilla (Acts 18, 18) The latter stay in Ephesus and meet Apollos who is going to Corinth (Acts 18, 24-28)		
	Caesarea Antioch		Acts 18, 22			
beginning 52	Galatia					beginning 3rd missionary journey
	Ephesus	3 months and 2 years (Acts 19, 8 and 10)		Timothy via Macedonia with Erastus to Corinth (Acts 19, 22 and I Cor. 16, 11)	Philippians Colossians Ephesians, Philemon I Corinthians	Paul in prison (I Cor. 15, 32)
	Corinth	II Cor. 1, 23 and 2, 1			"severe letter" (II Cor. 2, 4 and 7, 8)	intermediate visit

presumed date	places visited	indications of time	source	companions	letters	notes
	Ephesus			Titus to Corinth (with "severe letter") (II Cor. 2, 13; 7, 6-7 and 13-14)		
56/57	Macedonia		Acts 20, 1-2 cf. I Cor. 16, 5	Titus back; goes to Corinth (II Cor. 8)	II Corinthians	
	Corinth	3 months	Acts 20, 2-3	Timothy and others to Troas (Acts 20, 4)	Romans (cf. Rom. 16, 1)	
april 57	Philippi	days of unleavened bread (Acts 20, 5)	Acts 20, 6			20, 4-16 "we-passage" by Luke
	Troas		Acts 20, 4-6	Timothy and others join Paul		
	Miletus		Acts 20, 15			
	Tyre		Acts 21, 3			
May 57	Caesarea		Acts 21, 8			21, 1-18 "we-passage" by Luke
	Jerusalem	Pentecost (Acts 20, 16)	Acts 21, 17			
	Caesarea		Acts 23, 23			27, 1-28 "we-passage" by Luke
	Rome		Acts 28, 16			

C. THE INSCRIPTION AT DELPHI
WITH THE NAME OF GALLIO

The inscription found at Delphi containing Gallio's name consists of four fragments. From these the following text may be reconstructed:

Τιβέρ[ιος Κλαύδιος Καῖσ]αρ Σ[εβαστ]ὸς Γ[ερμανικός, δημαρχικῆς ἐξου]-
σίας [τὸ IB, αὐτοκράτωρ τ]ὸ ΚϚ', π[ατὴρ π]ατρί[δος, 11/16 letters χαίρειν.]
Πάλ[αι μὲν τ]ῆι π[όλει τῇ] τῶν Δελφ[ῶν ἦ ο]ὐ μό[νον εὔνους,
ἀλλ' ἐφρόντισα τῆς τύ]-
χης, ἀεὶ δ'ἐτήρη[σα τὴ]ν θρησκεί[αν τ]οῦ 'Από[λλωνος τοῦ Πυθίου.
'Επεὶ δὲ]
νῦν λέγεται καὶ [πολ]ειτῶν ἔρη[μο]ς εἶναι, ὥ[ς μοι ἄρτι ἀπήγγειλε
Λ. 'Ιού]-
νιος Γαλλίων ὁ φ[ίλος] μου κα[ὶ ἀνθύ]πατος, [βουλόμενος τοὺς Δελφοὺς]
ἔτι ἕξειν τὸν πρ[ότερον κόσμον ἐντελ]ῆ, ἐ[ντέλλομαί σε καὶ ἐξ ἄλ]-
λων πόλεων καλ[εῖν εἰς τοὺς Δελφοὺς νέους κατοίκους .... καὶ]
αὐτοῖς ἐπιτρέ[πειν 12 letters] πρεσ[βεῖα πάντα ἔχειν τὰ τῶν Δελ]-
φῶν ὡς πολε[ίταις γεγονόσιν. "Οσο]ι μὲν γὰρ τι[ὡς πολεί]-
ται μετῳκισ[αντο εἰς τούτους του]ς τόπους, κρίνω
[το]ύτους   ]ν πάντως ε[
                              ]σθη· οἵτινε[ς δὲ
                       ]ι καὶ τὸ συναύ[ξειν
                    ὥσπε]ρ ἐπὶ τῶν ἀνα[
ἀνα[φ]ημι [Τ]οῖς μέντ[οι
εἰς τῶν[   ]εια σε ἐντέλλομαι, ἵγ[α
κατὰ προ[σῆκον πάντων τ]ῶν ἐν αὐτῷ γεγραμ[μένων μηδὲν] ἐριστὸ[ν ἦι].

The translation reads:

Tiberius Claudius Caesar Augustus Germanicus, tribune of the people for the 12th time, imperator for the 26th time, father of the country ... greetings. I have already for a long time not only felt affection for the city of Delphi, but I have also looked after its well-being and have always fulfilled the service of the Pythian Apollo. Since it is now said that it also has a shortage of inhabitants, as my friend and proconsul L. Junius Gallio recently reported, who wishes that the Delphians will possess again the former full splendour, I command you, both to invite young citizens to Delphi from other cities and to provide them with all rights of Delphi as to born citizens. For all those ... as citizens moved to these places, I decide that ... who wholly ... is. And all those who ... and to contribute to the development ... as ... I say. But the ... to the ... of the ... I command you that ... as is proper, that nothing which is written in this is cause for disputes.

Literature: A Deismann, *Paulus*, Tübingen 1911, p. 159-177; A. Plassart, *L'Inscription de Delphes mentionnent le Proconsul Gallion*, in: "Revue des Études grecques" 80 1967, p. 372-378, and A. Plassart, *École Française d'Athénes — Fouilles de Delphes.* Tome III *Épigraphie.* Fascicule IV *Inscriptions de la Terrasse du Temple et de la Région Nord du Sanctuaire*, nos 276 à 350: *Les Inscriptions du Temple du IVe siècle*, Paris 1970, p. 26-32.

D. COMPARISON OF THE LETTERS
TO THE EPHESIANS AND
TO THE COLOSSIANS

The italicized words are found in the corresponding pericopes of Ephesians and Colossians. The underlined words have a parallel in other parts of these letters.

Eph. 1, 15-23
Διά τοῦτο κἀγώ, ἀκούσας . . . οὐ παύομαι εὐχαριστῶν
15-16. *Therefore I never cease to give thanks for you*
ὑπὲρ ὑμῶν
because I have heard of your faith in the Lord Jesus
and your love for all the saints.
I remember you in my prayers,
17. that the God of our Lord Jesus Christ, the Father of glory, may
σοφίας
give you the Spirit *of wisdom* and revelation
ἐν ἐπιγνώσει αὐτοῦ
to know Him.
18. May He illumine the eyes of your heart to know
what is the hope His call arouses,
τῆς κληρονομίας αὐτοῦ ἐν τοῖς ἁγίοις
how rich is the glory *of His heritage among the saints*
19. and how overwhelmingly great His power for us
who believe; in accordance with the action of the strength of His
power which He exerted in Christ
20. by raising Him from the dead
to place Him at his right hand in the heavenly realms
ὑπεράνω πάσης ἀρχῆς καὶ ἐξουσίας καὶ δυνάμεως καὶ κυριότητος
21. *above all dominion and might and power and government*
and all that has a name, not only in this age
but also in the age to come.
22. And He has put everything beneath His feet,

Col. 1, 9-20

Διὰ τοῦτο καὶ ἡμεῖς

9. *Therefore*, since the day *we*

ἠκούσαμεν

heard this, we never cease

ὑπὲρ ὑμῶν προσευχόμενοι

to pray for you and to ask that you may be filled with the

σοφία

knowledge of His will in all *wisdom* and spiritual insight.

περιπατῆσαι ἀξίως

10. to live a life worthy

of the Lord and to please Him in everything and

καρποφοροῦντες

to bear fruit in all sorts of good works and to

καὶ αὐξανόμενοι τῇ ἐπιγνώσει τοῦ θεοῦ

grow *in the knowledge of the Lord*

11. Thus you are strengthened with all power in the might of His glory to perseverance and patience.

12. Then you will joyfully give thanks to the Father, who has pre-

εἰς τὴν μερίδα τοῦ κλήρου τῶν ἁγίων

pared you to partake *in the heritage of the saints* in the light.

13. He has delivered us from the power of darkness and brought us into the kingdom of His dear Son,

ἐν ᾧ ἔχομεν

14. through whom we have the

        κεφαλὴν   τῇ ἐκκλησίᾳ
and given Him as a *head* above all that is *to the church*
       ἥτις ἐστιν τὸ σῶμα αὐτοῦ
23. *which is His body,*
τὸ πλήρωμα
the fullness of Him
         τὰ πάντα
who fills the *universe* in all its parts.

τὴν ἀπολύτρωσιν, τὴν ἄφεσιν τῶν ἁμαρτιῶν
redemption, the forgiveness of sins.

15. He who is the image of the invisible God, the firstborn of all creation.

16. For in Him all things were created, in the heavens and on earth, the visible and invisible things

εἴτε θρόνοι εἴτε κυριότητες
thrones or authorities or

εἴτε ἀρχαὶ εἴτε ἐξουσίαι
sovereignties or powers,

all things were created through Him and for Him.

17. And He is before everything and all things have their existence in Him.

ἡ κεφαλὴ τοῦ σώματος, τῆς ἐκκλησίας

18. And He is *the head of the body, the church,*

He is the beginning, the first born from the dead, that He might be the first in all things.

πλήρωμα

19. For it pleased the complete *fullness* to make its dwelling in Him.

τὰ πάντα ἀποκατάλλαξαι

20. And, through him he wished to reconcile *all things* with Himself

εἰρηνοποιήσας
restoring peace

τοῦ σταυροῦ αὐτοῦ
through the blood of his cross,

εἴτε τὰ ἐπὶ τῆς γῆς εἴτε τὰ ἐν τοῖς οὐρανοῖς
whether on earth or in heaven

ἀξίως περιπατῆσαι
Eph. 4, 1: . . . to live a worthy life . . .

καρποφορούμενον καὶ αὐξανόμενον
Col. 1, 6: . . . it bears fruit and grows . . .

ἐν ᾧ ἔχομεν τὴν ἀπολύτρωσιν
Eph. 1, 7: . . . through whom we have the redemption through His blood,

τὴν ἄφεσιν τῶν παραπτωμάτων
the forgiveness of tresspasses.

Eph. 2, 11-22

11. Remember therefore, that you, once gentiles in the flesh,
called "uncircumcised" by the so-called circumcision which is made
by human hands on the flesh,
12. that you were at that time without Christ,
ἀπηλλοτριωμένοι
excluded from the community of Israel
and aliens to the covenants of promise,
without hope and without God in the world.
13. But now you who were formerly far away
have come near through the blood of Christ.
14. For He is our peace,
which has made the two into one
and has broken down the dividing wall
that separated us,

$$\text{τὴν ἔχθραν}$$

15. because He has annulled in his flesh the *enmity*, that is: the law
of commandments consisting of decrees.
ποιῶν εἰρήνην
Thus He made peace
by creating out of the two a new man
    ἀποκαταλλάξη   δισ τοῦ σταυροῦ
16. to reconcile the two united in one body to God through the cross
                  τὴν ἔχθραν
on which He killed *the enmity*.
17. And when He came he proclaimed peace to you who were far
off and peace to those who were near.
18. For through Him we both have access in one Spirit to the
Father.
19. Thus you are no longer strangers and aliens,

ἀνακεφαλαιώσασθαι τὰ πάντα τὰ
Eph. 1, 10: . . . to effect the fullness of time in bringing everything under one
ἐπὶ τοῖς οὐρανοῖς καὶ ἐπὶ τῆς γῆς
head in Christ, whether it is in heaven or on earth.
ποιῶν εἰρήνην καὶ ἀποκαταλλαξῃ
Eph. 2,15-16 . . . thus He made peace . . . and reconciled the two into one body
διὰ τοῦ σταυροῦ
with God through the cross.

Col. 1, 21-23

ἀπηλλοτριωμένουν ἐχθροὺς
21. You also who were formerly *excluded* and *enemies* in your mind through your evil deeds,

ἀποκατήλλαξεν
22. *He has* now *reconciled* in His mortal body by his death
παραστῆσαι ὑμᾶς ἁγίους καὶ ἀμώμους . . . κατενώπιον αὐτοῦ
to place you before himself holy and unblemished and above reproach,

τεθεμελιωμένοι
23. But then you must be well founded and firm in the faith and not
τοῦ εὐαγγελίου
let yourselves be turned away from the hope of the gospel that you have heard.
and that has been proclaimed in the whole creation under heaven
οὗ ἐγενόμην ἐγὼ . . . διάκονος
and of which I, Paul, have become the servant.

ὑμᾶς ἁγίους καὶ ἀμώμους κατενώπιον αὐτοῦ
Eph. 1, 4: . . . that you may be holy and unblemished before Him
παραστήσῃ   ἁγία καὶ ἄμωμος
Eph. 5, 27: . . . so that he may place the church before himself holy and unblemished
τεθεμελιωμένοι
Eph. 3, 17: . . . rooted (cf. Col. 2, 7) and founded in love.
διὰ τοῦ εὐαγγελίου, οὗ ἐγενήθην διάκονος
Eph. 3, 7: . . . throught the gospel, of which I have become the servant. . .

but fellow citizens with the saints and the household of God,

ἐποικοδομηθέντες

20. built on the foundations of the apostles and prophets,

while Jesus himself is the corner stone.

21. In Him the building, well-bonded together,

αὔξει

grows into a temple holy in the Lord.

22. In Him you too are being built into a dwelling place for God in the Spirit.

ἐποικοδομούμενοι

Col. 2, 7 . . . rooted and built in Him . . .

Col. 2, 19 . . . the head from which the whole body, supported and bound

αὔξει τὴν αὔξησιν

together by tendons and ligaments, will receive its growth from God.

ἀποκαταλλάξαι

Col. 1, 20: through Him He wished to reconcile all things with himself . . .

εἰρηνοποιήσας　　　　　　　τοῦ σταυροῦ αὐτοῦ

restoring peace through the blood of His cross.

Eph. 5, 15-20

15. Be careful then how you conduct yourselves,

not as fools, but as wise men,

16. making use of the opportunity, for the days are evil.

17. Therefore do not be unwise,

but try to understand

what is the will of the Lord

18. And do not become drunk with wine,

which leads to dissipation,

but be filled with the Spirit.

19. And speak to one another

ψαλμοῖς καὶ ὕμνοις καὶ ᾠδαῖς πνευματικαῖς ᾄδοντες

in psalms and hymns and spiritual songs and sing

τῇ καρδίᾳ ὑμῶν τῷ κυρίῳ

and make music *to your Lord in your hearts,*

εὐχαριστοῦντες ὑπὲρ πάντων ἐν ὀνόματι τοῦ κυρίου ἡμῶν

20. *In the name of our Lord Jesus Christ give thanks* at all times

Col. 3, 16-17

16. May the word of Christ dwell in you abundantly, so that in all wisdom you may instruct and admonish each other.

ψαλμοῖς ὕμνοις ᾠδαῖς πνευματικαῖς

Sing to God with a thankful heart

ἐν τῇ χάριτι ᾄδοντες ἐν ταῖς καρδίαις

psalms, hymns and spiritual songs.

17. And whatever you do, in word or action,

ἐν ὀνόματι κυρίου 'Ιησοῦ εὐχαριστοῦντες

do everything *in the name of the Lord Jesus, giving thanks*

τῷ θεῷ πατρί

to God the Father through him.

'Ιησοῦ Χριστοῦ τῷ θεῷ καὶ πατρί
for everything to God the Father.

Eph. 6, 5-9
οἱ δοῦλοι, ὑπακούετε τοῖς κατὰ σάρκα κυρίοις
5. *Slaves, obey your earthly masters*
      μετὰ φόβου   ἐν ἁπλότητι τῆς καρδίας
with *fear* and trembling *in singleness of heart* as for Christ.
    μὴ κατ' ὀφθαλμοδουλίαν ὡς ἀνθρωπάρεσκοι
6. *Not as eye-servers to please men,*
                        ἐκ ψυχῆς
but as slaves of Christ doing God's will *whole-heartedly.*
           ὡς τῷ κυρίῳ καὶ οὐκ ἀνθρώποις
7. *Give service willingly as if to the Lord and not to men.*
    εἰδότες ὅτι
8. *For you know that* everybody, whether slave or free man,
κομίσεται
will be repaid by the Lord whatever good he has done.
       οἱ κύριοι
9. And *masters,* treat them the same way
εἰδότες ὅτι ὑμῶν ὁ κύριος ἔστιν ἐν οὐρανοῖς
You know that your master and theirs *is in heaven*
           προσωπολημψία οὐκ ἔστιν
and with Him *there is no partiality.*

Col. 3, 22-4, 1

οἱ δοῦλοι, ὑπακούετε . . . τοῖς κατὰ σάρκα κυρίοις

22. *Slaves, obey your earthly masters* in everything

μὴ ἐν ὀφθαλμοδουλίαις ὡς ἀνθρωπάρεσκοι

Not as eye-servers to please men,

ἐν ἁπλότητι καρδίας φοβούμενοι

but *in singleness of heart in the fear* of the Lord.

ἐκ ψυχῆς

23. Whatever you do, do your work *whole-heartedly,*

ὡς τῷ κυρίῳ καὶ οὐκ ἀνθρώποις

as if for the Lord and not for men.

εἰδότες ὅτι

24. *For you know that* the Lord will give you the heritage as a reward.

25. The Lord you are serving is Christ.

κομίσεται

For whoever does wrong *will receive* that wrong *in return.*

οὐκ ἔστιν προσωπολημψία

There is no partiality.

οἱ κύριοι

4, 1 *Masters,* be righteous and just toward your slaves.

εἰδότες ὅτι   κύριον ἐν οὐρανῷ

You know that you *have a Master in heaven.*

E. CANON MURATORI

In 1740 Muratori found, in the *Bibliotheca Ambrosiana*, a palimpsest (Cod. Ambros. J 101 sup.) from the eighth century containing a list of New Testament scriptures. This list must have been compiled around A.D. 200 in Rome, for which reason it is of particular significance for the history of the canon. It tells us not only which books were read in Rome at that time but also how they were rated. The Latin text is a very bad translation of a Greek original, for which reason the present translation has to be given with certain reservations here and there. The beginning and end of the text have been lost.

. . . quibus tamen interfuit et ita posuit. Tertium evangelii librum secundum Lucam. Lucas iste medicus post ascensum Christi cum eum Paulus quasi litteris studiosum secum adsumsisset nomine suo ex opinione conscripsit: Dominum tamen nec ipse uidit in carne, et ideo prout assequi potuit, ita et a natiuitate Iohannis incipit dicere. Quartum Evangeliorum Iohannis ex discipulis. Cohortantibus condiscipulis et episcopis suis dixit: Conieiunate mihi hodie triduo, et quid cuique fuerit reuelatum alterutrum nobis enarremus. Eadem nocte reuelatum Andreae ex apostolis, ut recognoscentibus cunctis, Iohannis suo nomine cuncta describeret.

Et ideo licet uaria singulis euangeliorum libris principia doceantur nihil tamen differt credentium fidei, cum uno ac principali spiritu declarata sint in omnibus omnia: de natiuitate, de passione, de resurrectione, de conuersatione cum discipulis suis, ac de gemino eius aduentu, primo in humilitate despectus, quod

. . . The third gospel book according to Luke. Since Paul had taken him in as a competent writer, the physician Luke wrote it down after the ascension of Christ under his own name (but) according to his (Paul's) views. Yet he himself did not see the Lord in the flesh either and therefore he too began his narrative, as far as he was able, with the birth of John. The fourth gospel is by John, one of the disciples. When his fellow-disciples and bishops urged him he said: Fast with me for three days from today and we shall tell each other what is revealed to each of us. That same night it was revealed to Andrew, one of the apostles, that John would write everything down under his name, and they were all to check it.

And therefore, although different prefaces (principles) are presented in the various gospel books, this still makes no difference for the faith of the believers, since everything is explained through the one leading

fuit, secundo in potestate regali prae-
claro, quod futurum est.
Quid ergo mirum si Iohannis tam
constanter singula etiam in epistulis
suis profert dicens in semetipsum:
Quae uidimus oculis nostris, et auribus
audiuimus, et manus nostrae pal-
pauerunt, haec scripsimus vobis. Sic
enim non solum uisorem se et audito-
rem, sed et scriptorem omnium mirabi-
lium Domini per ordinem profitetur.
Acta autem omnium apostolorum sub
uno libro scripta sunt. Lucas optimo
Theophilo comprendit, quae sub praesentia eius singula gerebantur, sicuti
et semota passione Petri euidenter
declarat, sed et profectione Pauli ab
urbe ad Spaniam profisciscentis.
Epistulae autem Pauli, quae, a quo
loco, uel qua ex causa directae sint,
uolentibus intellegere ipsae declarant.
Primum omnium Corinthis schisma
haereses interdicens, deinceps Galatis
circumcisionem, Romanis autem ordinem scripturarum, sed et principium
earum esse Christum intimans, proli-
xius scripsit, de quibus singulis
necesse est a nobis disputari; cum
ipse beatus apostolus Paulus, sequens
prodecessoris sui Iohannis ordinem,
nonnisi nominatim septem ecclesiis
scribat ordine tali: ad Corinthios
prima, ad Ephesios secunda, ad
Philippenses tertia, ad Colossenses
quarta, ad Galatas quinta, ad Thessa-
lonicenses sexta, ad Romanos septima.
Uerum Corinthiis et Thessalonicensi-
bus licet pro correctione iteretur, una
tamen per omnem orbem terrae ecclesia
diffusa esse dinoscitur; et Iohannis
enim in Apocalypsi, licet septem
ecclesiis scribat, tamen omnibus dicit.
Uerum ad Philemonem una et ad
Titum una, et ad Timotheum duae pro
affectu et dilectione; in honorem
tamen ecclesiae catholicae in ordina-
tionem ecclesiasticae disciplinae sanc-
tificatae sunt. Fertur etiam ad Laodi-

Spirit in all of them: concerning
the nativity, the passion, the resurrection, the association with his
disciples, and concerning his twofold
coming, the first time when, in low-
liness, he was despised, which has
taken place, the second time resplen-
dent in regal power, which is to
come. Is it surprising therefore if
John, so consistently brings the
various things forward also in his
letter, when he says of himself:
what we have seen with our eyes
and heard with our ears and touched
with our hands, that we have
written down for you. For thus he
introduces himself not only as a
spectator and hearer, but also as a
describer of all the miracles of the
Lord, in the (correct) order.

The Acts of all the apostles have
been written in one book. Luke sums
up for the excellent Theophilus
what successively took place in his
presence, as he makes clear by
omitting Peter's martyrdom and
also Paul's departure from the city
for Spain.

The letters of Paul themselves make
it clear, to anyone who wishes to
know, what (they are), from where
or for what reason they were sent.
The first of them all to the Corinthians, forbidding the heresy of the
schism; next to the Galatians, forbidding circumcision; then to the
Romans, explaining that Christ is
the rule of the Scriptures and their
principle, he wrote rather extensively
It is necessary for us to discuss
these one by one, since the blessed
apostle Paul, following the rule of
his predecessor John, wrote to only
seven congregations mentioned by
name, in this order: to the Corinthians, the first; to the Ephesians,
the second; to the Philippians, the
third; to the Colossians, the fourth;

*censes, alia ad Alexandrinos, Pauli
nomine finctae ad haeresem Marcionis,
et alia plura quae in catholicam
ecclesiam recipi non potest: fel enim
cum melle misceri non congruit.
Epistula sane Iudae et superscripti
Iohannis duae in catholica habentur;
et Sapientia ab amicis Solomonis in
honorem ipsius scripta. Apocalypses
etiam Iohannis et Petri tantum recipimus, quam quidam ex nostris legi in
ecclesia nolunt. Pastorem uero nuper-
rime temporibus nostris in urbe
Roma Hermas conscripsit, sedente
cathedra urbis Romae eclesiae Pio
episcopo fratre eius; et ideo legi eum
quidem oportet, se publicare uero in
ecclesia populo, neque inter prophetas,
completo numero, neque inter aposto-
los, in fine temporum potest.
Arsinoi autem seu Ualentini, uel
Miltiadis nihil in totum recipimus.
Qui etiam nouum psalmorum librum
Marcioni conscripserunt, una cum
Basilide, Asiano Cataphrygum con-
stitutore.*

to the Galatians, the fifth; to the
Thessalonians, the sixth; to the
Romans, the seventh. For when
(a letter is written) anew to the
Corinthians and Thessalonians to
reprove them, it is clear that there
is one church scattered over the
whole earth. For John also writes,
in his Revelation, to seven churches,
yet he speaks to all of them. But
one to Philemon, one to Titus and
two to Timothy (written) out of
affection and love have been held
sacred in honour of the catholic
church for the regulation of eccle-
siastic discipline. There is also in
circulation a letter to the Laodiceans
and another to the Alexandrians,
fakes in Paul's name for the sect
of Marcion and still others that
cannot be received in the catholic
church: for gall cannot be mixed
with honey. In addition a letter
from Jude and two with John's
subscription are preserved in the
catholic church; and the Wisdom
which was written by Solomon's
friends in his honour.

We have also included the Revelations of John and Peter, although
some of us will not let them be read
in church. Recently in our time
Hermas wrote the Pastor, in the city
of Rome, when his brother Pius
was seated as bishop on the throne
of the church of the city of Rome.
For this reason he should be read,
but he cannot be read to the people
in church, nor (be counted) among
the prophets, whose number is
complete, or among the apostles,
until the end of time.

We accept nothing at all by Arsi-
nous, or Valentine, or Miltiades.
They compiled a new book of psalms
for Marcion, together with Basilides,

of Asia Minor, the founder of the
Cataphrygians.

See H. Lietzmann, *Das Muratorische Fragment*, in: "Kleine Texte" 1,
Bonn 1921, p. 5-11.

F. TABLE OF FACTS
CONCERNING THE BOOKS
OF THE NEW TESTAMENT

Book	Author	Place of origin	Time	Addressed to
Gospel of Mark	Mark (?)	Rome (?)	c. 65	church and outsiders
Gospel of Matthew	a person in Matthew's circle	Antioch (?)	c. 75	the church
Gospel of Luke	Luke	Caesarea (?)	c. 80	Theophilus
Gospel of John	a person in the circle of the disciple John	Ephesus or Syria	c. 90	Jews and church
Acts	Luke	Caesarea	c. 80	Theophilus
Romans	Paul	Corinth	56-57	congregation at Rome
I Corinthians	Paul	Ephesus	55	congregation at Corinth
II Corinthians	Paul	Macedonia	56	congregation at Corinth
Galatians	Paul	Antioch in Syria	48	congregations in Galatia
Ephesians	Paul	Ephesus (prison)	53-54	gentile Christian congregations in Asia Minor, not founded by Paul
Philippians	Paul	Ephesus (prison)	53-54	congregation at Philippi
Colossians	Paul	Ephesus (prison)	53-54	gentile Christian congregation at Colossae not founded by Paul
I Thessalonians	Paul	Corinth	50	congregation at Thessalonica
II Thessalonians	Paul	Corinth	50	congregation at Thessalonica

Purpose	Sources
to prove by the story of his life that Jesus is the Christ	traditions derived from Peter and the church
to lead and console in giving the story of Jesus' life	traditions from Matthew (?), the gospel of Mark and traditions from the church
biography of Jesus as the Revelation of God to the whole world	gospel of Mark, traditions from eyewitnesses and from the church
to prove by the story of his life that Jesus is the Christ, the Son of God	traditions derived from the disciple John
second part of the gospel of Luke with a description of the spreading of the gospel as far as Rome	personal experience and church traditions
Paul asks for help for an intended journey to Spain. Discussion of the relations between Jewish and gentile Christians	16, 25-27 added when Paul's letters were combined into one volume
warnings on account of information from Corinth about parties and answers to practical questions	
expressing thankfulness for the good tidings brought from Corinth by Titus defence of Paul's apostleship and attack on Jewish-Christian ideas	chapters 10-13; part of "severe letter" (II, 2, 4 and 7, 8)
description of the wealth of Christians and of the Church in Jesus Christ	liturgy and exhortation derived from the church
letter of thanks for aid received from Philippi	
warning against a "gnostic" Jewish-Christian influence	liturgy and exhortation from the church
exhortation to a Christian way of life	
exhortation to a Christian way of life	

I Timothy	Paulinist	Asia Minor	c. 100	Pauline congregations
II Timothy	as I Tim.	as I Tim.	as I Tim.	as I Tim.
Titus	as I Tim.	as I Tim.	as I Tim.	as I Tim.
Philemon	Paul	Ephesus (prison)	53-54	Philemon, a Christian at Colossae
Hebrews	a person in Paul's circles	unknown	80 ?	unknown
James	James, the brother of the Lord	Palestine	c. 55	Palestine (-Syrian area)
I Peter	Peter	Babylon in Egypt or Rome	c. 65	gentile Christians in Asia Minor
II Peter	unknown	Antioch (or Rome ?)	90 ?	church in general
Jude	Jude, brother of James	Antioch	c. 65	church in general
I John	John, the disciple (?)	Ephesus	c. 80	Johannine circles
II John	John, the disciple (?)	as I John	c. 80	as I John
III John	John, the disciple (?)	as I John	c. 80	Gaius
Revelation	John, the disciple (?)	Patmos (Ephesus)	c. 90	seven churches in Asia Minor

advice for directing a congregation
as I Timothy
as I Timothy
commending Philemon's care his slave
Onesimus who has fled to Paul and whom
Paul is sending back to his master
homiletic exhortation to stand firm under
oppression

practical exhortations	words of the Lord and exhortations from the church
encouragement under oppression	liturgical and exhortative material from the church
attacking libertinism and those who scorn the Second Coming	Jude (and I Peter)
attacking libertinism	
exhortation, especially with respect to those who do not believe that Christ came in the flesh	exhortation partly derived from church teachings
as I John	
exhortation to take in strangers and warning against Diotrephes	
encouraging the oppressed church by reminding of the sovereignty and victory of Christ	influenced by Jewish apocalyptic tradition

BIBLIOGRAPHY

I New Testament Commentaries

Most commentaries are published in series, each having their own manner of interpreting the New Testament. One series may approach the text primarily by the historical-critical method, another may take a more theological or practical view of it. Some series have never been completed, of others the various volumes are continually reprinted. The state of affairs keeps changing. It is not possible, therefore, nor even desirable, to discuss each commentary separately. We shall restrict ourselves to a brief characterization of the different series.

One of the older series is the *Kommentar zum Neuen Testament* (Th. Zahn). The arrangement in these volumes is not always very clear, but the sources are scrupulously quoted and those volumes which were edited by Zahn still retain their usefulness. Another older series is *The International Critical Commentary* (I.C.C.), some volumes of which are below standard. The volumes devoted to Luke, Romans, Galatians and Revelation, however, are still valuable.

Among the modern series the English-speaking countries are well represented. *The Moffatt New Testament Commentary* is based on the New Testament translation by J. Moffatt. The aims of this series are defined as follows: "Everything ought to be subordinated to the aim of elucidating the religious content, of showing how the faith was held in such and such a way by the first Christians, and of making clear what that faith was and is". *Black's New Testament Commentaries* are "A series to meet the need for modern commentaries that are at once reliable in scholarship and relevant to the contemporary Church. Of moderate size, yet full enough for serious academic work ..." *The Anchor Bible* "a project of international and interfaith scope ... is aimed at the general reader with no special formal training in biblical studies; yet, it is written with the most exacting standards of scholarship". *The Cambridge Greek Testament Commentary* is convinced that "it became possible to devote increasing attention to the elucidation of the theological and religious contents of the New Testament, and to see it in the setting of the life and worship of Christian communities". *The Interpretor's Bible* (New Testament in volumes VII-XII) gives an "introduction to Scripture and the individual books, exegesis of the text, and relevant exposition", based on the King James Version and the Revised Standard Version. *Peake's Commentary on the Holy Scripture* (one volume) is introduced with these words: "The present work is designed to put before the reader in a simple form, without technicalities, the generally accepted results of Biblical Criticism, Interpretation, History and Theology ... It is not intended to be homiletic or devotional ..." *A Catholic Commentary on Holy Scriptures* (one volume) says, speaking of its collaborators: "Their endeavour has been to sum up the results of international scholarship during the last fifty years, and put them at the disposal not only of Catholics but also of all those who respect and would be glad to know more of the Catholic Church's teaching on Scripture and of the way in which her members interpret it". *The Tyndale New Testament Commentaries* try to avoid "the extremes of being unduly technical or unhelpfully brief". Finally we may mention *The New International Commentary*, a joint undertaking of Dutch, English and American New Testament scholars and the pocket size volumes in *Torch Bible Commentaries* and *Pelican New Testament commentaries*.

In the German language we have the *Theologischer Hand-Kommentar zum Neuen Testament mit Text und Paraphrase*, which is remarkable for its transparent arrangement. The *Handbuch zum Neuen Testament* is strongly influenced by the study of comparative religions. The various volumes are being republished. An important series will probably be *Herders Theologischer Kommentar zum Neuen Testament*, in which particular emphasis is placed on the theological significance of the different New Testament books.

Finally we may draw attention to *Evangelisch-Katholischer Kommentar zun Neuen Testament*.

Important French series are *Études Bibliques* with the excellent commentaries of Lagrange and the protestant *Commentaire du Nouveau Testament*.

A number of commentaries, not published in any series, must also be mentioned. A place of honour is due to J. B. Lightfoot with his commentaries on Galatians, Philippians, Colossians and Philemon, all of which date from the end of last century. These commentaries may still be consulted with profit. The same is true of C. G. Montefiore on the synoptic gospels (1909), pointing out numerous parallels in Jewish literature. V. Taylors' commentary on Mark and J. M. Creed's on Luke (both 1953) are both sound English works, inferior, however, to E. G. Selwyn's commentary on I Peter (1952). This last work is always stimulating and a joy to read.

The commentary on John by E. Hoskyns, edited by F. N. Davey (1947) shows clear traces of being unfinished, but is interesting because both author and editor are pioneers of English New Testament scholarship. C. K. Barrett's commentary on John (cheap edition 1956) has a high critical standard but in its theology it falls short. An interesting work is R. H. Lightfoot, *St. John's Gospel*, ed. by C. E. Evans, Oxford, 1960.

In conclusion we must mention four works with a character of their own. In the first place the work by Billerbeck (and Strack) in 7 volumes (the last two edited by J. Jeremias) with innumerable parallels from Jewish literature; a work covering the entire New Testament and, properly used, an inexhaustible source of information on the Jewish element in the New Testament. In the second place Foakes Jackson and Kirsopp Lake, *The Beginning of Christianity*. Assisted by many collaborators these authors discuss a very great number of problems concerned with the Acts of the Apostles. Their book, which appeared in the early twenties, contains in its five volumes numerous historical notes, a commentary and one volume of exposition on the text. And finally *Theologisches Wörterbuch zum Neuen Testament*, herausgegeben von G. Kittel, I-IV; V-X von G. Friedrich and *The New International Dictionary of New Testament Theology* I-III, translated, with additions and revisions, from the German *Theologisches Begriffslexikon zum Neuen Testament*.

It is not possible, obviously, to give a complete list of works on this subject. The value of a commentary depends on the individual reader's purpose and can only be determined by actual use.

2 Monographs on the various books of the New Testament

In addition to the commentaries which are concerned with details of text we should also mention the monographs concerned with an overall view of some New Testament book or author. Many, though not all, of these are of a theological nature.

Matthew

G. D. KILPATRICK, *The Origins of the Gospel of St. Matthew*, Oxford 1956.

K. STENDAHL, *The School of St. Matthew*, in: "Acta Sem. Neot. Upsal." 20, Upsala 1954, Philadelphia 1968.

W. TRILLING, *Das wahre Īsrael*, in: "Erfurter Theol. Stud." 7, Leipzig 1959.

G. BORNKAMM, G. Barth, H. J. Held, *Überlieferung und Auslegung im Matthäusevangelium*, in: "Wissensch. Monogr. z.A.u.N.T.", Neukirchen 1960.

G. STRECKER, *Der Weg der Gerechtigkeit*, in: "Forsch. z. Rel. u. Lit. des A.u.N.T." 82 1971[3].

R. HUMMEL, *Die Auseinandersetzung zwischen Kirche und Judentum im Matthäusevangelium*, in: "Betr. z. Evan. Theol." 33, 1963.

L'Évangile selon Matthieu. Rédaction et Théologie, par M. Didier a.o., in: "Bibl. Ephemeridum Theologicarum Lovaniensium" XXIX, Gembloux 1972.

Mark

W. WREDE, *Das Messiasgeheimnis in den Evangelien*, Göttingen 1901.

B. W. BACON, *The Gospel of Mark: its Composition and Date*, New Haven 1925.

R. H. LIGHTFOOT, *The Gospel Message of St. Mark*, Oxford 1950.

W. MARXSEN, *Der Evangelist Markus*, in: "Forsch. z. Rel. u. Lit. des A.u.N.T." 67 1956.

J. M. Robinson, *Das Geschichtsverständnis des Markus-Evangeliums*, in: "Abhandl. z. Theol. des A.u.N.T." 30 1956.

T. A. Burkill, *Mysterious Revelation*, Ithaca 1963.

E. Best, *The Temptation and the Passion. The Markan Soteriology*, in: "Soc. for N.T. Monograph Series" 2, Cambridge 1965.

R. P. Martin, *Mark: Evangelist and Theologian*, Exeter 1972 (1979).

L'Évangile selon Marc. Tradition et Rédaction, par M. Sabbe a.o., in: "Bibl. Ephemeridum Theologicarum Lovaniensium" XXXIX, Gembloux 1974.

Luke

H. Conzelmann, *Die Mitte der Zeit*, in: "Beitr. z. hist. Theol." 17 1954, 1962.

F. Rehkopf, *Die lukanische Sonderquelle*, in: "Wissensch. Unters. z. N.T." 5, Tübingen 1959.

C. K. Barrett, *Luke the Historian in recent Study*, London 1961.

H. Flender, *Heil und Geschichte in der Theologie des Lukas*, in: "Beitr. z. evang. Theol." 41, München 1965.

Studies in Luke Acts, Essays presented in honor of P. Schubert, ed. by L. E. Keck and J. L. Martyn, Nashville 1966.

I. H. Marshall, *Luke: Historian and Theologian*, Exeter 1970 (1979).

L'Évangile de Luc. Problèmes Littéraires et Théologiques. Mémorial L. Cerfaux, par F. Neirinck a.o., in: "Bibl. Ephemeridum Theologicarum Lovaniensium" XXII, Gembloux 1973.

John

W. F. Howard and C. K. Barrett, *The Fourth Gospel in recent Criticism and Interpretation*, London 1955.

C. H. Dodd, *The Interpretation of the Fourth Gospel*, Cambridge 1955.

A. Guilding, *The Fourth Gospel and Jewish Worship*, Oxford 1960.

C. H. Dodd, *Historical Tradition in the Fourth Gospel*, Cambridge 1963.

R. T. Fortna, *The Gospel of Signs*, in: "Soc. for N.T. Studies Monograph Series" 11, Cambridge 1970.

W. NICOL, *The Semeia in the Fourth Gospel*, in: "Supplements to Novum Testamentum", Leiden 1972.

O. CULLMANN, *Der Johanneische Kreis. Sein Platz im Spätjudentum, in der Jüngerschaft Jesu und im Urchristentum. Zum Ursprung des Johannesevangelium*, Tübingen 1975.

L. *Évangile de Jean. Sources, Rédaction, Théologie*, par M. de Jonge a.o., in: "Bibl. Ephemeridum Theologicarum Lovaniensium" XLIV, Gembloux 1977.

Acts

B. REICKE, *Glaube und Leben der Urgemeinde*, in: "Abhandl. z. Theol. des A.u.N.T." 32 1957.

W. GASQUE, *A History of the Criticism of the Acts of the Apostles*, in "Beitr. z. Geschichte der Bibl. Exegese" 17, Tübingen 1975.

Les Actes des Apôtres. Traditions, Rédaction, Théologie, par J. Kremer a.o., in: "Bibl. Ephemeridum Theologicarum Lovaniensium", Gembloux XLVIII 1979.

Pauline literature

A. SCHWEITZER, *Geschichte der paulinischen Forschung*, Tübingen 1911.

W. D. DAVIES, *Paul and Rabbinic Judaism*, London 1948.

J. MUNCK, *Paulus und die Heilsgeschichte*, in: "Acta Jutlandica" XXVI 1, Theologisk Serie 6, København 1954.

H. J. SCHOEPS, *Paulus*, Tübingen 1959.

E. E. ELLIS, *Paul and his recent Interpreters*, Grand Rapids 1961.

W. C. VAN UNNIK, *Tarsus or Jerusalem. The City of Paul's Youth*, London 1962.

D. E. H. WHITELEY, *The Theology of St. Paul*, Oxford 1974.

M. GRANT, *Saint Paul*, London 1976.

E. P. SANDERS, *Paul and Palestinian Judaism*, London 1977.

K. STENDAHL, *Paul among Jews and Gentiles and other Essays*, London 1977.

N. A. DAHL, *Studies in Paul. Theology for the Early Christian Mission*, Minneapolis 1977.

Hebrews

E. Käsemann, *Das Wandernde Gottesvolk*, in: "Forsch. z. Rel. u. Lit. des A.u.N.T." 37 1938, 1961[4].

R. Williamson, *Philo and the Epistle to the Hebrews*, in: "Arb. z. Lit. u. Gesch. des Hellenist. Judentums" IV, Leiden 1970.

I John

W. Nauck, *Die Tradition und Charakter des ersten Johannesbriefes*, in: "Wissensch. Unters. z. N.T." 3 1957.

K. Wengst, *Häresie und Orthodoxie im Spiegel des ersten Johannesbriefes*, Gütersloh 1976.

Revelation

A. Feuillet, *L'Apocalypse*, in: "Studia Neotest.", Subs. III 1962.

T. Holtz, *Die Christologie der Apokalypse des Johannes*, in: "Texte u. Unters." 85 1962.

A. Satake, *Die Gemeindeordnung in der Johannesapokalypse*, in: "Wissenschaftl. Monogr. z. A.u.N.T." 21, Neukirchen 1966.

3 Periodicals and Bibliographies

Copious literature refences are found in *Biblica*. Exclusively devoted to references (to articles in periodicals) is *Internationale Zeitschriftenschau* and *New Testament Abstracts*. Articles about Paul and Christ and the Gospels have been collected by B. M. Metzger, *Index to Periodical Literature on the apostle Paul*, Leiden 1960 and *Index to Periodical Literature on Christ and the Gospels*, Leiden 1966. The same author compiled the list of articles on textual criticism in *Annotated Bibliography of Textual Criticism of the New Testament 1914-1939*, Copenhagen 1955 and of those in "Festschritten" in *Index of Articles on the New Testament and the early church, published in Festschriften*, Philadelphia, 1951. A. J. Mattill Jr. and Mary Bedford Mattill compiled *A Classified Bibliography of Literature on the Acts of the Apostles*, Leiden 1966. Finally: *A Bibliography of New Testament Bibliographies*, compiled by J. C. Hurd Jr., New York 1966!

Exclusively concerned with New Testament studies are: *Zeitschrift für die neutestamentliche Wissenschaft, New Testament Studies, Novum Testamentum* and *Journal for the Study of the New Testament.*

A wide range of subjects is treated in: *Journal of Theological Studies, Journal of Biblical Literature, Biblische Zeitschrift, Theologische Zeitschrift,* and *Revue Biblique.*

The *Theologische Rundschau* is exclusively devoted to surveys of the state of affairs with respect to theological questions and the *Theologische Literaturzeitung* gives comprehensive reviews of literature.

INDEX

In this Index may be found the passages quoted from the Old Testament and the Fathers together with New Testament passages that occur in a chapter of which their book is not the subject.

Due